Please return/renew this item by the
last date shown to avoid a charge.
Books may also be renewed by phone
and Internet. May not be renewed if
required by another reader.

www.libraries.barnet.gov.uk

BARNET
LONDON BOROUGH

D1375520

LONDON BOROUGH OF BARNET

© Haynes Publishing, 2012

The right of Ian Welch to be identified as the author of this Work has been asserted by him in accordance with the Copyright, Designs & Patents Act 1988.

First published in 2012

A catalogue record for this book is available from the British Library

ISBN: 978-0-857331-79-3

Published by Haynes Publishing, Sparkford, Yeovil,
Somerset BA22 7JJ, UK
Tel: 01963 442030 Fax: 01963 440001
Int. tel: +44 1963 442030 Int. fax: +44 1963 440001
E-mail: sales@haynes.co.uk
Website: www.haynes.co.uk

Haynes North America Inc., 861 Lawrence Drive, Newbury Park, California 91320, USA

Images © Mirrorpix

Creative Director: Kevin Gardner
Designed for Haynes by BrainWave

Printed and bound in the US

Football
Football

RIVALS

ARSENAL

vs

SPURS

Classic
NORTH
LONDON
Derby Games

Ian Welch

CONTENTS

Introduction

For Arsenal and Spurs fans, the North London derby matches are the ones most keenly awaited when the fixture lists are published each July. Such is the intense rivalry between the two North London clubs that the pre-match build-up is a mixture of trepidation and anticipation in perhaps equal measure, depending on which team has recently had most success on the field.

The fixture itself dates back to November 1887, when Tottenham Hotspur entertained Royal Arsenal in a friendly that finished 2-1 to the home side. But it wasn't until December 1909 that the pair faced each other in a competitive match. Walter Lawrence scored the only goal, as Woolwich Arsenal recorded their first league victory over their neighbours. In the intervening years, the two clubs have met more than 160 times, in sometimes epic encounters that include League Cup and FA Cup semi-final ties.

To understand the depth of feeling between the rival sets of supporters you have to go back to the early 20th century. Arsenal moved from Plumstead to Highbury in 1913, with many Spurs fans resenting what they felt was an invasion of their territory. The bad feeling intensified when Arsenal – who had been relegated to the Second Division at the end of the 1912–13 season – were invited to become members of an enlarged First Division after the First World War. Spurs had finished the final prewar campaign of 1914–15 in 20th place, but, with the total number of clubs now rising from 20 to 22, there was space for two more participants in the top flight.

Chelsea, who had been relegated following Manchester United's fixed victory over Liverpool, which had ensured the Old Trafford club's place in the First Division, were reinstated. Bizarrely, though, instead of allowing Spurs to remain in the top flight as well, Arsenal chairman Sir Henry Norris' lobbying campaign succeeded in gaining his club promotion to the First Division on the grounds of their long service to the league. It was a decision that caused much resentment at the time, and has been a topic of debate ever since.

Controversy reared its head again in the 2005–06 season when it looked as though Spurs would finish in fourth place, above Arsenal in fifth, but miss out on a Champions League spot if the Gunners triumphed in that season's Champions League final. Tottenham chairman Daniel Levy was even considering legal action to prevent this happening after UEFA tightened their rules, having allowed a similar situation with Everton (fourth in the Premier League) and Liverpool (Champions League winners) the previous season. As events turned out, Arsenal lost 2-1 to Barcelona but still claimed fourth position in the Premier League, as Tottenham's players suffered a bout of food poisoning before losing 2-1 to West Ham United on the final day of the season.

While both Arsenal and Spurs can boast players who have represented both clubs in this fixture, there are two who appear in the following list of most derby appearances. Pat Jennings was a regular between the posts at White Hart Lane in the 1960s and 1970s, before a shock transfer to Highbury in 1977 saw him add an FA Cup winner's medal to his trophy collection. Sol Campbell also made the transition from Tottenham to Arsenal in the 21st century, but it is loyal, long-serving professionals who proliferate in the top five places. North London legends such as David O'Leary, Gary Mabbutt, Steve Perryman and Tony Adams dedicated the majority if not all in some cases, of their careers to plying their trade in the football capital.

Honours: Arsenal

Premier League winners 3
(1997–98, 2001–02, 2003–04)
Premier League runners-up 5
(1998–99, 1999–2000, 2000–01, 2002–03, 2004–05)
First Division winners 10
(1930–31, 1932–33, 1933–34, 1934–35, 1937–38, 1947–48, 1952–53, 1970–71, 1988–89, 1990–91)
First Division runners-up 3
(1925–26, 1931–32, 1972–73)
Second Division winners 0
Second Division runners-up 1
(1903–04)
FA Cup winners 10
(1930, 1936, 1950, 1971, 1979, 1993, 1998, 2002, 2003, 2005)
FA Cup runners-up 7
(1927, 1932, 1952, 1972, 1978, 1980, 2001)
League Cup winners 2
(1987, 1993)
League Cup runners-up 5
(1968, 1969, 1988, 2007, 2011)
Champions League winners 0
Champions League runners-up 1
(2005–06)
UEFA Cup winners 0
UEFA Cup runners-up 1
(1999–2000)
European Cup Winners' Cup winners 1
(1993–94)
European Cup Winners' Cup runners-up 2
(1979–80, 1994–95)
Fairs Cup winners 1
(1969–70)

Honours: Tottenham Hotspur

Premier League winners 0
Premier League runners-up 0
First Division winners 2
(1950–51, 1960–61)
First Division runners-up 4
(1921–22, 1951–52, 1956–57, 1962–63)
Second Division winners 2
(1919–20, 1949–50)
Second Division runners-up 2
(1908–09, 1932–33)
FA Cup winners 8
(1901, 1921, 1961, 1962, 1967, 1981, 1982, 1991)
FA Cup runners-up 1
(1987)
League Cup winners 4
(1971, 1973, 1999, 2008)
League Cup runners-up 3
(1982, 2002, 2009)
Champions League winners 0
Champions League runners-up 0
UEFA Cup winners 2
(1971–72, 1983–84)
UEFA Cup runners-up 1
(1973–74)
European Cup Winners' Cup winners 1
(1962–63)
European Cup Winners' Cup runners-up 0
Fairs Cup winners 0

Head to Head

League	P	W	D	L	F	A
Arsenal	148	60	41	47	228	202
Spurs	148	47	41	60	202	228

FA Cup	P	W	D	L	F	A
Arsenal	5	3	0	2	7	5
Spurs	5	2	0	3	5	7

League Cup	P	W	D	L	F	A
Arsenal	12	6	3	3	19	16
Spurs	12	3	3	6	16	19

Charity Shield	P	W	D	L	F	A
Arsenal	1	0	1	0	0	0
Spurs	1	0	1	0	0	0

Total	P	W	D	L	F	A
Arsenal	166	69	45	52	254	223
Spurs	166	52	45	69	223	254

Derby stars:

Player	Club	Years	Apps
David O'Leary	Arsenal	1973–93	35
Pat Jennings	Spurs & Arsenal & Spurs		
		1964–77, 1977–85, 1985–86	32
Gary Mabbutt	Spurs	1982–98	31
Steve Perryman	Spurs	1969–86	31
Tony Adams	Arsenal	1982–2002	30
George Armstrong	Arsenal	1961–77	27
Paul Davis	Arsenal	1978–95	23
Glenn Hoddle	Spurs	1975–87	23
John Radford	Arsenal	1962–76	23
Cyril Knowles	Spurs	1964–76	22
Kenny Sansom	Arsenal	1980–88	21
Paul Allen	Spurs	1985–93	20
Graham Rix	Arsenal	1974–88	20
Peter Simpson	Arsenal	1960–78	20
Alan Gilzean	Spurs	1964–74	19
Sol Campbell	Spurs & Arsenal		
		1992–2001, 2001–06, 2010	19
Robbie Keane	Spurs	2002–08, 2009–11	19
Phil Beal	Spurs	1962–75	18
Tony Galvin	Spurs	1978–87	18
Ledley King	Spurs	1998–	18
Maurice Norman	Spurs	1955–67	18
Pat Rice	Arsenal	1964–80	18
Peter Storey	Arsenal	1961–77	18

RIVALS

The 19th century

While football as a pastime had been around for a long time –
historians can trace the origins back to medieval Britain – it wasn't
until the formation of the Football Association (FA) in London in
October 1863 that the sport began to take on characteristics
and rules that more closely resemble the modern game. It was
Ebenezer Cobb Morley, a solicitor from Hull, who first drafted a
set of rules and, nine years later, the first FA Cup was contested
when the Football League kicked off its inaugural season in 1888.
These rules have evolved over the decades; one such change was
the introduction of the penalty kick, which came into effect for the
1891–92 season.

Although some professional clubs were in existence when the
FA was formed, an increase in the popularity of the game saw more
springing up around the country. The Hotspur Football Club was
formed in September 1882 by schoolboys who attended All Hallows
Church, but was renamed Tottenham Hotspur two years later to
avoid confusion with another team who were already using a similar
name. The fledgling club had been playing their home matches on
Tottenham Marshes, but moved to Northumberland Park in 1888,
where their facilities allowed them to charge spectators for the
privilege of watching them play.

Arsenal, meanwhile, had been founded in 1886 as Dial Square,
although that name was soon changed to Royal Arsenal, after the
armaments factory in Woolwich where the players were employed.
The club initially played their home matches on Plumstead Common,
but suffered a nomadic existence before eventually purchasing the
Manor Ground in 1893, when they also changed their name to
Woolwich Arsenal.

By this time, of course, the two clubs had contested their first
match, a friendly that took place on 19th November 1887, and

which had to be abandoned before the final whistle as the Arsenal team had arrived late. There is only one surviving commentary on the meeting, reproduced here from the *Tottenham Weekly Herald*:

Tottenham Hotspur 2 Royal Arsenal 1

This match was played at the ground of the former at Park, November 19th. The Spurs at once began to attack but ten minutes from the start, the Arsenal scored a lucky goal. From this point, the visitors were pressed throughout and, had it not been for the splendid defence of F Beardsley (Notts Forest) in goal, the score would have been much larger. Through darkness the game was stopped 15 minutes before time, the Spurs winning 2 goals to 1.

Fred Beardsley had previously turned out for Nottingham Forest, along with Morris Bates, and they managed to secure an old set of kit from their former club, thus beginning Arsenal's tradition of playing in red. Spurs, meanwhile, had already gone through several colour-scheme changes – from navy shirts to blue-and-white halved jerseys (such as worn by Blackburn Rovers during their FA Cup win of 1884) and other combinations, before finally settling on white shirts and navy shorts in emulation of Preston North End.

Two years later, Arsenal entered the FA Cup for the first time but they found it impossible to gain entry into the Football League, which had started out with members from only the Midlands and the north of England. As Arsenal soon found that their better players were being approached by professional teams trying to poach their prize assets, they attempted to instigate a southern equivalent of the Football League, but the intended competition failed to get off the ground. Their name change to Woolwich Arsenal coincided with the setting up of a limited liability company and a Football League invitation to join the newly formed Second Division in 1893, where they remained for the rest of the century.

After Arsenal suffered an FA Cup defeat at the hands of Millwall, the club decided to install Thomas Mitchell as their first professional manager. The Scot had already tasted success in the

FA Cup with Blackburn Rovers, as they dominated the competition with five wins between 1884 and 1891. His tenure as Arsenal manager lasted less than one season, however, as the club could only reach fifth in the Second Division, and he was replaced by William Elcoat, who resigned in February 1899, having had enough of the club's directors.

Spurs had turned professional in late 1895, gained entrance to the Southern League and also appointed their first manager. Information about Liverpool-born Frank Brettell is sparse, but it is known that he played for Everton as a full-back while working as a full-time reporter for the *Liverpool Mercury*. With his experience as club secretary and manager he moved to Bolton Wanderers in 1896, where he stayed for two years before joining Spurs in 1898. However, he was offered a more lucrative deal and left London for Portsmouth in February 1899, where he took the club to second place in the Southern League. Brettell left in 1901 and didn't hold another managerial position until he joined Plymouth Argyle in 1903. The club became established as professional under Brettell and he led them into the Southern League during the 1903–04 season. He retired from football management a year later.

By the end of the 19th century, Spurs had again moved home – this time to a former market garden that they developed into what became known as White Hart Lane. Like Association Football itself, Arsenal and Tottenham were still in their infancy, and both clubs were set for bigger and better things in the 20th century.

Record in the 19th century

Arsenal

Season	League	P	W	L	D	F	A	Pts	Pos
1888–89	Not a Football League member								
1889–90	Not a Football League member								
1890–91	Not a Football League member								
1891–92	Not a Football League member								
1892–93	Not a Football League member								
1893–94	Div 2	28	12	12	4	52	55	28	9
1894–95	Div 2	30	14	10	6	75	58	34	8
1895–96	Div 2	30	14	12	4	59	42	32	7
1896–97	Div 2	30	13	13	4	68	70	30	10
1897–98	Div 2	30	16	9	5	69	49	37	5
1898–99	Div 2	34	18	11	5	72	41	41	7
1899–1900	Div 2	34	16	14	4	61	43	36	8

FA Cup

1889–90	1-5 v Swifts (Fourth Qualifying Round)
1890–91	1-2 v Derby County (First Round)
1891–92	1-5 v Small Heath (First Round)
1892–93	0-6 v Sunderland (First Round)
1893–94	1-2 v Sheffield Wednesday (First Round)
1894–95	0-1 v Bolton Wanderers (First Round)
1895–96	1-6 v Burnley (First Round)
1896–97	2-4 v Millwall Athletic (Fifth Qualifying Round)
1897–98	1-3 v Burnley (First Round)
1898–99	0-6 v Derby County (First Round)
1899–1900	1-1, 0-0, 2-2, 1-1, 0-1 v New Brompton (Third Qualifying Round)

Tottenham Hotspur

Season	League	P	W	L	D	F	A	Pts	Pos
1888–89	Not a Football League member								
1889–90	Not a Football League member								

1890–91	Not a Football League member
1891–92	Not a Football League member
1892–93	Not a Football League member
1893–94	Not a Football League member
1894–95	Not a Football League member
1895–96	Not a Football League member
1896–97	Not a Football League member
1897–98	Not a Football League member
1898–99	Not a Football League member
1899–1900	Not a Football League member

FA Cup

1889–90	Did not enter
1890–91	Did not enter
1891–92	Did not enter
1892–93	Did not enter
1893–94	Did not enter
1894–95	2-2, 0-4 v Luton Town (Fourth Qualifying Round)
1895–96	0-5 v Stoke City (First Round)
1896–97	0-3 v Luton Town (Fifth Qualifying Round)
1897–98	3-4 v Luton Town (Fourth Qualifying Round)
1898–99	1-4 v Stoke City (Third Round)
1899–1900	0-1 v Preston North End (First Round)

The early 20th century

Both Arsenal and Tottenham had installed new managers in 1899 who were to bring success to the clubs in differing ways in the early years of the 20th century. For Spurs it was their first piece of silverware, while Arsenal finally gained promotion to the First Division.

Hailing from Ayr in Scotland, John Cameron (1872–1935) played as a forward for Queen's Park, Everton and Scotland before taking up the managerial reins. He was a prolific goalscorer and became player-manager of Tottenham in 1899, helping them win the Southern League title in 1900. Under Cameron, the club also won the FA Cup in 1901, becoming the first – and so far only – non-league team to win the competition. The FA Cup final was a draw, 2-2, against Sheffield United, with Sandy Brown scoring both the London club's goals. The replay, however, was a different matter and Cameron himself equalized the Blades' opener, with Tom Smith and Sandy Brown registering the other two goals in the 3-1 victory. The club went on to finish second in the Southern League in both 1902 and 1904. Despite his success story at Spurs, Cameron resigned as manager in March 1907 and joined Dresdner SC as coach.

Born in 1853, Henry "Harry" Bradshaw became secretary of Burnley in 1981, and chairman two years later. Although he was never a professional footballer he became first-team manager in 1896, but the squad were relegated from the First Division after losing play-offs at the end of his first campaign. The following season saw the club promoted back to the First Division, and they went on to finish third in the top flight in 1898–99. Bradshaw moved to Woolwich Arsenal in 1899 and led the Second Division team to promotion in 1903–04. Here the club became purveyors of a short passing game and a fluid style of play, courtesy of players such as Jimmy Jackson and Jimmy Ashcroft, but Bradshaw never managed the Gunners in the top flight as he moved to Fulham in the spring of 1904 as that club's first professional manager.

Bradshaw was succeeded in the managerial hot seat by Phil Kelso, and the former Hibernian manager established the club as a mid-table side and took them to two consecutive FA Cup semi-finals. With results and their league position declining, however, and with the club's finances under strain, Kelso resigned in February 1908 to run a hotel in Scotland; although, in an about turn, he took over the reins at Fulham the following year, a post he held until 1924.

Spurs, meanwhile, had appointed Fred Kirkham in April 1907. The announcement had come as a surprise to many because, while Kirkham was a well-known referee who had overseen the 1906 FA Cup final as well as international matches, he had never managed a football team before. His sojourn as White Hart Lane manager was brief as well as extremely unpopular, and he resigned in July 1908. Tottenham did bounce back, earning promotion from the Second Division as runners-up in 1908–09, but life was tough in the top flight and they were, more often than not, to be found in the bottom half of the table in the years preceding the First World War. Indeed, in the final prewar season of 1914–15 they finished bottom of the table and suffered the ignominy of relegation back to the Second Division.

By this time, Peter McWilliam had been installed as manager. Appointed in December 1912, the Scot had plied his trade with Inverness Thistle and Newcastle United, and he led Spurs through their most successful period so far. As previously mentioned, Arsenal were included in the enlarged postwar First Division – at Spurs' expense – but McWilliam had assembled a side that were brimming with talent and included Jimmy Cantrell. Like many of his era, Cantrell, the former Aston Villa and Notts County centre-forward, had had his career interrupted by the hostilities; however, he went on to lead the Spurs' attack in 1919–20 as they charged to the Second Division title with a then record 70 points.

George Morrell had taken over from Kelso as Arsenal manager in February 1908, but had struggled to maintain the momentum started by his predecessor, and found himself forced to sell stars such as Jimmy Ashcroft, Bert Freeman and Jimmy Sharp. He led the club to their best ever league finish of sixth in his first full season, but diced with relegation in 1909–10, and his side eventually fell through the trapdoor in 1912–13. Top five finishes in the two prewar seasons failed to bring about a return to the top flight, but Arsenal were invited to join the First Division elite straight after the war.

One of the biggest changes to occur in the prewar years was Arsenal's move to Highbury. It was instigated by chairman Sir Henry Norris – who was more than aware of the limitations of Woolwich Arsenal's home ground, and was keen to raise the level of income available to the club. He located what he thought was the perfect spot for a new stadium, in Highbury, but the move in the summer of 1913 coincided with the club's relegation from the First Division. It was decided to drop Woolwich from their name and just call themselves The Arsenal, although they became just plain Arsenal in November 1919.

Record in the early 20th century

Arsenal

Season	League	P	W	D	L	F	A	Pts	Pos
1900–01	Div 2	34	15	6	13	39	35	36	7
1901–02	Div 2	34	18	6	10	50	26	42	4
1902–03	Div 2	34	20	8	6	66	30	48	3
1903–04	Div 2	34	21	7	6	91	22	49	2
1904–05	Div 1	34	12	9	13	36	40	33	10
1905–06	Div 1	38	15	7	16	62	64	37	12
1906–07	Div 1	38	20	4	14	66	59	44	7
1907–08	Div 1	38	12	12	14	51	63	36	15
1908–09	Div 1	38	14	10	14	52	49	38	6
1909–10	Div 1	38	11	9	18	37	67	31	18
1910–11	Div 1	38	13	12	13	41	49	38	10

1911–12	Div 1	38	15	8	15	55	59	38	10
1912–13	Div 1	38	3	12	23	26	74	18	20
1913–14	Div 2	38	20	9	9	54	38	49	3
1914–15	Div 2	38	19	5	14	69	41	48	5
1919–20	Div 1	42	15	12	15	56	58	42	10

FA Cup

1900–01	0-1 v West Bromwich Albion (Second Round)
1901–02	0-2 v Newcastle United (First Round)
1902–03	1-3 v Sheffield United (First Round)
1903–04	0-2 v Manchester City (Second Round)
1904–05	0-0, 0-1 v Bristol City (First Round)
1905–06	0-2 v Newcastle United (Semi-final)
1906–07	1-3 v Sheffield Wednesday (Semi-final)
1907–08	0-0, 1-4 v Hull City (First Round)
1908–09	1-1, 0-1 v Millwall (Second Round)
1909–10	0-5 v Everton (Second Round)
1910–11	0-1 v Swindon Town (Second Round)
1911–12	0-1 v Bolton Wanderers (First Round)
1912–13	1-4 v Liverpool (Second Round)
1913–14	0-2 v Bradford City (First Round)
1914–15	0-1 v Chelsea (Second Round)
1919–20	0-1 v Bristol City (Second Round)

Tottenham Hotspur

Season	League	P	W	D	L	F	A	Pts	Pos
1900–01	Not a Football League member								
1901–02	Not a Football League member								
1902–03	Not a Football League member								
1903–04	Not a Football League member								
1904–05	Not a Football League member								
1905–06	Not a Football League member								
1906–07	Not a Football League member								
1907–08	Not a Football League member								
1908–09	Div 2	38	20	11	7	67	32	51	2

1909–10	Div 1	38	11	10	17	53	69	32	15
1910–11	Div 1	38	13	6	19	52	63	32	15
1911–12	Div 1	38	14	9	15	53	53	37	12
1912–13	Div 1	38	12	6	20	45	72	30	17
1913–14	Div 1	38	12	10	16	50	62	34	17
1914–15	Div 1	38	8	12	18	57	90	28	20
1919–20	Div 2	42	32	6	4	102	32	70	1

FA Cup

1900–01	2-2, 3-1 v Sheffield United (Final)
1901–02	1-1, 2-2, 1-2 v Southampton (First Round)
1902–03	2-3 v Aston Villa (Third Round)
1903–04	1-1, 0-2 v Sheffield Wednesday (Third Round)
1904–05	0-4 v Newcastle United (Second Round)
1905–06	1-1, 0-2 v Birmingham City (Third Round)
1906–07	0-4 v Notts County (Third Round)
1907–08	0-1 v Everton (First Round)
1908–09	0-0, 1-3 v Burnley (Third Round)
1909–10	2-3 v Swindon Town (Third Round)
1910–11	0-0, 0-2 v Blackburn Rovers (Second Round)
1911–12	0-3 v West Bromwich Albion (First Round)
1912–13	0-1 v Reading (Second Round)
1913–14	1-2 v Manchester City (Second Round)
1914–15	2-3 v Norwich City (Second Round)
1919–20	0-1 v Aston Villa (Fourth Round)

4th December 1909

First Division

Arsenal 1

Lawrence

Tottenham Hotspur 0

Attendance: **18,000**

Arsenal: *H L McDonald, D McDonald, Shaw, Ducat, Sands,*

McEachrane, Greenaway, Steven, Hoare, Lawrence, Neave.
Tottenham Hotspur: Joyce, Wilkes, Harris, Bentley, D Steel, Darnell, Curtis, Minter, I Brown, R Steel, Middlemiss.

The first ever competitive encounter between Arsenal and Spurs took place when the two sides contested a First Division match on 4th December 1909. It was also notable in that the new LCC tramway service ran direct to the ground from Woolwich Free Ferry for the first time. The visitors, who were still looking for their first league victory away from home that season, arrived in improved form and many forecast a draw ... especially seeing as the new Spurs goalkeeper – Tiny Joyce – had tasted success in previous meetings between his former club, Millwall, and Arsenal. As it turned out though, Walter Lawrence netted the only goal of the game eight minutes into the second half when he latched on to a cross from right-winger David Greenaway.

16th April 1910

First Division
Tottenham Hotspur 1
Curtis
Arsenal 1
McGibbon
Attendance: **39,800**
Tottenham Hotspur: Joyce, Coquet, Wilkes, Morris, D Steel, Bentley, Curtis, Minter, Humphreys, R Steel, Middlemiss.
Arsenal: H L McDonald, D McDonald, Shaw, Ducat, Thomson, McEachrane, Greenaway, Lewis, McGibbon, Lawrence, Heppinstall.

The return fixture saw both clubs languishing in the bottom half of the table, and the pre-match hype ensured a record crowd at White Hart Lane. It was Arsenal who – having been the better side in the opening exchanges – took the lead when Charlie McGibbon netted the first goal, although many spectators felt that Frank Heppinstall was clearly offside when he received the ball. The home side piled on the pressure after the break, but had to contend with some dangerous counter-attacks, one of which saw McGibbon find the back of the net again – although the goal was disallowed due to the use of a hand. Spurs began to monopolize the attacking play, and soon equalized when Jack Curtis shot past McDonald in a move that resulted in the injured McEachrane being forced to leave the field. The 10 men of Arsenal hung on to claim a draw but, despite losing their final game of the campaign (1-3 to Burnley), they had already done enough to secure their survival in the First Division. Spurs, meanwhile, recorded victories over Bolton (2-0) and Chelsea (2-1) to preserve their top-flight status, finishing one point and three places ahead of the Gunners.

3rd December 1910

First Division
Tottenham Hotspur 3
Darnell, Minter, Humphreys
Arsenal 1
Chalmers
Attendance: 16,000
Tottenham Hotspur: *Lunn, Coquet, Collins, Bentley, D Steel, Darnell, Curtis, Minter, Humphreys, R McTavish, Middlemiss.*
Arsenal: *Bateup, Gray, Shaw, Ducat, Thomson, McEachrane, Lewis, Common, Chalmers, Shortt, Neave.*

Spurs finally gained a league win over Arsenal when the two sides met in December 1910. The visitors had fared slightly better over the first few months of the campaign and were two points better off than Spurs, who, however, taking their recent form into account, started the game as slight favourites. Arsenal took the lead early in the game when Jackie Chalmers opened the scoring, although the home side was in front by half-time, courtesy of goals from Percy Humphreys and Jabez Darnell. Despite persistent pressure in the second half, Arsenal were unable to equalize, and found themselves further behind when Billy Minter registered a third for

Spurs that effectively killed off the game. Newspaper reports at the time suggested that Tom Collins, the full-back recently signed from Hearts for £825, failed to make a significant impact, although his counterpart, Ernie Coquet, acquitted himself well.

8th April 1911

First Division

Arsenal 2

Chalmers, Common

Tottenham Hotspur 0

Attendance: 24,583

Arsenal: *Burdett, Shaw, Gray, Ducat, Sands, McEachrane, Greenaway, Common, Chalmers, Hoare, Lewis.*

Tottenham Hotspur: *Lunn, Collins, Wilkes, Bentley, Rance, Darnell, Curtis, Minter, Tull, R Steel, Middlemiss.*

Little separated the two sides in the bottom third of the table, although both Arsenal and Spurs had already done enough to guarantee another season of top-flight football by the time they met at Plumstead in April 1911. In what turned out to be a disappointing performance from the visitors, goals from Chalmers and Alf Common (who became the first £1,000 transfer when he moved from Sunderland to Middlesbrough in 1905) secured the points, although Charlie Rance, Collins and Tommy Lunn were commended for limiting the score to just a two-goal deficit. Spurs finished the campaign with two defeats in their final three games, while Arsenal went on a run of three draws and two victories, which launched them up to a more respectable 10th in the table.

25th December 1911

First Division

Tottenham Hotspur 5

Darnell, J McTavish, Minter 2, Middlemiss

Arsenal 0
Attendance: 47,109
Tottenham Hotspur: *Lunn, Collins, Webster, D Steel, Rance, Darnell, J McTavish, Newman, Minter, R Steel, Middlemiss.*
Arsenal: *Crawford, Shaw, Peart, Ducat, Sands, McKinnon, Lewis, Common, Chalmers, Randall, Winship.*

Newspaper reports estimated that while a crowd of almost 50,000 witnessed Spurs put five goals past Arsenal without reply, another 10,000 were locked out of White Hart Lane, as the recently finished terraces struggled to cope with the numbers wanting to watch the Christmas Day spectacle. With Dick Roose being injured in Arsenal's previous league match and George Burdett ruled out with tonsillitis, reserve-team goalkeeper Harold Crawford found himself making his league debut between the posts, but could do little to stem the flow of goals. The home side quickly went into a three-goal lead, before adding another two early in the second half. Arsenal rallied towards the end of each 45-minute period, but were unable to score even a consolation goal.

26th December 1911

First Division
Arsenal 3
Lewis, Randall, Winship
Tottenham Hotspur 1
Minter
Attendance: 22,000
Arsenal: *Crawford, Shaw, Peart, Ducat, Sands, McEachrane, Lewis, Common, Chalmers, Randall, Winship.*
Tottenham Hotspur: *Lunn, Collins, Webster, D Steel, Rance, Darnell, J McTavish, Newman, Minter, R Steel, Middlemiss.*

The return fixture the following day saw just one change in the line-ups – with Roddy McEachrane replacing Angus McKinnon at left-half – but the result could not have been more of a contrast. Spurs had been struggling to find any consistent form in the preceding weeks, and their plight continued as they allowed Arsenal to open up a 2-0 advantage by half-time, with goals from Charlie Lewis and Charles Randall. Tommy Winship added a third after the interval as, while Minter replied for the visitors, the home side adapted better to the quagmire conditions that had followed overnight torrential rain.

14th December 1912

First Division

Arsenal 0

Tottenham Hotspur 3

R Steel, Cantrell 2 (1 pen)

Attendance: 13,000

Arsenal: *Crawford, Shaw, Peart, King, Thomson, McEachrane, Groves, Flanagan, Duncan, Spittle, Lewis.*

Tottenham Hotspur: *Joyce, Collins, Webster, Weir, Rance, Lightfoot, Tattersall, Minter, Cantrell, R Steel, Middlemiss.*

Harold Crawford began the 1912–13 season as the first-choice goalkeeper for Arsenal, but paid the price after Spurs' first away victory in a north London derby. He was dropped, and made only two further appearances for the club before joining Reading in June 1913. Both sides missed good chances to open the scoring in the first half, but it was Bobby Steel who netted the first goal of the game, just three minutes into the second half, when he got on the end of Findlay Weir's free-kick. Jimmy Cantrell scored the visitors' second from the penalty spot, after Steel's shot was handled on the line, and doubled his tally shortly before the final whistle.

19th April 1913

First Division

Tottenham Hotspur 1

Minter

Arsenal 1
Grant
Attendance: 20,000
Tottenham Hotspur: *Tate, Collins, Webster, Weir, Rance, Grimsdell, Walden, Minter, Cantrell, Bliss, Middlemiss.*
Arsenal: *H L McDonald, Shaw, Fidler, Grant, Thomson, Graham, Lewis, Spittle, Stonley, Devine, Burrell.*

There was very little to play for in the penultimate match of the 1912–13 campaign other than local pride. Spurs had secured their top-flight status and would finish in 17th position, while Arsenal were already doomed to Second Division football the following season. A dismal record of just three wins, coupled with 12 draws, had given them a paltry total of 18 points and rooted them to the bottom of the table. The home side gave debuts to two players: goalkeeper John Tate, and their latest signing, Fanny Walden (bought from Northampton Town for £1,700). Walden made a good impression at outside-right, and initial concerns that, at 5ft 2in tall, he was too small for First Division football were soon dismissed. He went on to play more than 200 league games for the club. The match itself was described as a very moderate one, with both goals coming from corners.

The 1920s

Arsenal had appointed Leslie Knighton as manager when peacetime football resumed, and he consolidated their position as a top-flight team, although they never came close to winning any silverware during his tenure. In fact, the club's league positions deteriorated after two respectable top 10 seasons, and they flirted with relegation in 1923–24 and 1924–25, which culminated in Knighton's sacking in the summer of 1925.

Spurs enjoyed further success under Peter McWilliam as they stormed to their second FA Cup win in 1921, with Jimmy Dimmock scoring the only goal, eight minutes after the interval, in the final against Wolves. They also ended their second season back in the top flight, as runners-up to Liverpool – their best ever league finish. However, it was the beginning of the end for this great Spurs team.

Jimmy Cantrell – who had collected an FA Cup winner's medal at the age of 38 – played his last match against Birmingham City just short of his 40th birthday, making him the oldest Spurs player to feature in a league match. It was a record that he held for 90 years, before being superseded by Brad Friedel. Cantrell played 176 times, and scored on 84 occasions in competitions between 1912 and 1922. He ended his career at Sutton United, before retiring in 1925.

Arsenal turned to Herbert Chapman in a bid to bring success to Highbury. He had played for a number of clubs at league and non-league levels, but his career remained unremarkable until he became Northampton Town manager in 1908. During his four years at the club he led them to a Southern League title and earned himself a reputation as a solid manager, which saw a move to Leeds City in 1912. For two years prior to the First World War, Chapman led and improved the club, but found himself out of a job, following the war, when Leeds City were implemented in a scandal that saw the club disbanded. Chapman was banned from football after the illegal payments scandal, but he appealed successfully, and moved on to Huddersfield Town.

Chapman arrived at Highbury having taken the Terriers to FA Cup glory in 1922, and having won back-to-back First Division titles between 1923 and 1925. One of his first signings for Arsenal was Charlie Buchan, and, between them, they responded to the change in the offside rule (that reduced the number of players an attacker needed between him and the opposition's goal from three to two) by changing the centre-half's role from that of a roving midfielder to that of a defensive stopper. This made provision for better, faster counter-attacks, as Chapman himself stated, "the most opportune time for scoring is immediately after repelling an attack, because opponents are then strung out in the wrong half of the field".

Chapman led Arsenal to runners-up position in the First Division in his first season in charge, behind his former club, who became the first team to win three consecutive league titles. However, this was not an immediate precursor to the success that Norris sought, as the rest of the 1920s saw them finish in mid-table. Arsenal reached their first FA Cup final the following year, but lost out to Cardiff City in the Wembley finale after goalkeeper Dan Lewis let a soft shot squirm into the net. They did, however, win their first trophy in 1930, when goals from Alex James and Jack Lambert gave them a 2-0 victory over Huddersfield Town.

By the time McWilliam left White Hart Lane – attracted by the offer of a £1,500 salary from Middlesbrough – Spurs were back to being in the lower half of the table team, and McWilliam's replacement, former club captain Billy Minter, was unable to revive the club's fortunes. Minter resigned in November 1929 due to ill health, and shortly after his side was relegated from the First Division.

Record in the 1920s

Arsenal

Season	League	P	W	D	L	F	A	Pts	Pos
1920–21	Div 1	42	15	14	13	59	63	44	9
1921–22	Div 1	42	15	7	20	47	56	37	17
1922–23	Div 1	42	16	10	16	61	62	42	11
1923–24	Div 1	42	12	9	21	40	63	33	19
1924–25	Div 1	42	14	5	23	46	58	33	20
1925–26	Div 1	42	22	8	12	87	63	52	2
1926–27	Div 1	42	17	9	16	77	86	43	11
1927–28	Div 1	42	13	15	14	82	86	41	10
1928–29	Div 1	42	16	13	13	77	72	45	9
1929–30	Div 1	42	14	11	17	78	66	39	14

FA Cup

1920–21	0-2 v Queens Park Rangers (First Round)
1921–22	1-1, 1-2 v Preston North End (Fourth Round)
1922–23	0-0, 1-4 v Liverpool (First Round)
1923–24	0-1 v Cardiff City (Second Round)
1924–25	0-0, 2-2, 0-1 v West Ham United (First Round)
1925–26	1-2 v Swansea Town (Sixth Round)
1926–27	0-1 v Cardiff City (Final)
1927–28	0-1 v Blackburn Rovers (Semi-final)
1928–29	0-1 v Aston Villa (Sixth Round)
1929–30	2-0 v Huddersfield Town (Final)

Tottenham Hotspur

Season	League	P	W	D	L	F	A	Pts	Pos
1920–21	Div 1	42	19	9	14	70	48	47	6
1921–22	Div 1	42	21	9	12	65	39	51	2
1922–23	Div 1	42	17	7	18	50	50	41	12
1923–24	Div 1	42	12	14	16	50	56	38	15
1924–25	Div 1	42	15	12	15	52	43	42	12
1925–26	Div 1	42	15	9	18	66	79	39	15

1926–27	Div 1	42	16	9	17	76	78	41	13
1927–28	Div 1	42	15	8	19	74	86	38	21
1928–29	Div 2	42	17	9	16	75	81	43	10
1929–30	Div 2	42	15	9	18	59	61	39	12

FA Cup

1920–21	1-0 v Wolverhampton Wanderers (Final)
1921–22	1-2 v Preston North End (Semi-final)
1922–23	0-1 v Derby County (Fourth Round)
1923–24	0-2 v Crystal Palace (First Round)
1924–25	2-2, 1-3 v Blackburn Rovers (Third Round)
1925–26	2-2, 0-2 v Manchester United (Fourth Round)
1926–27	2-3 v West Ham United (Third Round)
1927–28	1-6 v Huddersfield Town (Sixth Round)
1928–29	0-2 v Reading (Third Round)
1929–30	2-2, 1-4 v Manchester City (Third Round)

15th January 1921

First Division
Tottenham Hotspur 2
Cantrell, Bliss
Arsenal 1
Rutherford
Attendance: 39,221
Tottenham Hotspur: *Jacques, Clay, McDonald, Smith, Walters, Grimsdell, Walden, Seed, Cantrell, Bliss, Dimmock.*
Arsenal: *Williamson, Bradshaw, Hutchins, Baker, Butler, McKinnon, Rutherford, White, Pagnam, Blyth, Paterson.*

With both clubs having spent time in the Second Division, and the interruption of league football due to the First World War, the first north London derby for eight years saw just a handful of players who had previously appeared in the fixture taking the field. Jimmy Cantrell and Bert Bliss were both approaching the end of their playing careers, but both got their names on the scoresheet.

Cantrell scored his side's first goal in a match that was marred by foggy conditions as the game wore on. Although the visitors drew level through Jock Rutherford, a blistering 40-yard free-kick from inside-forward Bliss gave Ernie Williamson no chance, and condemned Arsenal to defeat.

22nd January 1921

First Division
Arsenal 3
Rutherford 2, White
Tottenham Hotspur 2
Cantrell, Smith
Attendance: **60,600**
Arsenal: *Dunn, Bradshaw, Hutchins, Baker, Butler, McKinnon, Rutherford, White, North, Blyth, Paterson.*
Tottenham Hotspur: *Jacques, Clay, McDonald, Smith, Walters, Grimsdell, Walden, Seed, Cantrell, Bliss, Dimmock.*

This game was notable in that it was the first north London derby to be played at Highbury – despite the fact that Arsenal had made it their home in 1913 – and it was fitting that the match resulted in a victory for the home side. Jock Rutherford opened the scoring with a soft shot that squirmed through Bill Jacques' hands in the 17th minute, before Jimmy Cantrell netted the equalizer with what turned out to be his last derby goal. Rutherford notched his second, which was played through by Jimmy Paterson as the Spurs defenders stood appealing for offside, and topscorer Henry White added Arsenal's third. Bert Smith scored a second for Spurs in the 68th minute, but the home side held out for the win, despite Jack Butler playing the majority of the second half with a damaged collarbone.

15th April 1922

First Division
Tottenham Hotspur 2
Grimsdell, Seed

Arsenal 0
Attendance: 40,394
Tottenham Hotspur: *Blake, Clay, McDonald, Smith, Walters, Grimsdell, Walden, Seed, Cantrell, Thompson, Dimmock.*
Arsenal: *Williamson, Bradshaw, Hutchins, Baker, Graham, Whittaker, Rutherford, White, Young, Boreham, Toner.*

The stakes could not have been much higher as both sides met towards the end of the 1921–22 campaign. Spurs were in second place in the First Division table, just five points behind Liverpool with five games to play, while Arsenal were in the second relegation spot and three points adrift of safety, with Manchester United already having been condemned to the drop. The Gunners put up a terrific fight but were unable to prevent Arthur Grimsdell opening the scoring after 15 minutes. Arsenal rallied in the second half but could not find a way past Herbert Blake in the Spurs goal, and the contest was settled 15 minutes from time when Jimmy Seed headed in Fanny Walden's corner. The result kept Spurs in with a slight mathematical chance of the league title, but left Arsenal in grave danger, although they did have a game in hand.

22nd April 1922

First Division
Arsenal 1
Graham (pen)
Tottenham Hotspur 0
Attendance: 42,000
Arsenal: *Williamson, Bradshaw, Hutchins, Baker, Graham, Whittaker, Rutherford, White, Earle, Boreham, Blyth.*
Tottenham Hotspur: *Blake, Clay, McDonald, Skinner, Walters, Grimsdell, Walden, Seed, Cantrell, Thompson, Dimmock.*

Arsenal gained their revenge in the return fixture, and had also improved their survival chances with two games against West Brom on the Monday (a 3-0 away win) and Tuesday (a 2-2 draw at Highbury), following their Saturday defeat at White Hart Lane. The match was a hard-fought affair, with Spurs seeming to suffer the most: Jimmy Cantrell was injured in the first half but was able to continue, whereas Arthur Grimsdell was absent for the majority of the game due to a badly kicked hip. The only goal of the game came from the penalty spot, with Alex Graham converting after Jimmy Dimmock had conceded the spot kick. Arsenal went on to win their two matches against Bradford City (2-0 away and 1-0 at home), which elevated them to 17th in the table and condemned the Bantams to the drop. Spurs, on the other hand, only managed one win in their final five league matches, and finished the campaign as runners-up, six points behind Liverpool.

23rd September 1922

First Division

Tottenham Hotspur 1

Lindsay

Arsenal 2

Boreham 2

Attendance: **40,582**

Tottenham Hotspur: *Blake, Clay, McDonald, Smith, Walters, Grimsdell, Walden, Seed, Lindsay, Bliss, Dimmock.*

Arsenal: *Dunn, Bradshaw, Hutchins, Baker, Voysey, Graham, Rutherford, White, Young, Boreham, Blyth.*

Arsenal recorded their first victory at White Hart Lane in the clubs' first clash of the 1922–23 campaign. Spurs had been tipped to emerge victorious from the derby match and, with Alex Lindsay replacing the injured Cantrell, had the better of the early chances, but the Arsenal defence held firm. Fanny Walden retired due to an injured thigh, and the visitors capitalized on their numerical supremacy when Reg Boreham opened the scoring early in the second half, with a left-foot drive that gave Herbert Blake a chance. Boreham doubled his side's lead half an hour later, before Lindsay broke through to reduce the deficit shortly before full-time. The fracas following Spurs' goal was described by one reporter as "the most disgraceful scene I have witnessed on any ground at any time. Players pulled the referee, blows with fists were exchanged, and all the dignity that appertains in the referee was rudely trampled on."

30th September 1922

First Division

Arsenal 0
Tottenham Hotspur 2

Dimmock 2

Attendance: 55,000

Arsenal: *Dunn, Bradshaw, Hutchins, Baker, Voysey, Graham, Rutherford, White, Young, Boreham, Blyth.*

Tottenham Hotspur: *Blake, Clay, McDonald, Smith, Walters, Grimsdell, Lindsay, Seed, Wilson, Dimmock, Brooks.*

Despite the fact that they were without the injured Cantrell, Bliss and Walden, Spurs had been enjoying their travels, and had actually played better football away from White Hart Lane than at it so far that season. So it was really no surprise that their patched-up team claimed the points at Highbury a week after their unexpected home defeat. Debutant Sam Brooks and Jimmy Dimmock formed a fantastic partnership on the left wing, with the latter netting both goals. Spurs played a clever, fast-paced game, although the referee – Mr W E Russell from Swindon – was inclined to err on the side of caution and, as a result, the game did not flow as smoothly as it could have. In the aftermath of the previous match's altercation, Bert Smith was suspended for a month, having been found guilty of using "filthy language", while Alex Graham and Stephen Dunn were both censured for their actions.

17th November 1923

First Division

Arsenal 1

Townrow

ARSENAL vs SPURS

Tottenham Hotspur 1
Seed
Attendance: **50,000**
Arsenal: *Robson, Mackie, Whittaker, Graham, Butler, Blyth, Rutherford, Townrow, Turnbull, Woods, Paterson.*
Tottenham Hotspur: *Maddison, Clay, Forster, Smith, Lowe, Grimsdell, Walden, Seed, Lindsay, Elkes, Handley.*

While official statistics put this game's attendance at 50,000, newspaper reports suggested that a much larger crowd of 60,000 was allowed into Highbury before the gates were locked. The match itself was "a delightful game to watch, the clever football of the visitors being matched by vigorous bustling play by the Arsenal". The home side took the lead after the interval, when a misunderstanding between full-back Matt Forster and goalkeeper George Maddison let Frank Townrow – making a rare league appearance for the Gunners – in to score. Arsenal were unable to protect their lead, however, with Jimmy Seed equalizing from a corner to ensure that the game finished with honours even.

24ᵗʰ November 1923

First Division
Tottenham Hotspur 3
Lindsay 2, Elkes
Arsenal 0
Attendance: **31,624**
Tottenham Hotspur: *Maddison, Clay, Forster, Smith, Lowe, Grimsdell, Walden, Seed, Lindsay, Elkes, Handley.*
Arsenal: *Robson, Mackie, Whittaker, Graham, Butler, Blyth, Rutherford, Townrow, Young, Baker, Paterson.*

In the return match a week later, Spurs were by far the cleverer side, and although the game was goalless at half-time, it seemed it was only a matter of time before they turned their dominance into goals. Arsenal's defence waivered and then collapsed in the second half, when Arthur Grimsdell sent Alex Lindsay through to open the scoring for the home side. Spurs sealed their victory with another goal from Lindsay, eight minutes from time, and a 30-yard belter from Jack Elkes.

25th October 1924

First Division
Arsenal 1
Brain
Tottenham Hotspur 0
Attendance: 51,000
Arsenal: *Robson, Mackie, Kennedy, Milne, Butler, John, Rutherford, Brain, Woods, Ramsay, Toner.*
Tottenham Hotspur: *Hinton, Forster, Poynton, Smith, Lowe, White, Osborne, Seed, Lindsay, Elkes, Dimmock.*

There were more than 50,000 people at Highbury to see Arsenal beat Spurs by a single goal, in a fast game in which both sets of defenders played well. Jock Rutherford was once again the outstanding figure on the field, and it was due to his clever run and centre that Jimmy Brain was able to head the only goal of the game. It was Brain's debut in an Arsenal shirt, following his arrival from Welsh club Ton Pentre, and the centre-forward would make a lasting impression on the Highbury faithful. During his eight years at Arsenal (before transferring to Spurs), Bristol-born Brain scored 139 goals, a feat since matched by Ted Drake but only bettered by Ronnie Radford, Cliff Bastin, Ian Wright and Thierry Henry.

28th February 1925

First Division
Tottenham Hotspur 2
Elkes, Dimmock
Arsenal 0
Attendance: 29,457
Tottenham Hotspur: *Hinton, Forster, McDonald, Smith, Skitt, Skinner,*

Thompson, Seed, Lane, Elkes, Dimmock.
Arsenal: *Robson, Mackie, Kennedy, Baker, Butler, John, Hoar, Neil, Brain, Blyth, Haden.*

Spurs bounced back from FA Cup disappointment two days earlier – when they lost a third-round replay against Blackburn Rovers – to register a 2-0 victory in the north London derby. Goals from Jack Elkes and Jimmy Dimmock consolidated their mid-table position, but did nothing to help Arsenal's plight near the foot of the table. Although there was a seven-point gap between them and Nottingham Forest in the relegation zone, Arsenal had come into this game on the back of five consecutive defeats. However, four wins and a draw in their remaining fixtures saw them secure their top-flight status, although it was the end of the line for manager Leslie Knighton.

29th August 1925

First Division
Arsenal 0
Tottenham Hotspur 1
Dimmock
Attendance: 53,183
Arsenal: *Robson, Mackie, Kennedy, Milne, Butler, John, Hoar, Buchan, Cock, Ramsay, Toner.*
Tottenham Hotspur: *Hinton, Clay, Forster, Skinner, Skitt, Grimsdell, Thompson, Seed, Lindsay, Handley, Dimmock.*

This game was an inauspicious start to Herbert Chapman's managerial reign at Highbury, but it did mark Charlie Buchan's Arsenal debut. The 33-year-old was signed from Sunderland for a fee of £2,000, plus £100 per goal, and went on to net 49 goals for the Gunners in 102 league appearances. Sadly for the Highbury faithful, neither Buchan nor his team-mates were able to find the back of the net in this match, and Jimmy Dimmock scored the only goal of the game 20 minutes into the second half. Both sides had plenty of chances but each defence outplayed the attackers, who seemed more content to hit the ball first time and let a team-mate chase it rather than trying to create opportunities themselves.

2nd January 1926

First Division
Tottenham Hotspur 1
Thompson
Arsenal 1
Baker
Attendance: 43,221
Tottenham Hotspur: *Hinton, Clay, Forster, B Smith, Skitt, Skinner, Thompson, Lindsay, Osborne, Handley, Dimmock.*
Arsenal: *Harper, Mackie, John, Baker, Butler, Blyth, Hoar, Buchan, Brain, Neil, Haden.*

With Arsenal pushing hard for their first ever league title, a win was imperative as they tried to keep ahead, in points, of Chapman's former club, Huddersfield Town. The pace of the game was so fast and the rivalry so keen that one reporter renamed the ground White Hot Lane. Spurs produced the more attractive football, and took an early lead when outside-right Andy Thompson opened the scoring. The second half was only 12 minutes old when the versatile Alf Baker equalized, following a free-kick. Despite moments of brilliance from Buchan and some fierce shots from Dimmock (to which Ted Harper was equal) neither side were able to add to their tally. By the end of the campaign, Arsenal registered their best ever league finish as runners-up to Huddersfield, who became the first club to win the First Division in three consecutive seasons.

18th December 1926

First Division
Arsenal 2
Butler, Brain

Tottenham Hotspur 4
Seed, Osborne 2, Handley
Attendance: 49,429
Arsenal: *Harper, Parker, John, Seddon, Butler, Blyth, Hulme, Brain, Buchan, Ramsay, Haden.*
Tottenham Hotspur: *J Smith, Clay, Forster, B Smith, Elkes, Lindsay, Thompson, Seed, Osborne, Handley, Dimmock.*

This game produced one of the fastest and cleanest local duels seen for many years. Right up to the last kick the pace was frenetic, and there could have been many more goals scored than the six that hit the back of the net. Spurs were immeasurably the better team in all departments, apart from Jimmy Smith in goal. Arsenal raced into a 2-0 lead, with goals from Jack Butler and Jimmy Brain, but then conceded four times, much to the dismay of the majority of the crowd. Jimmy Dimmock emerged as the man of the match, although Tommy Clay earned rave reviews by subduing Sammy Haden and keeping Buchan in check. Goals from Jimmy Seed and Charlie Handley, coupled with a brace from Frank Osborne, gave the visitors an emphatic 4-2 victory.

7th May 1927
First Division
Tottenham Hotspur 0
Arsenal 4
Brain 2, Tricker 2
Attendance: 29,555
Tottenham Hotspur: *Britton, Forster, Poynton, Skitt, Elkes, Grimsdell, Osborne, O'Callaghan, Sanders, Handley, Dimmock.*
Arsenal: *Moody, Parker, Kennedy, Roberts, Butler, John, Hulme, Blyth, Tricker, Brain, Peel.*

Arsenal and Spurs met at White Hart Lane, in the final match of the 1926–27 season, with nothing at stake except local bragging rights. Both sides were safely ensconced in mid-table, although

Arsenal had reached their first FA Cup final the previous month. In a one-sided game, Arsenal exacted revenge for the 4-2 defeat earlier in the season, by scoring four times without reply. Jimmy Brain and Reg Tricker both scored two goals apiece to ensure that Arsenal finished the campaign two places and two points better off than their north London rivals.

2nd January 1928

First Division

Arsenal 1

Hoar

Tottenham Hotspur 1

O'Callaghan

Attendance: 13,518

Arsenal: *Moody, Parker, Hapgood, Baker, Butler, John, Hulme, Buchan, Brain, Blyth, Hoar.*

Tottenham Hotspur: *Spiers, Forster, Richardson, Lowdell, Skitt, Grimsdell, Handley, O'Callaghan, Lindsay, Armstrong, Dimmock.*

As 1927 drew to a close, the harsh winter conditions hit the Football League programme badly, and the north London derby was just one of the many casualties. The rearranged game was played the day after New Year's Day, and a lowly crowd of just 13,518 braved the elements to watch their teams play out a draw. Spurs took the lead when Taffy O'Callaghan rounded Eddie Hapgood to net the opener, and continued to press in the second half. Their efforts came to no avail, however, after Sid Hoar equalized with a low shot that went in off the post.

7th April 1928

First Division

Tottenham Hotspur 2

O'Callaghan 2

Arsenal 0

Attendance: 39,193

Tottenham Hotspur: *Spiers, Forster, Poynton, Smith, Skitt, Grimsdell, Handley, O'Callaghan, Osborne, Sanders, Dimmock.*

Arsenal: *Lewis, Parker, John, Baker, Roberts, Blyth, Hulme, Shaw, Brain, Lambert, Hoar.*

The 1927–28 campaign turned out to be one of the most closely contested in history, and, as the season approached its finale, Spurs must have felt that they had taken a giant leap to safety with this impressive 2-0 victory over their near neighbours. Taffy O'Callaghan was by far the best player on the pitch, and it was fitting that he notched both his side's goals, to move them up to eighth in the First Division, only seven points behind leaders Everton. But with three of their last four games away from home, Spurs lost their matches against Sheffield Wednesday, Bury and Liverpool, while a draw against Burnley was not enough to secure their survival. The final league table demonstrated how close the season had been – just six points separated Derby County in fourth (on 44 points) and Spurs in 21st position (with 38).

The 1930s and 1940s

The fortunes of the two north London clubs could not have been more contrasting during the 1930s and 1940s. Herbert Chapman – one of the most successful and influential managers of the early 20th century – sowed the seeds for Arsenal to become the dominant force in English football throughout the 1930s, while Spurs spent the majority of their time in the Second Division, with only two seasons (1933–34 and 1934–35) in the top flight.

Chapman's obsession with counter-attacking football paid off when the First Division crown came to Highbury in 1930–31, but it also resulted in labels such as "Lucky Arsenal" or "Boring Arsenal" from detractors, who weren't won over by his team's style of play. It paid dividends, however, with the title-winning side scoring an incredible 127 league goals during the 42-game campaign – and Chapman was already looking to the future and to securing the first Double of the 20th century. Preston North End had achieved this by winning the FA Cup and Football League in the latter's inaugural season of 1888–89, and the feat was repeated by Aston Villa in 1897. Arsenal came close in 1931–32, being runners-up in the First Division and losing 2-1 to Newcastle United in the FA Cup final.

Arsenal reclaimed the league title the following season, although they were knocked out of the FA Cup in the third round in one of the biggest upsets of all time. Third Division North side Walsall managed to humiliate an Arsenal side that had been ravaged by injury and flu, to record a 2-0 victory that so enraged Chapman he promptly sold two of his team. Chapman then strengthened Arsenal with the addition of players such as Pat Beasley, Ray Bowden and Jimmy Dunne, and they went on to emulate Huddersfield's success by adding two more consecutive league titles (in 1933–34 and

1934–35). However, the manager did not live to see the hat-trick completed, as he contracted pneumonia and died in January 1934, at the age of 55.

But Chapman's legacy lived on under new manager George Allison, as the club claimed another FA Cup in 1936 (1-0 v Sheffield United), and the First Division title in 1937–38. Chapman had implemented great improvements at two clubs before his death, and is regarded as one of the forerunners of modern football. He was an innovative man who championed the use of floodlighting, numbered shirts and European club competitions, as well as introducing new ways of training and new tactics. As a result of his enormous contribution to football, Chapman was posthumously recognized with various honours.

Allison was a keen amateur footballer who failed to make the grade as a professional during his youth, but he did join Woolwich Arsenal as a programme editor shortly after his move to London in 1906. He stayed with the club when they moved to Highbury and were renamed Arsenal. Following the end of the First World War, Allison joined the board of directors, where he became club secretary, before taking responsibility as managing director. In the summer of 1934, he was appointed Arsenal manager following the death of Herbert Chapman, and went on to become the second longest-serving manager of the club. Allison had a hands-off approach, except with regard to relationships with the media and transfer policy, and preferred to leave the day-to-day management of the squad to Joe Shaw and Tom Whittaker. He was a well-liked manager, but many felt that he lacked deep knowledge of the game. The Second World War saw football suspended and, by the time the game resumed, many of Arsenal's more influential players (like Cliff Bastin and Ted Drake) had retired. The club was unable to repeat their prewar domination, and Allison decided to retire from his managerial position in May 1947.

Allison was succeeded by Tom Whittaker, who had resumed his coaching role at Highbury after serving as an ARP warden during the war. He was well versed in the Chapman way of doing things, having been appointed Arsenal's first-team trainer in 1927, when injury had forced a premature end to his playing career. In his first season in charge, his side won the club's sixth First Division title – seven points clear of second-placed Manchester United – while the FA Cup was also added to the trophy cabinet, as two Reg Lewis goals beat Liverpool 2-0.

Tottenham, meanwhile, appointed numerous managers during the 1930s and 1940s, who were charged with reviving the club's fortunes. Percy Smith arrived in January 1930 and enjoyed the most success, taking his side to runners-up position in the Second Division in 1932–33. Spurs built upon this by claiming second place in the First Division the following season, but ended up propping up the table in 1934–35, as their two-season stay in the top flight came to an end, with Smith paying the price for failure.

Jack Tresadern was the next to step up to the mark, but he was unable to secure a return to the First Division, and moved to Plymouth Argyle in April 1938, before the axe inevitably fell. Spurs turned to the tried and tested Peter McWilliam but – despite bringing youngsters such as Bill Nicholson through – promotion remained elusive, and the outbreak of the Second World War brought his tenure to an end. By the time peace returned, Joe Hulme was in the hot seat, and he put together a squad that would soon bring success, but not until he had gone; the board ran out of patience with the former Arsenal winger in May 1949 and appointed Arthur Rowe in his place.

Having been a regular for Spurs throughout the 1930s, until injury forced his retirement in 1939, Rowe was more than familiar with the Spurs ethos and style. The side he inherited proved more than a match for their opponents during the 1949–50 season, and they landed the Second Division title, winning 27 of their 42 games en route to promotion. At long last, the Spurs faithful had hope for the future ... and it wouldn't be long before success returned to White Hart Lane.

Record in the 1930s and 1940s

Arsenal

Season	League	P	W	D	L	F	A	Pts	Pos
1930–31	Div 1	42	28	10	4	127	59	66	1
1931–32	Div 1	42	22	10	10	90	48	54	2
1932–33	Div 1	42	25	8	9	118	61	58	1
1933–34	Div 1	42	25	9	8	75	47	59	1
1934–35	Div 1	42	23	12	7	115	46	58	1
1935–36	Div 1	42	15	15	12	78	48	45	6
1936–37	Div 1	42	18	16	8	80	49	52	3
1937–38	Div 1	42	21	10	11	77	44	52	1
1938–39	Div 1	42	19	9	14	55	41	47	5
1946–47	Div 1	42	16	9	17	72	70	41	13
1947–48	Div 1	42	23	13	6	81	32	59	1
1948–49	Div 1	42	18	13	11	74	44	49	5
1949–50	Div 1	42	19	11	12	79	55	49	6

FA Cup

1930–31	1-2 v Chelsea (Fourth Round)
1931–32	1-2 v Newcastle United (Final)
1932–33	0-2 v Walsall (Third Round)
1933–34	1-2 v Aston Villa (Sixth Round)
1934–35	1-2 v Sheffield Wednesday (Sixth Round)
1935–36	1-0 v Sheffield United (Final)
1936–37	1-3 v West Bromwich Albion (Sixth Round)
1937–38	0-1 v Preston North End (Fifth Round)
1938–39	1-2 v Chelsea (Third Round)
1945–46	0-6, 1-0 v West Ham United (Third Round over two legs)
1946–47	1-1, 1-1, 0-2 v Chelsea (Third Round)
1947–48	0-1 v Bradford Park Avenue (Third Round)
1948–49	0-1 v Derby County (Fourth Round)
1949–50	2-0 v Liverpool (Final)

Tottenham Hotspur

Season	League	P	W	D	L	F	A	Pts	Pos
1930–31	Div 2	42	22	7	13	88	55	51	3
1931–32	Div 2	42	16	11	15	87	78	43	8
1932–33	Div 2	42	20	15	7	96	51	55	2
1933–34	Div 1	42	21	7	14	79	56	49	3
1934–35	Div 1	42	10	10	22	54	93	30	22
1935–36	Div 2	42	18	13	11	91	55	49	5
1936–37	Div 2	42	17	9	16	88	66	43	10
1937–38	Div 2	42	19	6	17	76	54	44	5
1938–39	Div 2	42	19	9	14	67	62	47	8
1946–47	Div 2	42	17	14	11	65	53	48	6
1947–48	Div 2	42	15	14	13	56	43	44	8
1948–49	Div 2	42	17	16	9	72	44	50	5
1949–50	Div 2	42	27	7	8	81	35	61	1

FA Cup

1930–31   0-1 v West Bromwich Albion (Fourth Round)

1931–32   2-2, 1-3 v Sheffield Wednesday (Third Round)

1932–33   0-2 v Luton Town (Fourth Round)

1933–34   0-1 v Aston Villa (Fifth Round)

1934–35   1-1, 1-1, 0-2 v Bolton Wanderers (Fifth Round)

1935–36   1-3 v Sheffield United (Sixth Round)

1936–37   1-3 v Preston North End (Sixth Round)

1937–38   0-1 v Sunderland (Sixth Round)

1938–39   3-3, 1-1, 1-2 v West Ham United (Fourth Round)

1945–46   2-2, 0-2 v Brentford (Third Round)

1946–47   2-2, 0-1 v Stoke City (Third Round over two legs)

1947–48   1-3 v Blackpool (Semi-final)

1948–49   0-3 v Arsenal (Third Round)

1949–50   0-1 v Everton (Fifth Round)

16th September 1933

First Division

Tottenham Hotspur 1

Felton (pen)

Arsenal 1

Bowden

Attendance: 56,612

Tottenham Hotspur: *Nicholls, Felton, Whatley, T Evans, Rowe, Meads, McCormick, O'Callaghan, Hunt, G W Hall, W Evans.*

Arsenal: *Moss, Male, Hapgood, Hill, Roberts, John, Parkin, Jack, Bowden, James, Bastin.*

The first league meeting between the two north London rivals in five years was eagerly awaited by press and public alike, and the match certainly did not disappoint, with honours ending even. Both teams produced a dazzling display, but Spurs took the lead after Frank Hill was controversially adjudged to have fouled Willie Evans in the box. Billy Felton slotted the penalty home to register the only league goal of his Tottenham career, but the pace of the game was too frenetic for the home side to keep up. Following a surging run by David Jack, his shot was blocked, but the ball found its way to the unmarked Ray Bowden, who made no mistake from close range.

31st January 1934

First Division

Arsenal 1

Bastin

Tottenham Hotspur 3

W Evans 2 (1 pen), Howe

Attendance: 68,674

Arsenal: *Moss, Male, Hapgood, Jones, Roberts, John, Birkett, Bowden, Dunne, Bastin, Beasley.*

Tottenham Hotspur: *Nicholls, Felton, Whatley, Colquhoun, Rowe, Alsford, McCormick, Howe, Hunt, G W Hall, W Evans.*

Spurs visited the home of the defending First Division champions and dished out a footballing lesson in front of a record crowd. The visitors scored three times in the first half, with Willie Evans opening the scoring, courtesy of a seventh-minute penalty following Herbie Roberts' foul on George Hunt. Further goals from Les Howe, and a second from Evans, put paid to Arsenal's unbeaten home record that season, which had so far seen them win eight and draw four matches at Highbury. Although Cliff Bastin did get on the scoresheet for the home side, Joe Nicholls was in superb form between the posts to deny the opposition any chance of salvaging a draw.

20th October 1934

First Division
Arsenal 5
Beasley, T Evans (og), Drake 3
Tottenham Hotspur 1
G S Hunt
Attendance: **70,544**
Arsenal: *Moss, Male, Hapgood, Crayston, Roberts, John, Beasley, Bowden, Drake, James, Bastin.*
Tottenham Hotspur: *Nicholls, Channell, T Evans, Colquhoun, Rowe, Meads, McCormick, Howe, G S Hunt, G W Hall, W Evans.*

Arsenal gained revenge for the previous season's 3-1 home defeat with a fantastic display of attacking football in front of another record crowd. The opening half hour was full of chances at both ends, but it was Albert Beasley who netted the first goal. Arsenal's tally was doubled when Tom Evans turned an Alex James pass into his own net, and Ted Drake added a third before half-time. Drake – bought from Southampton earlier in the year for £6,500 – completed his hat-trick in the second half, while George Hunt scored a consolation goal for the visitors. Arsenal had evolved into a better side than they had been the previous year. They were superior to Spurs because of their craftsmanship and their quicker and more intelligent anticipation in both attack and defence.

6ᵗʰ March 1935

First Division
Tottenham Hotspur 0
Arsenal 6
Drake 2, Dougall, Kirchen 2, Bastin (pen)
Attendance: 47,714
Tottenham Hotspur: *Taylor, Channell, Whatley, Phypers, Howe,*
Alsford, McCormick, A G Hall, G S Hunt, D A Hunt, Burgon.
Arsenal: *Moss, Male, Compton, Crayton, Sidey, Copping, Kirchen,*
Davidson, Drake, Dougall, Bastin.

This encounter at White Hart Lane could not have been more crucial
for both sides, but for totally contrasting reasons. Spurs were deep
in relegation trouble, having failed to win a league match since
Boxing Day, while Arsenal were closing in on a third consecutive
First Division crown. It was the visitors who made the running, with
Spurs seemingly content to check the faster Arsenal side with an
offside trap and, in doing so, piling more weight on their already
overburdened shoulders. It might not have been so bad had the
home side the skill to exploit this trick – they succeeded up to a
point, then fell behind to a Ted Drake goal and yet were not able
to change tactics. Quite simply, Arsenal were a team in the fullest
sense of the word, while Spurs were a collection of individuals.
Peter Dougall and debutant Alf Kirchen made it 3-0 at the interval,
before second-half goals from Drake, Kirchen again, and a Cliff
Bastin penalty, completed the rout, to register the biggest victory
margin in a north London derby.

8ᵗʰ January 1949

FA Cup third round
Arsenal 3
McPherson, Roper, Lishman
Tottenham Hotspur 0
Attendance: 47,314
Arsenal: *Swindin, Barnes, Smith, Macaulay, L H Compton, Mercer,*

Roper, Logie, Rooke, Lishman, McPherson.
Tottenham Hotspur: *Ditchburn, Tickeridge, Buckingham, Nicholson, Woodward, Burgess, Cox, Gilberg, Rundle, Bennett, Jones.*

Despite the fact that Arsenal were a First Division side and Spurs were a tier lower in the Football League, when the two sides met for the first time in an FA Cup match, many of the visiting fans would have been hopeful of an upset – especially seeing as Spurs reached the semi-final the previous year. But a long cup run was not on the cards as the 1940s drew to a close, as winger Ian McPherson capitalized on an error by Spurs keeper Ted Ditchburn, to score with his head. Don Roper and Doug Lishman completed the scoring, while the Arsenal defence was superbly led by Leslie Compton. The newspapers blamed the dismal nature of the defeat on two things: team choice and tactics. Eddie Baily, one of Spurs' liveliest forwards, was omitted from the team, while the policy of instructing the inside-forwards to hang back and watch opposing wing-halves, Archie Macaulay and Joe Mercer, was heavily criticized.

The 1950s

The early 1950s saw Arsenal and Spurs both lay claim to the First Division title, as well as narrowly missing out on other silverware as the decade wore on. Tottenham – flying high after winning the Second Division title in 1949–50 using Arthur Rowe's "push and run" tactics, which involved making the ball do the work, with players running into space where they would be in a better position to receive a pass – went from success to success, and they finished the season as First Division champions. They ended the campaign four points ahead of second-placed Manchester United, thereby becoming the first postwar team to win back-to-back titles. The situation was reversed in 1951–52, with Matt Busby's side finishing four points ahead of runners-up Spurs, but it had been the best three years in the club's history and the fans would not have to wait as long for further success.

Buoyed by their achievements in the late 1940s, Arsenal were still one of the best teams in the country in the early part of the decade, and reached the FA Cup final in 1952, only to lose 1-0 to Newcastle United. Tom Whittaker continued to add to his collection of trophies, though, with the First Division title in 1952–53 on goal average from Preston North End. The whole club was stunned, however, when Whittaker died of a heart attack in October 1956 at the age of 58, and it was left to his assistant Jack Crayston to pick up the pieces.

Born in Grange-over-Sands in October 1910, Crayston was signed by Arsenal manager George Allison for a fee of £5,250 from Bradford Park Avenue in May 1934, and was an integral member of the 1934–35 title-winning team. The talented Crayston went on to win his first international cap for England in a 3-0 win against Germany in December 1935. Following the war, Crayston returned to Arsenal as a member of the coaching staff, and became assistant manager to Whittaker in June 1947. Crayston's reign lasted less than two years, as he resigned in May 1958 following a disappointing bottom half of the table finish, and was replaced by George Swindin.

Ill-health plagued the end of Arthur Rowe's time as manager, and he was eventually replaced in July 1955 by Jimmy Anderson, who had spent many years at Tottenham Hotspur as a member of the ground staff before he took up the reins as manager. He was well placed for the role, having worked as acting manager during the latter part of Rowe's reign. For three years, Anderson battled to bring the directors and supporters a First Division title – with the closest he came being runners-up in 1956–57 – but ill-health and an extremely public falling out with captain Danny Blanchflower put him under increasing pressure, and he retired from the club in October 1958. His decision to retire, it is believed by many, was further influenced by the up-and-coming Bill Nicholson, who progressed from player to manager and was seen as Rowe's chosen successor. During the three years that Anderson managed Spurs, Nicholson developed as a first-team coach, and was renowned for his influence both on and off the pitch. Appointed in October 1958, the same year that the use of substitutes was introduced, Nicholson's time was coming ...

His counterpart in north London was George Swindin. The former Arsenal goalkeeper took the club to third place in the First Division at the first attempt, but then mid-table mediocrity set in, despite the addition of players such as George Eastham and Tommy Docherty to the Highbury ranks.

Record in the 1950s

Arsenal

Season	League	P	W	D	L	F	A	Pts	Pos
1950–51	Div 1	42	19	9	14	73	56	47	5
1951–52	Div 1	42	21	11	10	80	61	53	3
1952–53	Div 1	42	21	12	9	97	64	54	1
1953–54	Div 1	42	15	13	14	75	73	43	12
1954–55	Div 1	42	17	9	16	69	63	43	9
1955–56	Div 1	42	18	10	14	60	61	46	5
1956–57	Div 1	42	21	8	13	85	69	50	5
1957–58	Div 1	42	16	7	19	73	85	39	12
1958–59	Div 1	42	21	8	13	88	68	50	3
1959–60	Div 1	42	15	9	18	68	80	39	13

FA Cup

1950–51	0-1 v Manchester United (Fifth Round)
1951–52	0-1 v Newcastle United (Final)
1952–53	1-2 v Blackpool (Sixth Round)
1953–54	1-2 v Norwich City (Fourth Round)
1954–55	0-1 v Wolverhampton Wanderers (Fourth Round)
1955–56	1-3 v Birmingham City (Sixth Round)
1956–57	2-2, 1-2 v West Bromwich Albion (Sixth Round)
1957–58	1-3 v Northampton Town (Third Round)
1958–59	2-2, 0-3 v Sheffield United (Fifth Round)
1959–60	2-2, 1-1, 0-2 v Rotherham United (Third Round)

Tottenham Hotspur

Season	League	P	W	D	L	F	A	Pts	Pos
1950–51	Div 1	42	25	10	7	82	44	60	1
1951–52	Div 1	42	22	9	11	76	51	53	2
1952–53	Div 1	42	15	11	16	78	69	41	10
1953–54	Div 1	42	16	5	21	65	76	37	16
1954–55	Div 1	42	16	8	18	72	73	40	16
1955–56	Div 1	42	15	7	20	61	71	37	18

1956–57	Div 1	42	22	12	8	104	56	56	2
1957–58	Div 1	42	21	9	12	93	77	51	3
1958–59	Div 1	42	13	10	19	85	95	36	18
1959–60	Div 1	42	21	11	10	86	50	53	3

FA Cup

1950–51	0-2 v Huddersfield Town (Third Round)
1951–52	0-3 v Newcastle United (Fourth Round)
1952–53	1-2 v Blackpool (Semi-final)
1953–54	0-3 v West Bromwich Albion (Sixth Round)
1954–55	1-3 v York City (Fifth Round)
1955–56	0-1 v Manchester City (Semi-final)
1956–57	1-3 v AFC Bournemouth (Fifth Round)
1957–58	0-3 v Sheffield United (Fourth Round)
1958–59	1-1, 0-1 v Norwich City (Fifth Round)
1959–60	1-3 v Blackburn Rovers (Fifth Round)

26ᵗʰ August 1950

First Division

Arsenal 2

Roper, Barnes (pen)

Tottenham Hotspur 2

Burgess, Walters

Attendance: 64,500

Arsenal: *Swindin, Barnes, Smith, Shaw, Compton, Mercer, Cox, Logie, Goring, Lishman, Roper.*

Tottenham Hotspur: *Ditchburn, Ramsey, Willis, Nicholson, Clarke, Burgess, Walters, Murphy, Duquemin, Baily, Medley.*

Elementary justice was fought and won a battle with outrageous fortune at Highbury to ensure that there should not be a loser in the great London clash between Arsenal and Spurs. The 2-2 draw was an eminently fair result to a tough but good-tempered game, bristling with thrills. Spurs' artistic use of the quick, short pass – with Baily as chief purveyor – had the Arsenal defence at full stretch in the opening stages. Then the stiff breeze which had been their ally played them false. A freak goal gave Arsenal an undeserved lead, when Don Roper swung over a speculative lobbed centre. Ted Ditchburn expected the ball to sail wide but a capricious gust of wind carried it under the bar. Far from being daunted, Spurs hit back, and Alf Ramsey placed a long free-kick perfectly for Ron Burgess to head home off a post. Arsenal struck their cup final form after the interval and, exploiting the long passing game, would have been a couple of goals ahead had Ditchburn not redeemed his earlier lapse. Then, what appeared to be a clear case of handball by Peter Murphy gave Spurs the lead, as their young inside-right – who had been blotted out by Joe Mercer – seemed to pull a Compton clearance down with his hand. The ball ran to Les Medley, and Sonny Walters side-footed the centre past George Swindin. It was Arsenal's turn to fight against adversity and, when Bill Nicholson fouled Doug Lishman 11 minutes from the end, Wally Barnes went through the formality of putting the ball on the spot with his hands, and into the back of the net with his foot. It was fitting that the scorers should include those two great Welsh ornaments of the game – Wally Barnes and Ron Burgess. Both contributed outstanding displays of polished craft to a game in which skill was not completely sacrificed to speed.

23rd December 1950

First Division
Tottenham Hotspur 1
Baily
Arsenal 0
Attendance: 54,898
Tottenham Hotspur: *Ditchburn, Ramsey, Willis, Nicholson, Clarke, Burgess, Walters, Bennett, Duquemin, Baily, Medley.*
Arsenal: *Swindin, Scott, Barnes, Forbes, Compton, Mercer, McPherson, Logie, Goring, Lishman, Cox.*

This Yuletide match between the two north London rivals was eagerly anticipated, with both clubs riding high in the table and vying for the title. Arsenal – who had occupied the top spot since 7th October – had slipped up at home to Burnley the previous week, and allowed Middlesbrough to leapfrog them. Lionel Smith missed out through injury, and was replaced by Laurie Scott, who partnered Wally Barnes at full-back, while Fred Cox, the former Spurs winger, was included in the Arsenal attack. In front of a crowd of almost 55,000, Eddie Baily scored the only goal of the game, to dash any hopes the visitors might have had of returning to the top of the table. In fact, with two defeats at the hands of Stoke City on Christmas Day and Boxing Day, Arsenal's form in December was extremely poor, as they only had one point to show from six matches.

29th September 1951

First Division
Arsenal 1
Holton
Tottenham Hotspur 1
Murphy
Attendance: **72,164**
Arsenal: *Swindin, Barnes, Smith, Forbes, Daniel, Mercer, Milton, Logie, Holton, Lishman, Cox.*
Tottenham Hotspur: *Ditchburn, Ramsey, Willis, Nicholson, Clarke, Burgess, Walters, Murphy, McClellan, Harmer, Medley.*

Tottenham's confidence was riding high when they visited Highbury in September 1951. Not only had they taken three out of a possible four points from the previous season's two league matches, but they had clinched their first First Division crown in May 1951. A postwar record attendance of 72,164 crammed into Highbury to see whether the defending champions could be brought to their knees. In the end, neither side was to be rewarded with a victory, as goals from Cliff Holton and Peter Murphy cancelled each other out.

9th February 1952

First Division

Tottenham Hotspur 1

Walters

Arsenal 2

Roper, Forbes

Attendance: **66,438**

Tottenham Hotspur: *Ditchburn, Ramsey, Withers, Nicholson, Clarke, Burgess, Walters, Baily, Duquemin, Harmer, Medley.*

Arsenal: *Swindin, Barnes, Smith, Forbes, Daniel, Mercer, Cox, Logie, Lewis, Lishman, Roper.*

Tottenham's defence of their First Division title faltered as 1951 came to a close and the new year began. This match proved to be their eighth defeat in the last 13 games, with only 11 points taken from a possible 26. A lone strike from Sonny Walters was not enough to secure any points, as two goals from Don Roper and Alex Forbes gave Arsenal their first victory at White Hart Lane since March 1935. Spurs again found more consistent form in the aftermath of this game, and went on an unbeaten run that extended until the end of the season. However, this wasn't enough to prevent Manchester United from winning the league by four points.

20th September 1952

First Division

Tottenham Hotspur 1

Harmer

Arsenal 3

Goring, Milton, Logie

Attendance: **69,247**

Tottenham Hotspur: *Ditchburn, Ramsey, Willis, Nicholson, Clarke, Burgess, Medley, Harmer, Duquemin, Baily, Robb.*

Arsenal: *Platt, Chenhall, Smith, Shaw, Daniel, Forbes, Milton, Logie, Goring, Lishman, Roper.*

With Jimmy Logie and Arthur Milton, Arsenal were all speed, determination and ruthless action towards goal, and on a mellow, Indian-summer afternoon before a vast crowd of nearly 70,000, Tottenham's 3-1 defeat was definite and complete. Spurs were not allowed to get started, and dependable players such as Bill Nicholson and Ron Burgess were being harried, harassed and overburdened with salvage work. Arsenal showed how to score goals without playing football when Logie snapped up a poor clearance and crossed for Peter Goring, to score rather typically with his knee. Arthur Milton then collected a ball around the halfway line and, with a shrug of his shoulders, was through the Spurs defence for an electrifying individual goal. In the second half, right-back John Chenhall made a long clearance out to Goring on the left wing. His quick pass found a semi-fit Logie in the middle of the pitch who, with the last of his strength, sent the ball past the flailing Ted Ditchburn. Tommy Harmer's snapped goal from 20 yards proved no inspiration to a Tottenham team that was well beaten, and they knew it.

7th February 1953

First Division

Arsenal 4

Holton 2, Lishman, Logie

Tottenham Hotspur 0

Attendance: **69,051**

Arsenal: *Kelsey, Wade, Smith, Forbes, Daniel, Mercer, Milton, Logie, Holton, Lishman, Roper.*

Tottenham Hotspur: *Ditchburn, Ramsey, Willis, Nicholson, Clarke, Brittan, Walters, Bennett, Duquemin, Baily, Medley.*

Many felt that Spurs had become slaves to their own style by the time the two sides met in February 1953. It looked good and, given the run of the ball, they were an effective and attractive side, but this match at Highbury proved once more that when the opposition was really resolute the system broke down and Spurs seemed to have nothing to replace it. While Cliff Holton scored twice and Doug Lishman added another, the goal which crowned Arsenal's high-powered display was a perfect example of their flair for turning cool defence into profitable attack. Goalkeeper Jack Kelsey flung the ball to Don Roper, who swung it across for Arthur Milton to provide a quick run and centre to Jimmy Logie, resulting in a goal.

10th October 1953

First Division
Tottenham Hotspur 1
Robb
Arsenal 4
Logie 2, Milton, Forbes
Attendance: **69,821**
Tottenham Hotspur: *Ditchburn, Ramsey, Withers, Nicholson, Clarke, Wetton, Walters, Bennett, Duquemin, Harmer, Robb.*
Arsenal: *Kelsey, Wills, Evans, Forbes, Dodgin, Mercer, Milton, Logie, Lawton, Lishman, Roper.*

With Arsenal having lost six out of their first eight games, it was the home side who took the field for this match with the better form, but the result did not favour them on the day. Spurs were easily beaten, with Jimmy Logie again proving a major thorn in Tottenham's side. Spurs supporters who saw Len Wills make an impressive debut as Arsenal's right-back against their team, were probably wondering how he ended up at Highbury instead of White Hart Lane. Wills was born in Hackney, the home town of many Spurs players. He used to play for Eton Manor, the amateur club coached by Alf Ramsey, but managed by former Arsenal player Len Thompson, who had advised the youngster to try his luck at Highbury.

27th February 1954

First Division
Arsenal 0
Tottenham Hotspur 3
Walters, Robb 2
Attendance: 64,311
Arsenal: *Kelsey, Wills, Barnes, Forbes, Dodgin, Mercer, Walsh, Logie, Holton, Lishman, Roper.*
Tottenham Hotspur: *Ditchburn, Ramsey, Willis, Marchi, Clarke, Wetton, Walters, Bennett, Dunmore, Baily, Robb.*

Spurs had not enjoyed much success against Arsenal in recent years, and fans would have had to cast their minds back to December 1950 to remember the last time that their club emerged victorious from a north London derby. But it was even further back, in January 1934, that Spurs had last won at the home of their old foes, while the last time that Arsenal had failed to score in the corresponding fixture was in August 1925. In February 1954, however, Spurs did manage to keep a clean sheet, and scored three times without reply. A Sonny Walters goal and a brace from George Robb was enough to send the White Hart Lane faithful home in a jubilant mood.

4th September 1954

First Division
Arsenal 2
Logie, Lishman
Tottenham Hotspur 0
Attendance: 53,977
Arsenal: *Kelsey, Wills, Barnes, Goring, Forbes, Bowen, Tapscott, Logie, Lawton, Lishman, Roper.*
Tottenham Hotspur: *Ditchburn, Ramsey, Withers, Wetton, Clarke, Brittan, Walters, Bennett, Dunmore, Baily, Robb.*

Unusually for a north London derby, both teams arrived for this game in poor form. The hosts had lost their first three games of the new season, before registering a 2-0 win at home to Everton, while their opponents had won two and lost two of their opening four matches. Arsenal inevitably raised their game for the clash with their neighbours, and emerged with their confidence boosted and a well-earned win, with goals from Jimmy Logie and Doug Lishman. Many eyes, however, were on the Gunners' upcoming friendly against Moscow Dynamo, which the Russians won 5-0.

15th January 1955

First Division
Tottenham Hotspur 0
Arsenal 1
Lawton
Attendance: 36,263
Tottenham Hotspur: *Reynolds, Ramsey, Hopkins, Blanchflower, Clarke, Marchi, Gavin, Baily, Dunmore, Brooks, Robb.*
Arsenal: *Kelsey, Barnes, Evans, Goring, Fotheringham, Bowen, Milton, Tapscott, Lawton, Lishman, Holton.*

Despite Spurs' centre-half Harry Clarke playing a blinder, and restricting Tommy Lawton to one real scoring chance, he ended up on the losing side as Arsenal did the double over their neighbours. Clarke was forced to climb to get to Cliff Holton's centre, but was unable to get enough on the ball to decisively clear the danger. The ball fell to Doug Lishman, who nodded it forward to give Lawton an unmissable chance. He quickly pivoted and sent a crisp shot flying past Ron Reynolds, to make the score 1-0 to Arsenal ... Spurs manager Arthur Rowe bemoaned the fact that "our approach play is as good as it was in our best days, but we're just not hitting that net".

10th September 1955

First Division
Tottenham Hotspur 3
Stokes 2, Baily
Arsenal 1
Roper
Attendance: 51,029
Tottenham Hotspur: *Ditchburn, Withers, Hopkins, Blanchflower, Clarke, Marchi, Walters, Brooks, Stokes, Baily, Robb.*
Arsenal: *Kelsey, Barnes, Evans, Goring, Fotheringham, Bowen, Clapton, Tapscott, Lawton, Roper, Walsh.*

The 1955–56 campaign got off to a dreadful start for Spurs, with one draw and five defeats in their first six matches, but they raised their game for Arsenal's visit, to record their first victory of the season. The Gunners hadn't fared much better in their opening matches, with one win, three draws and two defeats over the same period, and wouldn't register their next victory until 1st October, with a 1-0 win at home to Aston Villa. Two goals from Alfie Stokes and one from Eddie Baily – in what would prove to be his last north London derby match as the popular forward was sold to Port Vale in January 1956 for a fee of £7,000 – were enough to secure the points for Spurs, with Don Roper's reply really just a consolation effort.

14th January 1956

First Division
Arsenal 0
Tottenham Hotspur 1
Robb
Attendance: 60,606
Arsenal: *Kelsey, Wills, Evans, Forbes, Fotheringham, Holton, Clapton, Tapscott, Groves, Bloomfield, Nutt.*
Tottenham Hotspur: *Reynolds, Norman, Hopkins, Blanchflower, Clarke, Marchi, Dulin, Brooks, Duquemin, Smith, Robb.*

It had taken nearly half a century but Spurs finally recorded the double over Arsenal in the 1955–56 season. Arsenal welcomed Alex Forbes back to the fray, after a 10-month layoff that included a cartilage operation, and brought in Danny Clapton on the right wing and Gordon Nutt on the left, following injuries to Peter Goring and Mike Tiddy during the previous Thursday's FA Cup replay at Bedford Town. It was Spurs, though, who claimed the points and the kudos, with George Robb scoring the only goal of the game, to give them their 12th league win of the season.

20th October 1956

First Division
Arsenal 3
Herd 2, Haverty
Tottenham Hotspur 1
Smith
Attendance: 60,580
Arsenal: *Sullivan, Charlton, Evans, Wills, Dodgin, Holton, Clapton, Tapscott, Herd, Bloomfield, Haverty.*
Tottenham Hotspur: *Ditchburn, Baker, Henry, Blanchflower, Clarke, Marchi, Dulin, Harmer, Smith, Stokes, Robb.*

The form books were turned on their head by the end of this match. Spurs had arrived on the back of six straight league wins, while Arsenal had lost six of their first 13 games, but it was the home side who had the last laugh. Signed from Stockport County for £10,000 in 1954, David Herd bagged two goals as he established himself in the first team; he went on to be the club's top scorer for the next four seasons. Joe Haverty was the scorer of the other Arsenal goal, while Bobby Smith notched Spurs' only response.

13th March 1957

First Division
Tottenham Hotspur 1
Medwin

Arsenal 3
Bowen 2, Tapscott
Attendance: **64,555**
Tottenham Hotspur: *Reynolds, Baker, Norman, Blanchflower, Ryden, Marchi, Medwin, Harmer, Smith, Brooks, Robb.*
Arsenal: *Kelsey, Wills, Evans, Holton, Dodgin, Bowen, Clapton, Tapscott, Herd, Bloomfield, Haverty.*

On the run of play Arsenal hardly deserved one point from this match, but on their opportunism they deserved both. The Spurs forwards thrilled the crowd – a record attendance for a floodlit match at White Hart Lane – with fast and intricate movements, prompted by the genius of Tommy Harmer. Yet Arsenal held out against the opening storm until Terry Medwin popped up on the left and smashed in a great shot. Arsenal's answer was an out-of-the-blue goal from left-half Dave Bowen, who equalized with a dipping drive from 35 yards. His goal meant that every Arsenal player, apart from goalkeeper Jack Kelsey, had now scored at some point that season. Two minutes into the second half, Spurs' left-back, Peter Baker, gave the ball straight to Derek Tapscott with a misguided backpass, and the inside-right made it 2-1. Spurs recovered their poise and searched for an equalizer, until Bowen robbed Harmer, glanced up and found the back of the net with a 25-yard piledriver. The sad news for Arsenal was that this win over their neighbours came on the same day that former manager George Allison died, following a heart attack at the age of 73.

12th October 1957

First Division
Tottenham Hotspur 3
Medwin 2, Smith
Arsenal 1
Holton
Attendance: **60,671**
Tottenham Hotspur: *Ditchburn, Baker, Hopkins, Blanchflower, Ryden,*

Iley, Medwin, Harmer, Smith, Stokes, Brooks.
Arsenal: *Kelsey, Charlton, Evans, Holton, Dodgin, Bowen, Tapscott, Groves, Herd, Bloomfield, Tiddy.*

The big news in the run-up to this match was the return of Ted Ditchburn between the posts for Spurs. The 36-year-old former England keeper had seriously thought of retiring and devoting all his time to his flourishing grocery business, after he had lost his place as first choice following the 4-3 home defeat against Chelsea the previous February. However, he replaced Ron Reynolds in a Spurs defence that had leaked more goals than any other First Division side so far that season. The tactic worked, with Spurs running out 3-1 winners, with goals from Terry Medwin (2) and Bobby Smith.

22nd February 1958

First Division
Arsenal 4
Henry (og), Clapton, Herd, Nutt
Tottenham Hotspur 4
Smith 2, Harmer 2 (1 pen)
Attendance: **59,116**
Arsenal: *Kelsey, Charlton, Evans, Ward, Fotheringham, Petts, Clapton, Groves, Herd, Bloomfield, Nutt.*
Tottenham Hotspur: *Ditchburn, Hills, Henry, Blanchflower, Norman, Ryden, Medwin, Harmer, Smith, Brooks, Jones.*

Cliff Jones, Spurs' recent signing from Swansea Town, looked like a kid who was anxious to get himself into a game with the big chaps in the park when he made his debut in the February 1958 derby match. In the rain, sleet and snow which swirled around Highbury, the Welsh left-winger had only a few chances to show the form that had persuaded Bill Nicholson to part with £35,000. At times he was an onlooker, trying to figure out what he should do and where he should be, but there were flashes of brilliance that were enough to show that – on better pitches and with time to gain more understanding – Jones was going to be the crowd-pulling match-winner that Spurs anticipated. Meanwhile, eight goals generally means a thrilling game, but they didn't make this a great one. Arsenal's attack was so bad when it came to shooting that one reporter suggested that they all be sent to Whale Island … the Royal Navy Gunnery School! They should have had the match won by half-time but both sides scored unorthodox goals. A long high cross from Arsenal's left-winger Gordon Nutt found its way into the net off the head of the Spurs left-back Ron Henry. Bobby Smith equalized at the second attempt, after his first shot had been blocked by Jack Kelsey, before outside-right Danny Clapton put Arsenal in front again after two incredible misses. Spurs fought back when inside-right Tommy Harmer extracted the ball from a desperate mass of players and popped it into the net while everyone else was wondering where it had gone. Arsenal then took a 4-2 lead through Nutt and David Herd, which looked to have settled the match in the home side's favour, but Spurs had other ideas. Arsenal left-back Dennis Evans needlessly tried to intercept a cross from Johnny Brooks, and gave away a penalty for handball, which Harmer coolly put away. Just one minute later, the scores came level once again when Smith timed a shot to perfection, which gently rolled through the slush to curl just inside the far post.

13th September 1958

First Division
Arsenal 3
Nutt, Herd 2
Tottenham Hotspur 1
Clayton
Attendance: **65,565**
Arsenal: *Kelsey, Wills, Evans, Ward, Dodgin, Docherty, Clapton, Groves, Herd, Bloomfield, Nutt.*
Tottenham Hotspur: *Hollowbread, Baker, Hopkins, Blanchflower, Norman, Iley, Medwin, Harmer, Smith, Clayton, Robb.*

Despite crushing their rivals 3-1, manager George Swindin was still not satisfied, although he was delighted that Arsenal headed the First Division table. Less than one year previously, his team had been almost hopelessly struggling, but Swindin had inspired them to play "delightful soccer" ... and play it flat out for 90 minutes. The only addition to the side was Tommy Docherty, bought from Preston for £28,000 in August 1958. David Herd struck two spectacular goals that John Hollowbread in the Spurs goalmouth hardly saw, while Gordon Nutt added to the side's tally. Meanwhile, Eddie Clayton netted the visitors' goal for a Spurs side that seemed to be completely lacking in confidence.

31ˢᵗ January 1959

First Division
Tottenham Hotspur 1
Smith
Arsenal 4
Groves, Herd, Henderson 2
Attendance: **60,241**
Tottenham Hotspur: *Hollowbread, Baker, Hopkins, Dodge, Norman, Iley, Brooks, Harmer, Smith, Dunmore, Jones.*
Arsenal: *Kelsey, Wills, Evans, Docherty, Dodgin, Bowen, Clapton, Groves, Herd, Julians, Henderson.*

Tommy Docherty produced a spectacular display in what would be his last match before starting a 14-day suspension. The Scottish right-half linked with skipper Dave Bowen on the left to take an iron grip on the game and drive their own forwards on to victory at White Hart Lane. Arsenal's brilliant display mesmerized Spurs, and only the sending off of Len Julians in the second half marred a near perfect performance. Only an occasional burst by centre-forward Bobby Smith or speedy left-winger Cliff Jones ever promised any joy for Spurs, and when the former scored his side's only goal two minutes from time, it was far too late to inspire a comeback. Arsenal had ripped in four by then, the first three inside half an hour.

Inside-right Vic Groves got the first when John Hollowbread failed to hold a fast, hard cross sent over by David Herd. Dave Bowen began the second deep in his own half, a brilliant move carried on by Julians and Groves to give Herd a clear run on goal. Outside-left Jackie Henderson scored the visitors' two other goals and he definitely deserved them. He did the work of two men, roaming from wing to wing after Julians' dismissal and after Herd was injured by pulling a thigh muscle.

5th September 1959

First Division
Arsenal 1
Barnwell
Tottenham Hotspur 1
Medwin
Attendance: 61,011
Arsenal: *Standen, Wills, McCullough, Charles, Dodgin, Docherty, Clapton, Barnwell, Herd, Bloomfield, Haverty.*
Tottenham Hotspur: *Brown, Baker, Hopkins, Blanchflower, Norman, Marchi, Medwin, Harmer, R Smith, Dunmore, Jones.*

The headlines after this match claimed "Mel scores great goal that wasn't"; it was a game that left Spurs still unbeaten that season, with Arsenal chasing their first home win. It was a torrid game played in the hot sun that could easily have been a 10-4 special either way. Arsenal would have won, in fact, had it not been for one of several strange decisions given by referee Les Tirebuck. Mel Charles hit home a brilliant free-kick from outside the edge of the penalty area in the 22nd minute but it was disallowed. Although no one would give any official statement afterwards, news filtered through that the referee had done so because he personally was not ready for the kick to be taken. Seven minutes later and Spurs had the lead through outside-right Terry Medwin, although John Standen worked wonders at keeping the score to 1-0. The visitors' best player was Bill Brown, although the goalkeeper was beaten by a drive from inside-right John Barnwell in the first minute of the second half.

16th January 1960

First Division
Tottenham Hotspur 3
R Smith, Allen 2
Arsenal 0
Attendance: 58,962
Tottenham Hotspur: *Brown, Baker, Henry, Blanchflower, Norman, Mackay, White, Harmer, R Smith, Allen, Jones.*
Arsenal: *Standen, Magill, Evans, Wills, Snedden, Barwell, Clapton, Herd, Julians, Bloomfield, Haverty.*

While Tottenham were riding high in the table, enjoying a purple patch that had only seen them beaten four times so far that season, Arsenal were struggling to find any consistency, having won just three times in the league since the end of September. But it didn't get any better for the Gunners, as Bobby Smith and Les Allen (with two goals) piled on the misery. Arsenal keeper Jim Standen – who had deputized for the injured Jack Kelsey during the 1958–59 season – was unable to prevent the opposition from scoring. He would leave for Luton Town the following October, having made just 35 league appearances for the club since joining in 1953.

The 1960s

The 1960s brought even more avenues for success with the introduction of the League Cup in time for the 1960–61 season (although many of the bigger clubs elected not to compete initially), and the growing popularity of European competition. While Tottenham fans had been forced to watch as their north London rivals conquered all in the 1930s, the 1960s saw a reversal of fortunes, with the White Hart Lane club making the headlines. Under the stewardship of Bill Nicholson, the 1960s would prove an extremely rewarding decade for Spurs.

Ironically, given the proliferation of football on television in the 21st century, the debate about live football was raging furiously in September 1960, with Spurs directors deciding not to allow their match against Aston Villa on 24th September to be broadcast until the league had called an extraordinary general meeting to discuss the issue. Wolves, West Brom, Villa and Birmingham had already announced that they would not take part in televised matches played on Saturdays, so the league were hoping to switch as many of their televised matches as they could to a Friday night, in order to save the £150,000 deal.

Spurs sprinted out of the blocks with victories in their first 11 league games and, by the end of the league campaign, they scored 115 goals in their 42 games to bring the First Division title back to north London. They also fought their way through to the FA Cup final, where goals from Bobby Smith and Terry Dyson earned them a 2-0 win over Leicester City, thereby making them the first team to achieve the Double in the 20th century. Smith was again on target in the following season's FA Cup final, along with Jimmy Greaves and Danny Blanchflower, as Spurs swept aside the challenge of Burnley in May 1962.

Arsenal had been forced to change their manager when George

Swindin resigned the same month – and they brought in Billy Wright. The former Wolves and England legend led his side to seventh place in the First Division in 1962–63 (as Spurs finished runners-up to Everton), a position that brought European qualification for the following season, although they only progressed to the second round of the Inter-Cities Fairs Cup, where they lost 4-2 on aggregate to FC Liège. Wright also brought players of the calibre of Bob Wilson and Frank McLintock to the club, both of whom would prove to be loyal servants.

Spurs, meanwhile, had already begun their European adventure, with a run to the semi-final of the European Cup in 1961–62 that was ended by Benfica. Their second foray into European waters culminated in them meeting Atlético Madrid in Rotterdam in May 1963. Goals from Jimmy Greaves (2), John White and Terry Dyson (2) gave Spurs a 5-1 win in the final of the European Cup Winners' Cup, and earned the club the distinction of being the first British club to win a major European trophy. Spurs continued pressing in a bid to bring more silverware to White Hart Lane, but the best they could achieve in the league was third in 1966–67. The same season, however, they reached the final of the FA Cup, where goals from Jimmy Robertson and Frank Saul saw off the challenge of Chelsea.

With the Arsenal board watching enviously as their neighbour's trophy cabinet was filling up, Billy Wright found himself sacked in the summer of 1966 and replaced by Bertie Mee, who had been employed as the club's physiotherapist since 1960. It was a strange move, but Mee enlisted the help of Dave Sexton and Don Howe, and the club's fortunes took an almost immediate upturn. They reached the final of the League Cup in 1968 (losing 1-0 to Leeds United) and 1969 (losing 3-1 to Swindon Town), before ending on a high with victory in the Inter-Cities Fairs Cup. Trailing to a first-leg 3-1 deficit, goals from Eddie Kelly, John Radford and Jon Sammels earned the Gunners a 4-3 aggregate win over Anderlecht, and their first European trophy.

Record in the 1960s

Arsenal

Season	League	P	W	D	L	F	A	Pts	Pos
1960–61	Div 1	42	15	11	16	77	85	41	11
1961–62	Div 1	42	16	11	15	71	72	43	10
1962–63	Div 1	42	18	10	14	86	77	46	7
1963–64	Div 1	42	17	11	14	90	82	45	8
1964–65	Div 1	42	17	7	18	69	75	41	13
1965–66	Div 1	42	12	13	17	62	75	37	14
1966–67	Div 1	42	16	14	12	58	47	46	7
1967–68	Div 1	42	17	10	15	60	56	44	9
1968–69	Div 1	42	22	12	8	56	27	56	4
1969–70	Div 1	42	12	18	12	51	49	42	12

FA Cup

1960–61	1-2 v Sunderland (Third Round)
1961–62	0-1 v Manchester United (Fourth Round)
1962–63	1-2 v Liverpool (Fifth Round)
1963–64	0-1 v Liverpool (Fifth Round)
1964–65	1-2 v Peterborough United (Fourth Round)
1965–66	0-3 v Blackburn Rovers (Third Round)
1966–67	0-1 v Birmingham City (Fifth Round)
1967–68	1-1, 1-2 v Birmingham City (Fifth Round)
1968–69	0-1 v West Bromwich Albion (Fifth Round)
1969–70	1-1, 2-3 v Blackpool (Third Round)

League Cup

1960–61	Did not enter
1961–62	Did not enter
1962–63	Did not enter
1963–64	Did not enter
1964–65	Did not enter
1965–66	Did not enter
1966–67	1-3 v West Ham United (Third Round)

1967–68   0-1 v Leeds United (Final)
1968–69   1-3 v Swindon Town (Final)
1969–70   0-0, 0-1 v Everton (Third Round)

Europe

1960–61   Did not qualify
1961–62   Did not qualify
1962–63   Did not qualify
1963–64   Inter-Cities Fairs Cup: 1-1, 1-3 v FC Liège (Second Round)
1964–65   Did not qualify
1965–66   Did not qualify
1966–67   Did not qualify
1967–68   Did not qualify
1968–69   Did not qualify
1969–70   Inter-Cities Fairs Cup: 1-3, 3-0 v Anderlecht (Final)

Tottenham Hotspur

Season	League	P	W	D	L	F	A	Pts	Pos
1960–61	Div 1	42	31	4	7	115	55	66	1
1961–62	Div 1	42	21	10	11	88	69	52	3
1962–63	Div 1	42	23	9	10	111	62	55	2
1963–64	Div 1	42	22	7	13	97	81	51	4
1964–65	Div 1	42	19	7	16	87	71	45	6
1965–66	Div 1	42	16	12	14	75	66	44	8
1966–67	Div 1	42	24	8	19	71	48	56	3
1967–68	Div 1	42	19	9	14	70	59	47	7
1968–69	Div 1	42	14	17	11	61	51	45	6
1969–70	Div 1	42	17	9	16	54	55	43	11

FA Cup

1960–61   2-0 v Leicester City (Final)
1961–62   3-1 v Burnley (Final)
1962–63   0-3 v Burnley (Third Round)
1963–64   1-1, 0-2 v Chelsea (Third Round)
1964–65   0-1 v Chelsea (Fifth Round)

1965–66	1-2 v Preston North End (Fifth Round)
1966–67	2-1 v Chelsea (Final)
1967–68	1-1, 1-2 v Liverpool (Fifth Round)
1968–69	0-1 v Manchester City (Sixth Round)
1969–70	0-0, 0-1 v Crystal Palace (Fourth Round)

League Cup

1960–61	Did not enter
1961–62	Did not enter
1962–63	Did not enter
1963–64	Did not enter
1964–65	Did not enter
1965–66	Did not enter
1966–67	0-1 v West Ham United (Second Round)
1967–68	Did not enter
1968–69	0-1, 1-1 v Arsenal (Semi-final)
1969–70	0-1 v Wolverhampton Wanderers (Second Round)

Europe

1960–61	Did not qualify
1961–62	European Cup: 1-3, 2-1 v Benfica (Semi-final)
1962–63	European Cup Winners' Cup: 5-1 v Atlético Madrid (Final)
1963–64	European Cup Winners' Cup: 2-0, 1-4 v Manchester United (First Round)
1964–65	Did not qualify
1965–66	Did not qualify
1966–67	Did not qualify
1967–68	European Cup Winners' Cup: 0-1, 4-3 v Lyon (Second Round)
1968–69	Did not qualify
1969–70	Did not qualify

10th September 1960

First Division

Arsenal 2

Herd, Ward

Tottenham Hotspur 3

Saul, Dyson, Allen

Attendance: **60,088**

Arsenal: *Kelsey, Wills, McCullough, Ward, Snedden, Docherty, Clapton, Bloomfield, Herd, Kane, Henderson.*

Tottenham Hotspur: *Brown, Baker, Henry, Blanchflower, Norman, Mackay, Medwin, White, Saul, Allen, Dyson.*

Spurs were on a roll and had begun the season with six consecutive wins, but the build-up to this game centred around the absence of two Spurs players. Winger Cliff Jones had passed a fitness test the previous day but was given a trial run with the reserves rather than coming straight back into the first team. Centre-forward Bobby Smith was still missing through injury, and 17-year-old Frank Saul – in what would be just his second game – was named as his replacement. Arsenal manager George Swindin delayed naming his line-up until the day itself, when he could check the condition of the pitch, and eventually included Danny Clapton at outside-right. Inevitably, it was Saul who struck first after 12 minutes, and then set up Terry Dyson for the visitors' second. David Herd and Gerry Ward equalized for the Gunners before Les Allen latched on to a pass from Danny Blanchflower, with 20 minutes to go, and lobbed Jack Kelsey to claim the victory that kept up an unbeaten streak, which continued until mid-November.

21st January 1961

First Division

Tottenham Hotspur 4

Allen 2, Blanchflower (pen), R Smith

Arsenal 2
Henderson, Haverty
Attendance: 65,251
Tottenham Hotspur: *Brown, Baker, Henry, Blanchflower, Norman, Mackay, Jones, White, R Smith, Allen, Dyson.*
Arsenal: *McClelland, Magill, McCullough, Neill, Young, Docherty, Clapton, Eastham, Herd, Henderson, Haverty.*

Spurs beat Arsenal handsomely at White Hart Lane, with Bill Nicholson extremely pleased with the way his wingers – Cliff Jones and Terry Dyson – operated so effectively. They were hailed as the best pair of wingers in the English game at the time, being described as "little men who drop back to fight fearlessly for the ball in their own goal area. And the exceptional speed of Jones once he has won possession creates havoc among their opponents." Arsenal's last chance of beating Spurs was shattered when Jones performed his quick-fire defence-into-attack trick. Twice he had the Gunners in such a state that, although they knew they must turn back to stop him, their legs were still going forward ... and they stumbled over themselves in confusion. George Swindin, accepting that Spurs deserved their victory, was nevertheless delighted with the performance of reserve goalkeeper John McClelland, who made his debut in this game.

26th August 1961

First Division
Tottenham Hotspur 4
Allen, Dyson 3
Arsenal 3
Skirton, Charles 2
Attendance: 59,371
Tottenham Hotspur: *Brown, Baker, Henry, Blanchflower, Norman, Marchi, Jones, J Smith, R Smith, Allen, Dyson.*
Arsenal: *McClelland, Magill, McCullough, Brown, Snedden, Neill, MacLeod, Eastham, Charles, Henderson, Skirton.*

Reg Leafe, the respected referee, let Spurs off the hook at White Hart Lane with a decision that amazed thousands of fans. Spurs, rocked by two wonder headers from mighty Mel Charles in the 67th and 72nd minutes, were tumbling to a 3-2 home defeat when tiny winger Terry Dyson appeared to palm down a corner kick before hooking it, right-footed, into the net. It was a goal that never should have been. Charles was one of the angry Arsenal players who swarmed around Leafe protesting. Two minutes later he swooped again, this time without a trace of doubt, to snap up a superb delayed pass from Danny Blanchflower and lash it home, left-footed, for a sensational winner, thus completing his own hat-trick. Arsenal no doubt claimed that the referee cost them both points, but some of the blame lay with their own defence, which lacked experience. The near-60,000 crowd got their first taste of blood in the 15th minute when Cliff Jones, in wonderful form for Spurs, opened the way for deputy inside-right John Smith to centre. Les Allen powered the ball home with his head. Five minutes later, Arsenal's defence – distracted by Jones – let Dyson in on a Blanchflower free-kick to score with another header. The Gunners hit back when George Eastham, competing with Jones as the game's top forward, schemed a great goal for left-winger Alan Skirton. Then Charles nodded home centres from Johnny MacLeod and Eastham, to give the Gunners that shock lead with just seven minutes to go. All the game needed was a finish, and the fans got it with that last-gasp burst of Spurs fire and efficiency that, combined with Mr Leafe's amazing decision, earned them the points.

23rd December 1961

First Division
Arsenal 2
Charles, Skirton
Tottenham Hotspur 1
Mackay
Attendance: **63,440**
Arsenal: *Kelsey, Bacuzzi, McCullough, Clamp, Brown, Snedden,*

MacLeod, Barnwell, Charles, Eastham, Skirton.
Tottenham Hotspur: Brown, Baker, Henry, Blanchflower, Norman, Mackay, Medwin, White, Allen, Greaves, Jones.

This match was notable in that it was recent signing Jimmy Greaves' first taste of the north London derby. Signed after a short spell with AC Milan, having made his name as a youngster with Chelsea, the England centre-forward would not experience victory today, and failed to get on the scoresheet. A bumper crowd was expected for this Yuletide game and the turnstiles didn't disappoint, with more than 63,000 turning out to watch the spectacle. After Spurs' recent dominance in the fixture, Gunners fans were sent home ecstatic when goals from Mel Charles and Alan Skirton gave them maximum points for the first time since January 1959.

6th October 1962

First Division
Tottenham Hotspur 4
Mackay, White, Jones 2
Arsenal 4
Court 2, MacLeod, Strong
Attendance: 61,749
Tottenham Hotspur: Brown, Baker, Henry, Blanchflower, Norman, Mackay, Medwin, White, Allen, Clayton, Jones.
Arsenal: McClelland, Magill, McCullough, Snedden, Brown, Groves, MacLeod, Strong, Court, Eastham, Skirton.

Spurs and Arsenal played out a blazing 4-4 draw with a brilliant display from George Eastham. Arsenal were on their knees at half-time, with only bad luck and a brilliant display by goalkeeper John McClelland keeping a fantastic Spurs attack down to four goals – although youngster David Court had responded with two goals. After goals from Dave Mackay, John White and a brace from Cliff Jones, many expected the avalanche to continue in the second half, but Spurs failed to build on their lead and it was then that Eastham and Vic Groves, captain courageous in his first league game since March, stamped their authority and experience on the match. As the Spurs machine slowed down so Arsenal quickened, gathering confidence with every move. At the end, Arsenal were the dominant side, and they earned a draw with second-half goals from Johnny MacLeod and Geoff Strong.

23rd February 1963

First Division

Arsenal 2

Strong, Baker

Tottenham Hotspur 3

R Smith, Jones, Marchi

Attendance: 59,980

Arsenal: *McClelland, Magill, McCullough, Barnwell, Brown, Snedden, MacLeod, Strong, Baker, Eastham, Armstrong.*

Tottenham Hotspur: *Brown, Baker, Henry, Marchi, Norman, Mackay, Medwin, White, R Smith, Greaves, Jones.*

The topic of debate after this game was who should be England's first-choice number 9, as selectors for the national team watched Joe Baker and Bobby Smith from the stands? The two players faced an artificial "contest" at Highbury, when they went on show in front of almost 60,000 fans as rival centre-forwards in the north London derby that ended with Spurs beating Arsenal 3-2. Smith may not have been as quick as Baker, nor did he have the poise or pace from a standing start to match the Arsenal man, but he did have the edge at Highbury on a surface that ranged from ice to slush. They each got a goal, they each missed chances, but Smith – despite the rugged attentions of centre-half Laurie Brown – made a bigger contribution to Spurs' attacks than his counterpart. Smith had opened the scoring in the first half, while Cliff Jones doubled the visitors' lead after the interval, before Geoff Strong made it 2-1. Then Spurs got in a third in the 70th minute. A mishit Tony Marchi shot dribbled past McClelland to restore Spurs' two-goal advantage and, despite a late rally following Baker's goal, the visitors held on for the victory.

15th October 1963

First Division

Arsenal 4

Eastham 2 (1 pen), Baker, Strong

Tottenham Hotspur 4

Greaves, R Smith 2, Mackay

Attendance: 67,986

Arsenal: *McKechnie, Magill, McCullough, Brown, Ure, Groves, MacLeod, Strong, Baker, Eastham, Armstrong.*

Tottenham Hotspur: *W Brown, Baker, Henry, Blanchflower, Norman, Mackay, Jones, White, R Smith, Greaves, Dyson.*

Angry Spurs players swarmed around Birmingham referee Dennis Howell after Arsenal had snatched an amazing last-minute equalizer at Highbury. A minute after the game had finished, Spurs centre-forward Bobby Smith – already booked for protesting against inside-right Geoff Strong's equalizer – was still arguing with Howell. Smith claimed a foul on goalkeeper Bill Brown ... but a breathless 67,986 had already accepted the result. Sensationally, Spurs had grabbed the lead through Greaves after only 90 seconds. Danny Blanchflower's bullet free-kick touched left-winger Terry Dyson's head, and then flew like a rocket off Greaves and into the top far corner. Spurs were 2-0 up in the 18th minute when White crossed from the left, Cliff Jones ducked, and Smith battered the ball into the net. The first Arsenal goal was a giveaway though as Dyson – back to his own penalty area – pushed Arsenal winger George Armstrong, before George Eastham coolly slotted home the penalty. Spurs restored their two-goal cushion within 90 seconds when Dave Mackay broke on the left. Jones and John White carried the move on, for Mackay to burst into the box and shoot left-footed past Ian McKechnie. Arsenal reduced the deficit again when Blanchflower failed to clear a corner and his header fell to Eastham, who flicked the ball up with his right foot and exploded a superb left-foot volley past Brown. Again Spurs responded in the only way they knew how – Jones and White broke open the Arsenal defence for the inside-right to lay on a cross that was smashed home by Smith. With Spurs leading 4-2 at half-time, the Gunners were able to settle into a controlled rhythm because of injuries to Jimmy Greaves and Brown. Greaves was a lone figure on the halfway line for long periods, as Spurs pulled back their men to quench Arsenal's fire. It looked as though it was all over with just six minutes to go when centre-forward Joe Baker swivelled past two defenders to cut Spurs' lead to 4-3. Then, in two final minutes of breathless tension, Arsenal gave everything in search of an equalizer. Spurs scrambled away one corner, conceded another ... and every Arsenal player crowded in. Over came the corner kick, which Strong headed into the roof of the net, while Smith and his colleagues protested for the foul on Brown.

22nd February 1964

First Division

Tottenham Hotspur 3

Greaves (pen), Jones 2

Arsenal 1

Strong

Attendance: 57,261

Tottenham Hotspur: *Hollowbread, Baker, Hopkins, Beal, Norman, Marchi, Jones, White, L Brown, Greaves, Dyson.*

Arsenal: *McClelland, Clarke, McCullough, Groves, Ure, Snedden, MacLeod, Strong, Baker, Eastham, Armstrong.*

There was hardly a man in the near-60,000 crowd who was ready to back Laurie Brown as a centre-forward before this match. But there were plenty to acclaim the former half-back – signed the previous Friday from Arsenal for £40,000 – in his new role 90 minutes later when Spurs had won 3-1. Spurs' answer to a 43rd-minute Geoff Strong header came seconds later from Brown. A corner kick brought a triple challenge from Brown, Maurice Norman and spring-heeled winger Cliff Jones. Brown was left free, and his looping header was fisted from under the bar by right-back Fred Clarke, with Jimmy Greaves making no mistake from the spot. The pay-off came with two Jones specials ... his first goals for eight weeks.

10th October 1964

First Division

Tottenham Hotspur 3

Robertson, Greaves, Saul

Arsenal 1

Baker

Attendance: 55,959

Tottenham Hotspur: *Jennings, Knowles, Henry, Mullery, Norman, Marchi, Robertson, Greaves, Saul, Jones, Dyson.*

Arsenal: *Furnell, Howe, Clarke, McLintock, Ferry, Simpson, Anderson, Strong, Baker, Eastham, Armstrong.*

Goalscorer supreme Jimmy Greaves may have only got one in this game, but it marked a milestone in the Spurs–Arsenal encounters. It was the 100th goal that Spurs had scored in league matches against their north London rivals. Two half-backs, reported to be jointly worth £152,000, were on view – Frank McLintock, Arsenal's recent £80,000 import from Leicester, and Alan Mullery, Spurs' £72,000 buy from Fulham. Mullery looked the far better constructive player as McLintock could only strive to fit into an Arsenal plan that made him neither defender nor attacker. The match hinged on the half-backs though. Arsenal brought in Peter Simpson at left-half, but Greaves soon had his measure. Against this unbalanced defence, Spurs pitted a sound half-back line in which Tony Marchi – almost written off the previous season – played some outstanding football. George Eastham was Arsenal's inside-forward star; he tried hard to bring some sort of blend to the attack but it was all in vain. Spurs scored after 10 minutes, a goal which exposed the shakiness of the Arsenal defence. Left-back Fred Clarke failed to clear, and a move inspired by Marchi, linked by a pass to Jones, helped Jimmy Robertson to tap the ball home. After 23 minutes, Greaves – playing a constructive game but always looking for scoring chances – cashed in on a free-kick to score. Keeper Jim Furnell dived over the ball, when better timing would have brought him right on to it. It was not a class game, but one which could only be described as hard-working rather than glamorous. Exciting incidents kept the crowd occupied, particularly when Frank Saul capped an energetic display with the third Spurs goal. It was in the 75th minute that Arsenal at last showed what more cohesive, settled football could do for them, when a fine combined movement ended with Joe Baker scoring their only goal. While Eastham strove throughout the entire game to give Arsenal the confidence and blend they clearly lacked, Greaves helped Spurs to all the confidence going in this game ... Greaves the scorer was also Greaves the tactician.

23rd February 1965

First Division
Arsenal 3
Radford, Baker 2
Tottenham Hotspur 1
Gilzean
Attendance: **48,367**
Arsenal: *Burns, Howe, McCullough, Neill, Ure, Court, Tawse, Radford, Baker, Eastham, Armstrong.*
Tottenham Hotspur: *W Brown, Knowles, Henry, Mullery, Norman, Marchi, Robertson, Greaves, Gilzean, Clayton, Jones.*

Arsenal gained their revenge for their earlier 3-1 defeat against Spurs by matching the scoreline in the reverse fixture at Highbury. John Radford and Joe Baker each scored, to give the home side a 2-0 half-time advantage in this midweek game. Goals from Alan Gilzean and a second for Baker completed the scoring by the time the final whistle had been blown. The result placed Arsenal sixth, one place behind Spurs, who had a game in hand but were level in points. Both clubs would endure a torrid run-in to the end of the season, with Spurs losing five of their last 11 games to finish in sixth place. The Gunners, meanwhile, also lost five of their final 10 games, and were sequestered in 13th spot.

11th September 1965

First Division
Tottenham Hotspur 2
Gilzean, Saul
Arsenal 2
Baker, L Brown (og)
Attendance: 53,962
Tottenham Hotspur: *W Brown, Norman, Knowles, Mullery, L Brown, Mackay, Greaves, Clayton, Gilzean, Saul, Possee (Low).*
Arsenal: *Furnell, Howe, McCullough, McLintock, Neill, Court, Armstrong, Radford, Baker, Sammels, Eastham.*

When the two sides met early in the 1965–66 season, Arsenal were unchanged from the side that had beaten Nottingham Forest four days earlier, with skipper George Eastham retaining his place on the left wing, and new £65,000 centre-half Ian Ure again restricted to the touchline. Spurs were on an unbeaten home run that had seen them avoid defeat in 27 league matches since they lost to Liverpool on 27th March 1964. The streak would last until Sheffield Wednesday became the first side to come away from White Hart Lane with two points on 13th November. By the end of the 90 minutes, honours were even, with strikes from Alan Gilzean and Frank Saul cancelling out a Joe Baker goal and a Laurie Brown own goal.

8th March 1966

First Division
Arsenal 1
Court

Tottenham Hotspur 1
Possee
Attendance: 51,805
Arsenal: *Furnell, Storey, McCullough, Neill, Ure, Court, Skirton,
Sammels, Radford, Eastham, Armstrong.*
Tottenham Hotspur: *Jennings, Mullery, Knowles, Clayton, L Brown,
Mackay, Robertson, Greaves, Saul, Gilzean, Possee.*

Arsenal and Spurs fought themselves to a standstill in a blazing
duel of strength in the midweek encounter at Highbury. In the end
they found equality, and perhaps satisfaction, out of the thundering
tackles and long-ball bombardments. In the middle of it all, Jimmy
Greaves and George Eastham stood shoulder to shoulder in a
moment of injury hold-up – two little men of great skill symbolizing
their search for a place in a duel where artistry was at a premium
and seldom wanted. Eastham, returning to a thundering roar from
the fans who, on Saturday, had demanded his recall, fought as hard
as any of them and as much as his frail frame would allow. Greaves,
producing one wicked shot that was at last a flash of his old self,
was willing to plunge himself into tackles that had previously played
no part in his game. Ambition governs this type of team planning,
but on the night it was beyond the capabilities of the men who
had to play. Spurs, settling into a new strategy after their cup exit
at Preston, moved wing-half Alan Mullery to right-back and ranged
three men in midfield. But they were almost immediately under
fire, with tension tugging at their tactics. A wicked half volley from
Arsenal left-winger George Armstrong was brilliantly tipped over,
one-handed, by Pat Jennings. After two flashes of Eastham skill,
Arsenal went in front in the ninth minute. A mix-up in the Spurs
defence allowed Alan Skirton two bites at the ball, and at the
second he sent it to David Court, who flashed a fierce shot past an
unsighted Jennings. Arsenal piled it on and Spurs seemed unsure
of themselves and of their football. It wasn't until the second half
that a note of command came into their game, as Arsenal lost their
grip in midfield. Dour defensive play by Ian Ure and Terry Neill kept

Spurs at bay, but confidence began to flow into Spurs' football. Greaves shot inches wide, Alan Gilzean forced a fine save out of Jim Furnell, and then Spurs were level in the 62nd minute. The move began deep in their own half. The ball went wide to Gilzean, via Eddie Clayton, before Frank Saul tried his luck with a shot. The ball broke free for hard-working left-winger Derek Possee to hit home. Arsenal might have won it when Eastham, breaking fast with Ure on his right, gave the Scottish international a chance, but Jennings was equal to the shot. Spurs might also have won it when Greaves created a chance for Saul, who hammered the ball high over the bar.

3rd September 1966

First Division

Tottenham Hotspur 3

Greaves 2, Jones

Arsenal 1

Sammels

Attendance: 56,271

Tottenham Hotspur: *Jennings, Kinnear, Knowles, Beal, England, Mackay, Robertson, Greaves, Gilzean, Venables, Jones.*

Arsenal: *Furnell, Court, Simpson, McLintock, Ure, Neill, Coakley, Baldwin, Radford, Sammels, Armstrong.*

Arsenal arrived at White Hart Lane with three wins and a draw from the opening four games of the campaign, while their hosts had won three and lost one of their corresponding fixtures. Form was therefore fairly similar, but it was the home side who emerged on top at the end of this encounter. Two goals from Jimmy Greaves and one from Cliff Jones easily outweighed the solitary John Sammels strike that was all the Gunners could muster. Arsenal's early season title ambitions took a massive blow following this game, as they only managed to win three more league matches before Christmas, while Spurs' form was indifferent until the New Year.

7th January 1967

First Division

Arsenal 0

Tottenham Hotspur 2

Robertson, Gilzean

Attendance: **49,851**

Arsenal: *Furnell, McNab, Storey, McLintock, Simpson, Ure, Neilson, Radford, Graham, Sammels, Armstrong.*

Tottenham Hotspur: *Jennings, Beal, Knowles, Mullery, England, Clayton, Robertson, Greaves, Gilzean (Saul), Venables, Weller.*

Former Chelsea team-mates Terry Venables and George Graham lined up against each other for the first time as Arsenal entertained Spurs. The pair – who were sold for £155,000 – added their own little bit of spice to the contest by agreeing a bet of a fiver a goal. As it turned out, neither got their name on the scoresheet, but Venables would have been the happier of the two with his side registering a 2-0 victory at Highbury, courtesy of goals from Jimmy Robertson and Alan Gilzean. Venables skippered his new side in the absence of Dave Mackay (who had failed a fitness test on his injured ankle), with Eddie Clayton taking his place in the half-back line. Arsenal were also without their captain, Terry Neill, who failed to make the starting line-up, despite being declared fit after jarring his heel.

16th September 1967

First Division

Arsenal 4

Radford, Neill (pen), Graham, Addison

Tottenham Hotspur 0

Attendance: **62,836**

Arsenal: *Furnell, Storey, Simpson, McLintock, Neill, Ure, Radford, Addison, Graham, Sammels, Armstrong.*

Tottenham Hotspur: *Jennings, Kinnear, Knowles, Mullery, England, Beal, Robertson, Greaves, Gilzean, Venables, Saul.*

Arsenal's £70,000 Scottish centre-forward George Graham prepared for this match by getting married just a few hours before kick-off, with Terry Venables as his best man. The wedding party headed to Highbury after the ceremony, where the groom notched one of his side's four goals in a convincing win over their north London rivals. John Radford opened the scoring, while a Terry Neill penalty doubled their advantage and Colin Addison completed the rout that had one reporter claiming that "Everything went so much Arsenal's way ... that if they had charged their fans for coming out of Highbury they would have got away with it."

20th January 1968

First Division

Tottenham Hotspur 1

Gilzean

Arsenal 0

Attendance: 57,885

Tottenham Hotspur: *Jennings, Kinnear, Knowles, Mullery, Beal, Mackay, Robertson, Gilzean, Chivers, Venables, Greaves.*

Arsenal: *Furnell, Simpson, McNab, McLintock, Neill, Ure, Radford, Jenkins (Rice), Graham, Sammels, Armstrong.*

The speculation before the game was more about whether Mike England would get through a comeback game for the third team against Chelmsford, than the upcoming derby or the unveiling of recent £125,000-signing Martin Chivers. In his absence, the Spurs defence lacked both height and decision and was wary of the aerial threat posed by the Arsenal attack, but they were determined to make amends for the four-goal drubbing they had suffered at Highbury earlier in the season. But Spurs needn't have worried, as a sole Alan Gilzean goal was enough to secure the points and restore some pride back to the white half of north London.

10ᵗʰ August 1968

First Division

Tottenham Hotspur 1

Greaves

Arsenal 2

Radford, Beal (og)

Attendance: 56,280

Tottenham Hotspur: *Jennings, Beal, Knowles, Mullery, England, Collins, Robertson, Greaves, Chivers, Venables, Pearce.*

Arsenal: *Wilson, Storey, McNab, McLintock, Neill, Simpson, Radford, Sammels, Graham, Court, Jenkins.*

The pre-match hype over whether Burnley winger Willie Morgan would choose Arsenal or Spurs dominated the newspaper columns in the run-up to this match. While Bertie Mee admitted "Obviously we will be interested in a player of Morgan's calibre", Spurs' interest in Morgan was undoubtedly heightened following the 2-1 defeat at home to Arsenal, which underlined the need for more progressive forwards. But Arsenal were looking as though they could have their best season in years and that created an awkward situation for Frank McLintock and Jon Sammels, who had both expressed their desire to leave Highbury, as they felt there was little chance of success. Both had had their transfer requests turned down by the club and appeals to the Football League overruled. The match was a great display of defensive depth that brought a win for the visitors. Their running on the ball was superb, and the quick breaks from defensive positions were carried out with cunning. Two such moves led to their goals: Phil Beal turned a difficult cross into his own goal before John Radford ran in for a splendid second, while Jimmy Greaves scored Spurs' only response. As to where Willie Morgan ended up ... Manchester United.

20th November 1968

League Cup semi-final first leg
Arsenal 1
Radford
Tottenham Hotspur 0
Attendance: 55,237
Arsenal: *Wilson, Storey, McNab, McLintock, Ure, Simpson, Radford, Court, Sammels, Graham (Gould), Armstrong.*
Tottenham Hotspur: *Jennings, Kinnear, Knowles, Mullery, Collins, Beal, Pearce, Greaves, England, Venables, Gilzean.*

Arsenal – aiming for their second successive League Cup final – were intending to set up a two-goal advantage from this first leg match, with skipper Frank McLintock explaining: "Defensively, we are a better side than we were a year ago and we are still improving. If we finish two goals in front at Highbury, I can't see Tottenham pulling that back at White Hart Lane." Ian Ure replaced the injured Terry Neill in Arsenal's defence, and he held out to keep a clean sheet. Unfortunately for the pre-match prediction, they could only score one goal. John Radford netted that with just 40 seconds left on the clock, and it was a shattering disappointment for Spurs, who had turned their backs on tradition to assemble the deepest of defences. Spurs did not have a crack at goal until Jimmy Pearce shot wide five minutes from the end, but their strategy had looked like paying off, as Arsenal hurled over centres and fired in shots that rarely suggested they would be productive.

4th December 1968

League Cup semi-final second leg
Tottenham Hotspur 1
Greaves
Arsenal 1
Radford
Attendance: 55,923
Tottenham Hotspur: *Jennings, Kinnear, Knowles, Mullery, Collins,*

Beal, Pearce, Greaves, England, Venables, Gilzean.
Arsenal: *Wilson, Storey, McNab (Graham), McLintock, Ure, Simpson, Radford, Court, Sammels, Gould, Armstrong.*

Skipper Alan Mullery talked about the task that faced Tottenham as they went into the home leg of their League Cup semi-final against Arsenal. He said: "They must stop us scoring. And the longer it goes without us managing to break them down, the harder it will be for us." Arsenal's slim advantage – a Radford 89th-minute goal from the first leg at Highbury – was considered as anything but enough. But Arsenal had conceded only seven goals in 10 away league games in a successful season, and only Leeds had scored twice against them. Tottenham kept Mike England at centre-forward, and this would have a bearing on the side Arsenal boss Bertie Mee announced just prior to the start. Radford (rested) and Terry Neill and George Graham (injured) were absentees the previous week when Arsenal won 1-0. Their return for this match meant David Court and Bobby Gould were in danger of missing the big clash although, Peter Simpson was assured of a place in the starting line-up. Arsenal reached the final of the League Cup for the second year running with a dramatic 87th-minute goal from John Radford at White Hart Lane. Radford, who had scored Arsenal's goal in the first leg two weeks' previously, sent his club to Wembley with a header from a left-wing corner. It cancelled out a goal by Jimmy Greaves in the 67th minute, and gave Arsenal a 2-1 aggregate victory. Arsenal sensibly refused to sit back on their one-goal lead from the first leg, and they surprised Spurs with the speed of their counter-attacks. The game was vigorous, the tackling at times dangerous, and Bobby Gould, who started in place of George Graham, was warned after a foul on Peter Collins. The first positive move of the game ended with Spurs forward Terry Venables volleying just over after Ian Ure had headed clear. Arsenal keeper Bob Wilson was hurt following a Greaves corner and had to have treatment. With a Wembley place at stake, the pressure was intense and it began to show in skirmishes and private feuds. In the first half the game was fought out in a tight midfield area, and Arsenal proved too busy for Spurs, winning more of the ball and making better use of it. With tension building, the inevitable explosion came when Spurs full-back Cyril Knowles clashed with Radford. And when Mullery vigorously intervened, the referee spoke to him and Radford. Almost immediately, Knowles was booked for a wild challenge on Radford, and Alan Gilzean shot narrowly wide from a chance made for him by England. The best opportunity of the first half went to Arsenal, but their forwards completely missed in front of the goal, after winger George Armstrong had deceived Jon Kinnear. Venables shaved the bar with a long-range shot, while Arsenal began to flag in the second half and Spurs, showing greater precision, got more into the match. In the 67th minute, they at last broke down Arsenal's defence. After a throw-in on the left, Mullery switched the ball across the field to Jimmy Pearce, who centred for Greaves to volley into the roof of the net. It was the 25th goal of the season for Greaves, and perhaps his most vital. The pressure was now on Arsenal, but with three minutes left they won a corner which was to settle the match. Radford met the corner on the near post among a ruck of Spurs defenders, and headed the ball home off the underside of the bar.

24th March 1969

First Division

Arsenal 1

Sammels

Tottenham Hotspur 0

Attendance: 43,972

Arsenal: *Wilson, Storey (Graham), McNab, McLintock, Ure, Simpson, Radford, Sammels, Court, Gould, Armstrong.*

Tottenham Hotspur: *Jennings, Evans, Want, Mullery, Pratt, Collins, Pearce (Jenkins), Greaves, Gilzean, Venables, Johnson.*

Arsenal's bold pledge to win all their remaining matches seemed more like a whispered promise at Highbury in March 1969. A goal struck from long range by Jon Sammels at least gave Arsenal the satisfaction of north London supremacy. Winning at White Hart Lane on the opening day of the season, and unbeaten in two League Cup encounters, they completed the hand without due trouble. There was little to console Spurs. Weakened by illness and injury they gave the youth a chance. Tony Want at left-back emphasized the promise he had shown just a year before, while on the other flank 18-year-old Roy Evans showed on his debut that he had a lot to work with. But, although some of the faces on the pitch were unfamiliar, Spurs' faults were all too familiar. Hopeful, cluttered, indecisive football, which didn't bring them one clear-cut chance, was how the team's game could be described. Arsenal were little better. Although they were as sound as ever in midfield, they were short of true quality in attack. A fixture with a tradition of urgent, committed effort hardly offered a moment worthy of recall, according to match reports at the time. A crowd drawn more by the past than by the present, waited in vain for the game to come alive. Five minutes before half-time Arsenal worked through on the right and the ball rebounded to Sammels. He hit it from 25 yards, and a late swerve took it wide of Jennings' right hand as he dived. Spurs brought on David Jenkins for Jimmy Pearce, and Arsenal eventually replaced Peter Storey with George Graham. But although a left-wing corner had Arsenal's crowd gasping with anxiety as Spurs sought an equalizer, the game finished as most of it had been played – on a note of mediocrity.

16th September 1969

First Division
Arsenal 2
Robertson, Radford
Tottenham Hotspur 3
Gilzean, Chivers, Pratt
Attendance: 55,280
Arsenal: *Webster, Storey, McNab, McLintock, Neill, Simpson, Robertson, George, Radford, Graham, Sammels.*
Tottenham Hotspur: *Jennings, Beal, Knowles, Mullery, England, Collins, Chivers (Want), Greaves, Gilzean, Pratt, Morgan.*

Arsenal gave a debut to 18-year-old goalkeeper Malcolm Webster, whose biggest game so far in his career had been a Junior World Cup match for England against Czechoslovakia the previous May. With Bob Wilson injured, the youngster was now in line to face Spurs, Manchester United, Everton and Chelsea in the space of 12 days. It was a baptism of fire for Webster, though, as Spurs ran into a 3-0 first-half lead with goals from Alan Gilzean, Martin Chivers and John Pratt. Jimmy Roberston reduced the deficit before John Radford added a second for the home side six minutes before the end. Despite pushing for an equalizer, Arsenal were unable to notch a third, and Spurs registered another victory at Highbury.

2nd May 1970
First Division
Tottenham Hotspur 1
Gilzean
Arsenal 0
Attendance: 46,969
Tottenham Hotspur: *Jennings, Evans, Knowles, Mullery, England, Beal, Gilzean, Pearce, Chivers, Peters, Morgan.*
Arsenal: *Wilson, Storey, McNab, Kelly (Kennedy), Roberts, Simpson, Armstrong, Sammels, Radford, George, Graham.*

This Spurs–Arsenal fixture was more than just a match that brought down the final curtain on a hectic league season. The close rivalry between the north London giants suggested that 50,000 fans were poised to pack White Hart Lane, and Arsenal's fine feat in winning the Fairs Cup the previous Tuesday almost guaranteed it. With England poised to leave for the World Cup in Mexico, Alan Mullery, Martin Peters and Bob McNab were all desperate to be involved. Mullery explained "If it was Tottenham against any team other than Arsenal I'd probably be content to sit it out or finish my Mexico packing. But Arsenal – that's different! It's an important gamer for the boss – Bill Nicholson. It's one our fans will very much want us to win. And it's a match with extra meaning for Tottenham's players.

We don't begrudge Arsenal their trophy. I'm genuinely pleased for them. But we feel our form in the last weeks of the season promises great things for the future." John Roberts deputized for the injured Frank McLintock in another match, where Alan Gilzean scored the only goal of the game to ensure that Spurs finished ahead of Arsenal in the league table.

The 1970s

The new decade began with a change in rules that would have often dramatic consequences, as 1970 saw the introduction of the use of red and yellow cards to punish serious offences. Arsenal and Spurs, meanwhile, remained on the trophy trail …

Emulating the feat achieved by their north London rivals a decade earlier, Arsenal registered only the second Double of the 20th century in 1970–71. The league campaign was an extremely close-fought affair, with Leeds United pushing Arsenal all the way to the final day of the season. The Gunners needed to either beat or draw 0-0 with Spurs to claim the title on goal average, and an 87th-minute Ray Kennedy strike – the only goal of the game – secured the club's first league title in 18 years. The FA Cup final was a dramatic affair, where the score was goalless after 90 minutes, but the 100,000 crowd was thrilled with three extra-time goals. Steve Heighway notched the first for Liverpool, before Eddie Kelly equalized, and Charlie George sent the Arsenal fans into rapture nine minutes from the end.

Spurs had also won more silverware in a tremendous season for north London, as two Martin Chivers goals against Aston Villa brought the League Cup to White Hart Lane. Chivers was again on target, with another brace, in the first leg of the following season's UEFA Cup final. In an all-British affair with Wolves, Spurs won the away leg 2-1, and fought out a 1-1 draw in the return match to win their second European trophy.

Both Arsenal and Spurs endured near misses as the 1970s wore on, with the Gunners narrowly missing out on a successful defence of the FA Cup when they lost the 1972 final to Leeds United, before finishing the 1972–73 season as First Division runners-up to Liverpool. Although players such as Alan Ball were signed, the Double-winning team began to be broken up, with Charlie George,

George Graham and Frank McLintock leaving the club.

Tottenham were also under new stewardship following Bill Nicholson's resignation in August 1974. He was disappointed in the poor start his side had made to the new campaign, but was also troubled by the rioting that had marred the 1974 UEFA Cup final with Feyenoord, who had emerged 4-2 winners on aggregate. His replacement was Terry Neill, the former Arsenal stalwart who had earned his managerial spurs with Hull City. Neill managed to stave off the threat of relegation in his first season in charge, and improve the team so they were ninth by the time he left in June 1976.

He succeeded Bertie Mee as Arsenal manager, and made impressive signings such as Malcolm Macdonald and Pat Jennings. He led the club to four finals in four years – Arsenal won the 1979 FA Cup once (3-2 against Manchester United) and finished runners-up twice (1-0 against Ipswich Town in 1978 and 1-0 against West Ham in 1980). They also ended the 1979–80 season as European Cup Winners' Cup runners-up to Valencia. The match finished 0-0, with the Spaniards going on to win the penalty shootout 5-4.

Keith Burkinshaw took over the reins at White Hart Lane, and went on to become Spurs' second most successful manager – despite an inauspicious start – signing the popular Argentine duo of Ossie Ardiles and Ricardo Villa in 1978. Burkinshaw's first season in charge ended in relegation from the First Division, with Spurs propping up the rest of the table, having won just 12 of their 42 league games. They bounced back at the first attempt, having finished third in the Second Division table, amassing the same number of points as fourth-placed Brighton, but with the White Hart Lane club boasting the better goal difference. It was time to resume the north London rivalry on a regular basis, with further success just around the corner.

Record in the 1970s

Arsenal

Season	League	P	W	D	L	F	A	Pts	Pos
1970–71	Div 1	42	29	7	6	71	29	65	1
1971–72	Div 1	42	22	8	12	58	40	52	5
1972–73	Div 1	42	23	11	8	57	43	57	2
1973–74	Div 1	42	14	14	14	49	51	42	10
1974–75	Div 1	42	13	11	18	47	49	37	16
1975–76	Div 1	42	13	10	19	47	53	36	17
1976–77	Div 1	42	16	11	15	64	59	43	8
1977–78	Div 1	42	21	10	11	60	37	52	5
1978–79	Div 1	42	17	14	11	61	48	48	7
1979–80	Div 1	42	18	16	8	52	36	52	4

FA Cup

1970–71	2-1 v Liverpool (Final)
1971–72	0-1 v Leeds United (Final)
1972–73	1-2 v Sunderland (Semi-final)
1973–74	1-1, 0-2 v Aston Villa (Fourth Round)
1974–75	0-2 v West Ham United (Sixth Round)
1975–76	0-3 v Wolverhampton Wanderers (Third Round)
1976–77	1-4 v Middlesbrough (Fifth Round)
1977–78	0-1 v Ipswich Town (Final)
1978–79	3-2 v Manchester United (Final)
1979–80	0-1 v West Ham United (Final)

League Cup

1970–71	0-0, 0-2 v Crystal Palace (Fourth Round)
1971–72	0-0, 0-2 v Sheffield United (Fourth Round)
1972–73	0-3 v Norwich City (Fifth Round)
1973–74	0-1 v Tranmere Rovers (Second Round)
1974–75	1-1, 1-2 v Leicester City (Second Round)
1975–76	2-2, 0-1 v Everton (Second Round)
1976–77	1-2 v Queens Park Rangers (Fifth Round)

1977–78   1-2, 0-0 v Liverpool (Semi-final)
1978–79   1-3 v Rotherham United (Second Round)
1979–80   1-1, 3-4 v Swindon Town (Fifth Round)

Europe
1970–71   Fairs Cup: 2-1, 0-1 v Cologne (Quarter-final)
1971–72   European Cup: 1-2, 0-1 v Ajax (Quarter-final)
1972–73   Did not qualify
1973–74   Did not qualify
1974–75   Did not qualify
1975–76   Did not qualify
1976–77   Did not qualify
1977–78   Did not qualify
1978–79   UEFA Cup: 0-1, 1-1 v Red Star Belgrade (Third Round)
1979–80   European Cup Winners' Cup: 0-0 (4-5 pens) v Valencia (Final)

Tottenham Hotspur

Season	League	P	W	D	L	F	A	Pts	Pos
1970–71	Div 1	42	19	14	9	54	33	52	3
1971–72	Div 1	42	19	13	10	63	42	51	6
1972–73	Div 1	42	16	13	13	58	48	45	8
1973–74	Div 1	42	14	14	14	45	50	42	11
1974–75	Div 1	42	13	8	21	52	63	34	19
1975–76	Div 1	42	14	15	13	63	63	43	9
1976–77	Div 1	42	12	9	21	48	72	33	22
1977–78	Div 2	42	20	16	6	83	49	56	3
1978–79	Div 1	42	13	15	14	48	61	41	11
1979–80	Div 1	42	15	10	17	52	62	40	14

FA Cup
1970–71   0-0, 0-1 v Liverpool (Sixth Round)
1971–72   1-2 v Leeds United (Sixth Round)
1972–73   1-1, 3-5 v Derby County (Fourth Round)
1973–74   0-1 v Leicester City (Third Round)

1974–75	1-1, 0-1 v Nottingham Forest (Third Round)
1975–76	1-1, 1-2 v Stoke City (Third Round)
1976–77	0-1 v Cardiff City (Third Round)
1977–78	2-2, 1-2 v Bolton Wanderers (Third Round)
1978–79	1-1, 0-2 v Manchester United (Sixth Round)
1979–80	0-1 v Liverpool (Sixth Round)

League Cup

1970–71	2-0 v Aston Villa (Final)
1971–72	2-3, 2-2 v Chelsea (Semi-final)
1972–73	0-1 v Norwich City (Final)
1973–74	0-1 v Queens Park Rangers (Second Round)
1974–75	0-4 v Middlesbrough (Second Round)
1975–76	1-0, 1-3 v Newcastle United (Semi-final)
1976–77	1-2 v Middlesbrough (Second Round)
1977–78	2-3 v Coventry City (Third Round)
1978–79	2-2, 1-3 v Swansea City (Second Round)
1979–80	1-3 v Manchester United (Second Round)

Europe

1970–71	Did not qualify
1971–72	UEFA Cup: 2-1, 1-1 v Wolverhampton Wanderers (Final)
1972–73	UEFA Cup: 0-1, 2-1 v Liverpool (Semi-final)
1973–74	UEFA Cup: 2-2, 0-2 v Feyenoord (Final)
1974–75	Did not qualify
1975–76	Did not qualify
1976–77	Did not qualify
1977–78	Did not qualify
1978–79	Did not qualify
1979–80	Did not qualify

5th September 1970

First Division

Arsenal 2

Armstrong 2

Tottenham Hotspur 0
Attendance: 48,713
Arsenal: *Wilson, Rice, McNab, Kelly, McLintock (Nelson), Roberts, Armstrong, Storey, Radford, Kennedy, Graham.*
Tottenham Hotspur: *Hancock, Kinnear, Want, Mullery, England, Beal, Gilzean, Perryman, Chivers, Peters, Morgan.*

The headlines in the run-up to this match centred around Graeme Souness. The homesick 17-year-old had walked out and returned to Edinburgh after discussions with the club had broken down. "Mr Nicholson offered me more money," explained the young Scot, "but better wages are not important. I'm homesick for Scotland." As it turned out, Souness made just one appearance for Spurs, as a substitute in a UEFA Cup tie, before a £30,000 transfer to Middlesbrough in 1972. The 1970–71 campaign had begun indifferently for both clubs, but it was Arsenal who showed the resilience to win this game 2-0, with both goals coming from George Armstrong.

3rd May 1971

First Division
Tottenham Hotspur 0
Arsenal 1
Kennedy
Attendance: 51,992
Tottenham Hotspur: *Jennings, Kinnear, Knowles, Mullery, Collins, Beal, Gilzean (Pearce), Perryman, Chivers, Peters, Neighbour.*
Arsenal: *Wilson, Rice, McNab, Kelly, McLintock, Simpson, Armstrong, Graham, Radford, Kennedy, George.*

Arsenal won the League Championship in glorious style in May 1971, beating Spurs in their final match to settle an incredibly close race with Leeds. It was impossible to contain thousands of their supporters when referee Kevin Howley, in the last match of his career, blew the whistle which signaled Arsenal's triumph by one point. And no one could deny Arsenal their reward. They played better than they had for months, keeping their heads, but with their hearts blazing throughout the contest. With the gates locked and thousands of supporters left in the streets outside, Arsenal settled down quickly to reveal the mood they had managed to whip up for another great moment. There was no question of any Arsenal player labouring, with Wembley on his mind, and three fouls by the team in the opening two minutes showed Spurs that they had a real battle on their hands. It was Arsenal who nearly went in front in the sixth minute. Charlie George turned on a pass from full-back Pat Rice to hit a marvellous shot that nearly caught Pat Jennings by surprise. George leapt excitedly, believing he had scored, but Jennings deflected the ball into the massed ranks of supporters behind his goal. Playing with great determination and showing the more positive approach, Arsenal continued to take the game forward. But they were thrown back at last when a move by Spurs gave Steve Perryman the chance to strike a fearsome volley, which might have beaten Bob Wilson if it had not struck a defender. Then, when Alan Gilzean centred cleverly, Wilson and Martin Peters were hurt as they challenged for the ball. When Spurs were caught offside for the fifth time in quick succession, it brought a slow handclap from the crowd. Although this Arsenal tactic was clearly irritating, it served to inhibit their opponents. It forced Spurs to lengthen their passes in an attempt to play over the top of Arsenal's defence, but it took the rhythm out of their play. An untidy volley from George Graham, which sent the ball high in the air, was Arsenal's next threatening gesture. But they were under pressure themselves when Jennings boomed an enormous free-kick into Arsenal's penalty area. A bad foul by Peter Simpson on Martin Chivers revealed the "needle", which began to creep into the match. It was then that Peters produced a stroke of genius, to come close to scoring a great goal. Chivers laid the ball back to him and, with Arsenal expecting Peters to pass, he took it on the volley. It completely beat Wilson – only to rebound from the stanchion behind the crossbar. Arsenal went forward again and Frank McLintock, up in support for a corner, had a point-blank shot blocked two yards from goal by Phil Beal's urgent challenge. At that stage, Arsenal were in almost complete command – forcing four corners in succession before Spurs managed to work the ball clear. Yet Peters – again – this time with a shot on the turn – nearly took a goal. Wilson, alert to the danger, got his fingertips to the ball and turned it away for a corner. As the second half opened, it was clear that there was even more tension building, in what was surely the most momentous match ever staged at White Hart Lane. Wilson was hurt as he came out bravely to fall at Kinnear's feet, and then Arsenal had their greatest let-off of the night when Gilzean missed from two yards, after a low cross from Knowles had scythed through the penalty area. Charlie George, a strange mixture of adult temperament and childish petulance, came into the game with sensible passes, and Arsenal settled down to play their best football of the night. They took control and then gloriously – with just two minutes left – Ray Kennedy, who began the season as a reserve, scored the goal which gave Arsenal the title. A scramble in the Spurs' goalmouth led to a centre and Kennedy, at last finding some freedom in the air, headed the ball in, off the underside of the bar. There was one last despairing Spurs attack, but Arsenal survived to be swamped by a hysterical chanting crowd at full-time.

24th November 1971

First Division
Tottenham Hotspur 1
Chivers
Arsenal 1
Kennedy
Attendance: 52,884
Tottenham Hotspur: *Jennings, Evans, Knowles, Coates, England, Beal, Neighbour, Perryman, Chivers, Peters, Gilzean.*
Arsenal: *Wilson, Rice, McNab, Storey, Roberts, McLintock, Armstrong, Kelly, Radford, Kennedy, Graham.*

Arsenal rediscovered their character in November 1971, to survive a frenzied, scowling encounter with Spurs at White Hart Lane. In a match of breathtaking incidents, but little memorable football, they were still clinging precariously to a one-goal lead with only 10 minutes left. Then full-back Pat Rice committed a disastrous error, which gave Martin Chivers the chance to score a glorious equalizer. Rice, under no pressure, chose to roll the ball back to goalkeeper Bob Wilson, but Chivers pounced and sent his shot into the far side of the goal. It was no more than Spurs deserved from a second half in which they had put Arsenal under siege with continuous pressure. Yet, for a long while, Arsenal, whose confidence had been undermined by a succession of defeats, threatened to win again on the ground where they had clinched the League Championship in the previous season. Ray Kennedy had already had two fiercesome blows blocked by Spurs defenders before he shot Arsenal ahead in the 33rd minute. He beat Beal's challenge and sent a firm right-foot shot into the top corner of the net. In that moment, Arsenal had justified a decision to play without Charlie George, potentially their most dangerous player. George was left out because Arsenal felt they needed more effort in midfield. It led to the reintroduction of Eddie Kelly, but it was the recall of full-back Bob McNab which proved most significant. His astute covering restored order to Arsenal's defence. Yet, in the end, it was Wilson's agility and courage that blocked Spurs from an avenging victory. Referee Keith Walker's indulgent decisions kept players from both teams out of trouble, when more than one of them deserved a caution. Peter Storey was booked for a foul on Ralph Coates, but Alan Gilzean might have followed him for a challenge which left Wilson unconscious. Wilson's catching was commendable enough but it was a superb one-handed save from a Peters' header that stood out from the rest of his work. Even when under pressure, Arsenal threatened whenever Radford and Kennedy were given possession, but a decision to concede the middle of the field nearly cost them dearly, when a Steve Perryman shot was turned over the bar. Charlie George and Sammy Nelson were both dropped by Arsenal for the big London clash. George was replaced by Scot Eddie Kelly, and Nelson gave way for England full-back Bob McNab. Bertie Mee stated that Charlie had not been playing well.

11ᵗʰ May 1972

First Division

Arsenal 0

Tottenham Hotspur 2

Mullery, Coates

Attendance: **42,038**

Arsenal: *Barnett, Rice, McNab, Nelson, McLintock, Roberts, Armstrong, Simpson (Marinello), Radford, Kennedy, Graham.*

Tottenham Hotspur: *Jennings, Kinnear, Knowles, Mullery, England, Beal, Gilzean, Perryman, Pearce, Pratt, Coates.*

Ralph Coates scored one of the great goals of 1972 in the closing minute of the final First Division game of the season. By any standard it was a cracker. But the fact that it was only Coates' second league goal since his £190,000 move from Burnley 12 months ago made it even more memorable. From an Arsenal corner kick, the ball came to Coates, who raced more than 70 yards, before striking a vicious left-foot shot wide of keeper Geoff Barnett. Arsenal played like a team feeling the effects of losing the FA Cup final and their third game in six days. Yet, for more than an hour, it looked as though the 42,038 fans were going to see the first goalless draw in 72 league clashes between these north London giants. Then a long Joe Kinnear cross from the left was flicked on by Alan Gilzean, and Alan Mullery, lurking unmarked at the far post, blasted the ball in. Arsenal, at the end of this tiring, too-long season, raised their game, as George Graham lashed a drive inches wide and John Radford hit a searing shot that was saved superbly by goalkeeper Pat Jennings. But there was no denying that Spurs looked the team with more urgency and determination, and Coates signed off their season in a grand manner.

9th December 1972

First Division

Tottenham Hotspur 1

Peters

Arsenal 2

Storey, Radford

Attendance: **47,515**

Tottenham Hotspur: *Jennings, Evans, Knowles, Pratt, England, Naylor, Neighbour (Coates), Perryman, Chivers, Peters, Pearce.*

Arsenal: *Wilson, Rice, McNab, Storey, Blockley, Simpson (McLintock), Armstrong, Ball, Radford, Kennedy, Kelly.*

There was satisfaction, but no smugness, in Bob Wilson's voice in December 1972, when he relived two games that had resurrected his own and Arsenal's future. After successive wins over Leeds and Tottenham Hotspur, crisis was the last word to be heard around the marble walls of Highbury. And, as Arsenal reasserted themselves following crushing defeats by Norwich and Derby, for goalkeeper Wilson the satisfied feeling went particularly deep. His comeback after injury started with a five-goal hiding at Derby. But he said: "I've proved to myself in these last two games that I can still do my stuff. The signs were there against Leeds – though I didn't have too much to do that day," he continued. "At Tottenham, I was much more involved. And I had the confidence to do what needed doing. I'm delighted with the way things have gone – for me as well as Arsenal – these past two games, but I won't be entirely happy until this season is finished – and I've come through it OK." Wilson, it was stated, had done no training the previous week and, up to the Saturday morning, it was doubtful he would play in the Tottenham game. Geoff Barnett had been pulled from the Friday night reserve fixture as a precaution, and went with the squad to White Hart Lane. But Wilson emphasized that his doubtful position had nothing to do with his knee, which was described at the time as being in terrific shape. While Tottenham talked of the strain of a third tough match in six days, Arsenal could point out that George

Armstrong and Ray Kennedy played despite heavy colds. Armstrong was magnificent with his defending and attacking, he never stopped running and was prominent in both Arsenal goals. Peter Storey ran bravely and intelligently to head home Armstrong's long cross after 66 minutes. Four minutes later the tigerish midfield man was at the centre of yet another Arsenal goal controversy as they went two up. This time he moved back from a definite offside position – that had a linesman raising his flag – as Alan Ball and Armstrong sent John Radford streaking in to score. Fortune, it seemed was continually favouring Arsenal. Referee Roy Capey argued that Storey hadn't interfered with play. But Tottenham manager Bill Nicholson told the newspapers that four of the defenders stopped dead in their tracks when the ball was played through. They all thought that Storey was offside, and so did the opposing manager. Martin Peters ensured a fighting Tottenham finish, with a fine goal eight minutes form the end. But an excellent Wilson save from substitute Coates denied them a point. What of Arsenal's deposed stars asked the press? George Graham, wanted by Stoke and Leicester, could have got the nod to go, but Charlie George and skipper Frank McLintock were earmarked to stay.

14th April 1973

First Division

Arsenal 1

Storey

Tottenham Hotspur 1

Chivers

Attendance: 50,863

Arsenal: *Wilson, Rice, McNab, Storey, Blockley, Simpson, Armstrong, Ball, Radford, Kennedy, Kelly (George).*

Tottenham Hotspur: *Jennings, Kinnear, Knowles, Coates (Evans), England, Beal, Gilzean, Perryman, Chivers, Peters, Pratt.*

Not-so-neighbourly Spurs virtually destroyed Arsenal's fading title chances, and with it the Gunners' only gateway to Europe, the following season in the last league match of the season at Highbury in April 1973. But Arsenal remained adamant that they could win the title. Their coach, Steve Burtenshaw, was confident that the squad could finish top. Before the match, more than 50,000 Highbury fans rose sportingly to congratulate Spurs' keeper Pat Jennings on being voted Player of the Year, but Arsenal themselves gave the acrobatic Irishman few real opportunities to display the glorious goalkeeping talents that deservedly won him the award. Highbury's final curtain came down on a strange mixture of a match. Some of Arsenal's football was superb, but when they reached the penalty box, they became even more frustrated than the Tottenham defence was, at times, confused. Arsenal forced 11 corners to Tottenham's two, yet it was Spurs who created the better scoring chances. Chivers shot Tottenham into a 57th-minute lead with a magnificent drive from a Peters assist, and it looked as if one goal would be enough. But Arsenal, who could never be accused of lacking guts, came back with an immediate counter punch, which brought about a superb equalizer. Storey finished the move with a shot from Armstrong's pass. Not even Jennings could stop that one. But the big fellow did give the crowd one brief glimpse of his glorious goalkeeping. It came midway though the second half when he rose to a long Kelly free-kick and plucked the ball majestically out of the air, one-handed. The crowd gasped, so did Kelly, but, alas, Arsenal gave Jennings little more to do. They pushed on George for Kelly nine minutes from time, and Tottenham countered by sending Evans on for Coates soon after. But in the end a draw was fair enough.

13th October 1973

First Division

Tottenham Hotspur 2

Gilzean, Chivers

Arsenal 0

Attendance: 41,856

Tottenham Hotspur: *Daines, Evans, Knowles, Pratt, England, Beal,*

Gilzean, Perryman, Chivers, Peters, McGrath.
Arsenal: *Wilson, Rice, McNab, Storey, Simpson, Kelly, Armstrong, George, Radford (Batson), Kennedy, Brady.*

Arsenal came into this game with £420,000-worth of talent on the casualty list. Struggling to reassert themselves among the country's top clubs, they received more bad news the day before, when it was announced that centre-half Jeff Blockley was ruled out of their next two games. Blockley had limped off with a knee injury in the previous week's match against Birmingham, and was later found to have suffered ligament damage. With midfield star Alan Ball also in plaster with damaged ligaments, Bertie Mee gave 17-year-old Liam Brady his full debut. Regardless, it was Bob Wilson who kept Arsenal in the game, as Spurs threatened to run riot with early saves from Martin Peters. The second half continued much in the same vein, but Wilson was unable to prevent the opening goal when Alan Gilzean got on the end of a loose free-kick to slot the ball home. Arsenal finally got their act together, and their attacking play limited Spurs to looking to double their lead with counter-attacks, which they did when Chivers headed home Cyril Knowles' free-kick.

16th February 1974

First Division
Arsenal 0
Tottenham Hotspur 1
McGrath
Attendance: 38,804
Arsenal: *Wilson, Rice, Nelson, Storey, Simpson, Kelly, Armstrong, Ball, Radford, Kennedy, Brady.*
Tottenham Hotspur: *Jennings, Evans, Naylor, Pratt, England, Beal, McGrath, Perryman, Chivers, Gilzean, Coates.*

There was little at stake by the time Arsenal hosted Spurs in February 1974. The visitors were 11th in the First Division table, 19 points behind runaway leaders Leeds United, with Arsenal four positions and two points further back. The shock transfer news was Arsenal's loan signing of goalkeeper Jimmy Rimmer from Manchester United, which left reserve keeper Geoff Barnett shocked and bewildered. Arsenal were without skipper Bob McNab for this fixture, as he was struggling with a hamstring injury, while Spurs were missing Mike England and Martin Peters. Winger Chris McGrath, who had made his debut in the derby clash the previous October, scored the only goal of the game, as Spurs heaped more misery on Highbury.

19th October 1974

First Division

Tottenham Hotspur 2

Perryman, Chivers

Arsenal 0

Attendance: 36,294

Tottenham Hotspur: Jennings, Evans, Knowles, Pratt, England, Naylor, Neighbour, Perryman (Coates), Chivers, Peters, Jones.

Arsenal: Rimmer, Storey, Nelson, Kelly, Powling, Simpson, Armstrong, Ball, Radford, Brady, Kidd.

Arsenal and Tottenham were given a stark reminder that they were very much the fallen giants of the First Division, as thousands of tickets for the derby game were left unsold. It was no surprise really, when you consider that Arsenal were bottom of the table for the first time since 1946, and Spurs were immediately above them on the strength of a fractionally better goal average. "The situation is serious for both clubs," admitted Spurs manager Terry Neill. "Anyone who talks about this game as being other than vital to the immediate future is dodging the issue. Equally important, we've got to give those who come something to entice them back again." One stark and frightening second-half moment spotlighted the difference between a side prepared to battle fearlessly for vital points, and a team who surrendered far too easily. Steve Perryman, a non-stop bundle of midfield energy, had the pain and a black eyepatch as a reminder of it for a few days afterwards. Midway through the second half, he put his head to the ball at the same time as Liam Brady tried to make contact with his boot. The price Perryman paid was a cut, swollen and black left eye, plus double vision for several hours afterwards. Martin Chivers cut his lip badly scoring Tottenham's second goal in the 70th minute, after Perryman had put them in front with a superb shot at 35 minutes. The biggest criticism of Arsenal was the way that, after looking the better side before Perryman scored, endeavour then dropped out of their game.

26th April 1975

First Division

Arsenal 1

Kidd

Tottenham Hotspur 0

Attendance: 43,752

Arsenal: *Barnett, Rice, Nelson, Storey, Mancini, Simpson, Ball, Brady, Hornsby, Kidd, Armstrong.*

Tottenham Hotspur: *Jennings, Kinnear, Knowles, Beal, Osgood, Naylor, Conn, Perryman, Jones, Duncan, Neighbour (Pratt).*

In April 1975, Spurs went into what must have been the most desperate match of their previous 25 years against Leeds at White Hart Lane. The squad's mental condition was described as the worst possible, having just lost 1-0 to Arsenal. How could they expect to survive against the then potential European champions after failing so miserably against a side as ordinary as Arsenal? That was the reaction from almost everyone involved at Highbury at the Saturday match. Even Tottenham manager Terry Neill seemed resigned and philosophical, as he talked vaguely about picking players "up from the floor". Yet some journalists disagreed, and felt that Spurs had a great chance of beating Leeds. Giving small comfort was the fact that Leeds' injury list was extensive. During the match with Arsenal, Tottenham had piled into frantic action with no discernible tactics, formation or marking. In the first 20-minute spell, when Brian Kidd scored the only goal, the accurate passes could be counted on one hand, while still leaving enough fingers for a rude gesture. Tottenham's self-pitying assertion was that a nightmare miss by Alfie Conn in front of an open goal cost them the point they desperately needed. Arsenal skipper Alan Ball, whose own performance contained uncharacteristic lethargy and reluctance – possibly because he accepted at the time that his career at Highbury was coming to an end – put it into perspective. "We always had the feeling that if they did score we could go and get another ourselves at any time. It was difficult to raise any enthusiasm." Even at a casual half-pace, Ball still managed to create three chances for colleagues in the last couple of minutes, to add to two other dramatic moments – a first-half attempt by Kidd that was blocked on the line, and a Peter Storey thump, which hit a post. Tottenham's young centre-half, Keith Osgood, looked inept, and struggled to cope with the thrusts from Kidd. And all Neill's praise for the effort and energy his players expended was overshadowed by their failure to marry those assets to any skill. The only Tottenham men who performed with much merit were the near-veterans Cyril Knowles and Phil Beal, defenders who had learned to live with the tension that had such a crushing effect on the younger men around them. If Neill had reflected on that, he might have considered calling back another man of experience for a one last-chance gamble – centre-forward Martin Chivers.

27th September 1975

First Division

Tottenham Hotspur 0
Arsenal 0

Attendance: 37,064

Tottenham Hotspur: *Jennings, Naylor, Knowles, Pratt, Young, Osgood, McNab, Perryman, Duncan (Chivers), Jones, Neighbour.*
Arsenal: *Rimmer, Rice, Nelson, Kelly, Mancini, O'Leary, Ball, Cropley, Stapleton, Kidd, Rostron (Brady).*

Another below-average crowd turned out for this encounter,

showing, it seemed, that fickle north London fans were only interested in a winning team; Tottenham and Arsenal were far from that in September 1975. Tottenham fled the country after this dour goalless draw, as Terry Neill took his men to Pont-l'Abbé in France to play a friendly against Le Stade Rennais. Arsenal would have been well advised to find themselves a disguise or two, after conspiring with Spurs to bore the pants off London's biggest crowd of the season. Neill did have the honesty to express disgust and apologize to everyone, after a game that had less entertainment value than a party political broadcast.

3rd April 1976

First Division
Arsenal 0
Tottenham Hotspur 2
Pratt, Duncan
Attendance: 42,134
Arsenal: *Rimmer, Rice, Nelson, Ross, Mancini, Powling, Armstrong, Ball, Radford, Kidd, Brady.*
Tottenham Hotspur: *Jennings, Naylor, McAllister, Pratt, Young, Osgood, Jones, Perryman, Chivers, Duncan, Neighbour.*

While Arsenal still languished near the bottom of the First Division, Spurs had at least restored some pride, with a run of results that would see them finish in the top half of the table. Alex Cropley was back in the Arsenal squad for the first time since breaking a bone in his foot the previous November, with the midfielder replacing Peter Simpson as substitute. Pat Jennings returned in goal for Spurs, replacing Barry Daines, but Ralph Coates was still out with a knee injury, with Chris Jones taking his place. As is often the case, the team with the momentum makes and takes its chances, with John Pratt and John Duncan scoring the goals to give Spurs the victory.

27th December 1976

First Division

Tottenham Hotspur 2

Young, Duncan

Arsenal 2

Macdonald 2

Attendance: 47,751

Tottenham Hotspur: *Jennings, Naylor, Gorman, Hoddle (Pratt), Young, Osgood, Conn, Perryman, Duncan, Coates, Taylor.*

Arsenal: *Rimmer, Rice, Powling, Ross, O'Leary, Simpson, Storey, Brady, Macdonald, Stapleton, Rostron.*

This was Terry Neill's first derby as Arsenal manager, following his shock move from White Hart Lane to Highbury in June 1976. His replacement, Keith Burkinshaw, introduced a youngster by the name of Glenn Hoddle to this fixture for the first time. Spurs lost defender Willie Young – already banned from international matches – when he was sent off in the 67th minute after two fouls on Frank Stapleton. A punch-up followed between players of both sides, but Spurs, after trailing to two Malcolm Macdonald goals, got a point with goals from Young and John Duncan. Another blow for Arsenal, in addition to losing that 2-0 lead, was that long-scoring winger George Armstrong had told the club that he no longer wanted to play for them.

11th April 1977

First Division

Arsenal 1

Macdonald

Tottenham Hotspur 0

Attendance: 47,432

Arsenal: *Rimmer, Rice, Matthews, Price, O'Leary, Young, Rix (Brady), Hudson, Macdonald, Stapleton, Armstrong.*

Tottenham Hotspur: *Daines, Naylor, Holmes, Pratt, Osgood, Perryman, Jones, Hoddle, Armstrong, Coates, Taylor.*

By the time the two sides met in April 1977, Spurs were deep in the relegation mire, and one of three London clubs in the bottom five in the First Division. But the capital did have one leader: Arsenal striker Malcolm Macdonald scored his 26th goal of the season in the 1-0 win over Spurs, thereby overtaking Aston Villa's Andy Gray to become the First Division's top marksman. Under fire, manager Keith Burkinshaw had the backing of the board, with chairman Sidney Wale stating, "We've got a long way to go before we're out of trouble. But we've got a fighting chance. It hasn't been an easy season for [Keith]. I've sat in the directors' box and had coins and paper cups thrown at me. It wasn't very pleasant. But we've put no pressure on Keith. We're not that sort of club."

23rd December 1978

First Division
Tottenham Hotspur 0
Arsenal 5
Sunderland 3, Stapleton, Brady
Attendance: 42,273
Tottenham Hotspur: *Kendall, Naylor, Gorman, Holmes, Lacy, Perryman, Pratt (Jones), Ardiles, Lee, Hoddle, Taylor.*
Arsenal: *Jennings, Rice, Walford, Price, O'Leary, Young, Brady, Sunderland, Stapleton, Gatting, Rix.*

Malcolm Macdonald's hopes of making his First Division comeback were dashed before this match, when a specialist ordered him to rest his troublesome left knee. Arsenal's £333,000 striker had made just one appearance for the club – as a substitute against Red Star Belgrade in the UEFA Cup – and played a handful of reserve games since a cartilage operation at the end of August. "The knee feels fine," explained Macdonald, "but I sometimes get fluid on it after playing." The injury would ultimately bring a premature end to his career at the end of the season, but Arsenal did not need his talents to win this match. A hat-trick from Alan Sunderland, plus goals from Frank Stapleton and Liam Brady, sealed a 5-0 rout on Pat Jennings' return to White Hart Lane, following his August 1977 transfer.

10th April 1979

First Division

Arsenal 1

Stapleton

Tottenham Hotspur 0

Attendance: **53,896**

Arsenal: *Jennings, Rice, Walford, Talbot, O'Leary, Young, Brady, Sunderland, Stapleton, Price, Rix.*

Tottenham Hotspur: *Daines, Naylor, McAllister, Holmes, Miller, Perryman, Pratt, Taylor, Jones, Hoddle, Villa.*

Liam Brady, the midfield master who made Arsenal tick, was back to boost their bid for a place in Europe. Brady returned for a home clash against neighbours Tottenham, after missing five games with a knee injury. In the Republic of Ireland star's absence, Arsenal's league form had slumped. In fact, their only win without him was against Wolves in the FA Cup semi-final. Although the competition offered the Gunners one possible route into European football the following season, they had to make sure by clinching a high First Division placing. They needed all the points they could get. Brady replaced Steve Gatting, who was relegated to substitute. Steve Walford continued at left-back for the suspended Sammy Nelson. Barry Daines stood by to take over in Spurs' goal from Mark Kendall, for what would be his first senior game for nearly six months. Centre-half John Lacy was banned, so teenager Paul Miller was in line for his first-team debut. "I've got to do something to put some fire and fight back in the side," said manager Keith Burkinshaw. The return of Brady was as welcome to Arsenal as the decision by Tottenham to drop Osvaldo "Ossie" Ardiles was surprising. Without Brady, Arsenal had failed to win seven successive league games. With him, there was more skill in their midfield, but they still found Tottenham determined opponents. A superb Ricardo Villa pass saw

Peter Taylor brush past two Arsenal defenders before sending a fierce shot narrowly wide. But Arsenal battled back, in a match fought at a frantic pace. Daines did well to turn a Frank Stapleton blast for a corner, then he did even better to push away a tremendous Brady free-kick. Taylor continued to look the man most likely to break down Arsenal. When Glenn Hoddle sent him through, Taylor sent a low drive inches wide. But Stapleton scored with a last-minute header, to give FA Cup finalists Arsenal the points.

26th December 1979

First Division

Arsenal 1

Sunderland

Tottenham Hotspur 0

Attendance: 44,560

Arsenal: *Jennings, Devine, Rice, Talbot, O'Leary, Young, Brady, Sunderland, Stapleton, Hollins, Rix.*

Tottenham Hotspur: *Aleksić, Hughton, McAllister, Yorath, Smith, Perryman, Ardiles, Jones, Armstrong (Galvin), Hoddle, Pratt.*

Alan Sunderland shot the Boxing Day goal that left Arsenal stubbornly insisting they would maintain a southern challenge to the northern domination of the First Division title chase. But Tottenham left Highbury convinced this should never have been another defeat in their latest lean spell. Seven minutes from the end of a game that will hardly go down as a classic, Ossie Ardiles was brought down by David O'Leary. Ardiles chased referee Brian Daniels to register his protest at the refusal to give a penalty. And Tottenham manager Keith Burkinshaw, following four defeats in five games, bluntly said: "There looked no doubt from where I was that it was a penalty." Arsenal manager Terry Neill commented: "If I'd been in Keith's position I might have shouted." Once again Arsenal, after going in front through Sunderland in the 15th minute, failed to show championship qualities at Highbury. Neill admitted: "We certainly haven't played as well at home as we have away this season.

We get a little bit hurried." The winning goal understandably left Burkinshaw far from happy. He said: "You've got to fault our keeper. The ball bounced out of Milija Aleksić's hands and left Sunderland plenty of time." The threat of the axe hung over the Tottenham strikers, as Burkinshaw finally ran out of patience and vowed to step up his search for reinforcements. He had been looking for a top-class striker for some time. But he refused to pay what he called "ridiculous" money to get one. However, his hand was being forced by a depressing run that had seen Spurs slide down the table, after losing four of their five previous games. Burkinshaw was known to be reviewing Clive Allen from QPR, Alan Biley of Cambridge, Liverpool's David Fairclough, and Scottish pair Steve Archibald and Andy Ritchie. He was reluctant to gamble on an untried player from the lower divisions.

7ᵗʰ April 1980

First Division

Tottenham Hotspur 1

Jones

Arsenal 2

Vaessen, Sunderland

Attendance: 41,365

Tottenham Hotspur: *Daines, Miller, Hughton, Yorath, McAllister, Perryman, Ardiles, Jones, Pratt, Hoddle, Galvin.*

Arsenal: *Barron, Rice, Walford, Talbot, O'Leary, Young, Brady (Sunderland), Devine, Vaessen, Hollins, Davis.*

Arsenal kept an important route to Europe open in April 1980, as they made it plain that their real priority in a crowded week lay in cup action on two fronts. The bulk of the team lining up to face Juventus and Liverpool missed a match that embarrassed Tottenham as much as it encouraged Arsenal. Juventus, who dashed from Gatwick to see the side they expected to face in the European Cup Winners' Cup semi-final at Highbury, were left to puzzle over the demands made on English League players. Sammy

Nelson and David Price – both definitely injured – as well as Pat Jennings, Alan Sunderland, Frank Stapleton and Graham Rix were all absent, though Sunderland substituted for Liam Brady in the second half. Manager Terry Neill expressed his delight at the way his kids had performed, and added: "The question as to whether we fielded an under strength side was answered on the pitch. I have never anticipated the League asking us about it." Full-back Nelson (with a hamstring strain) remained the one serious doubt among the Arsenal players for the week's cup matches. Burkinshaw tried to put a brave face on the defeat, but his disappointment was clear to see. Paul Davis, a 17-year-old forward making his first-team debut for Arsenal, won praise from both managers for a most promising performance. Tottenham keeper Barry Daines saved well from John Hollins and Paul Vaessen, but as time wore on a goalless draw seemed inevitable. Finally, in the 84th minute, Arsenal went in front. Brian Talbot's corner was headed across by David O'Leary, and Vaessen nodded through from close range. A linesman who signaled a goal kick was overruled by referee Ray Toseland, for the corner that led to that opening goal. Two minutes later, Sunderland put Arsenal further in front with a lob from a full 30 yards. Then, two minutes from the end, Chris Jones headed a goal for Tottenham – but it could not prevent Arsenal winning a game that kept alive their insurance policy of European football the following season, through a high placing in the league.

The 1980s

Spurs kicked off the 1980s with four cup finals under Keith Burkinshaw. They claimed the FA Cup in 1981 after a two-match epic against Manchester City, but it almost didn't come to fruition. City had taken the lead in the 30th minute through Tommy Hutchison, but Spurs were given a lifeline when the same player scored an own goal 11 minutes before the end of normal time. Extra-time could not separate the two sides, who met in a replay five days later, when two goals from Ricky Villa and one from Garth Crooks gave the men from London a 3-2 victory. They successfully defended their trophy the following season, but were again taken to a replay, this time by Queens Park Rangers. It took a Glenn Hoddle penalty to secure their second successive FA Cup trophy.

The same season saw Spurs reach Wembley again, this time in the League Cup. For most of the match, it looked as though Steve Archibald's 11th-minute goal was going to provide the White Hart Lane side with a unique double cup triumph, but Ronnie Whelan equalized for Liverpool with just three minutes to go. The Reds were the stronger side in extra-time, with Whelan netting his second and Ian Rush adding his side's third to break Tottenham hearts. There was yet another piece of silverware added to the White Hart Lane trophy cabinet, though, with the 1984 UEFA Cup. With the two-legged tie resulting in 1-1 draws in both London and Anderlecht, it was Spurs who held their nerve, to win the penalty shootout 4-3; however, this would prove to be Burkinshaw's last game in charge after a falling out with the board. He was replaced in quick succession by Peter Shreeves and David Pleat (who took Tottenham to the 1987 FA Cup final, where they lost 3-2 to less-fancied Coventry City), before Terry Venables saw the decade out.

Terry Neill, meanwhile, had made way for Don Howe in the Highbury hot seat, but Howe was unable to win any trophies, and resigned in March 1986, to be replaced by George Graham. The Scot cleared out many of his predecessors' players, and instead chose to build his team around the likes of Tony Adams, Lee Dixon, Paul Merson and Nigel Winterburn. Success in the 1987 League Cup final against Liverpool (runners-up the following year to Luton Town) was simply the precursor to the best part of a decade of success under Graham, which really began with the dramatic finale to the 1988–89 First Division campaign. Arsenal went to Anfield needing to win by two goals in the last game of the season – and a Michael Thomas strike in the last minute brought the league title to Highbury. Up until then, though, the two north London rivals had had little to shout about in the league throughout the 1980s, despite the introduction of three points for a win in 1981, in an effort to increase attacking football.

Record in the 1980s

Arsenal

Season	League	P	W	D	L	F	A	Pts	Pos
1980–81	Div 1	42	19	15	8	61	45	53	3
1981–82	Div 1	42	20	11	11	48	37	71	5
1982–83	Div 1	42	16	10	16	58	56	58	10
1983–84	Div 1	42	18	9	15	74	60	63	6
1984–85	Div 1	42	19	9	14	60	47	66	7
1985–86	Div 1	42	20	9	13	49	47	69	7
1986–87	Div 1	42	20	10	12	58	35	70	4
1987–88	Div 1	40	18	12	10	58	39	66	6
1988–89	Div 1	38	22	10	6	73	36	76	1
1989–90	Div 1	38	18	12	8	54	38	62	4

FA Cup

1980–81	0-2 v Everton (Third Round)
1981–82	0-1 v Tottenham Hotspur (Third Round)
1982–83	1-2 v Manchester United (Semi-final)
1983–84	2-3 v Middlesbrough (Third Round)

1984–85	0-1 v York City (Fourth Round)
1985–86	2-2, 0-3 v Luton Town (Fifth Round)
1986–87	1-3 v Watford (Sixth Round)
1987–88	1-2 v Nottingham Forest (Sixth Round)
1988–89	2-2, 0-1 v West Ham United (Third Round)
1989–90	0-0, 0-2 v Queens Park Rangers (Fourth Round)

League Cup

1980–81	0-1 v Tottenham Hotspur (Fourth Round)
1981–82	0-0, 0-3 v Liverpool (Fourth Round)
1982–83	2-4, 1-2 v Manchester United (Semi-final)
1983–84	1-2 v Walsall (Fourth Round)
1984–85	2-3 v Oxford United (Third Round)
1985–86	1-1, 1-2 v Aston Villa (Fifth Round)
1986–87	2-1 v Liverpool (Final)
1987–88	2-3 v Luton Town (Final)
1988–89	1-1, 0-0, 1-2 v Liverpool (Third Round)
1989–90	1-3 v Oldham Athletic (Fourth Round)

Europe

1980–81	Did not qualify
1981–82	UEFA Cup: 0-1, 2-1 v FC Winterslag (Second Round)
1982–83	UEFA Cup: 2-3, 2-5 v Spartak Moscow (First Round)
1983–84	Did not qualify
1984–85	Did not qualify
1985–86	English clubs banned from European competition
1986–87	English clubs banned from European competition
1987–88	English clubs banned from European competition
1988–89	English clubs banned from European competition
1989–90	English clubs banned from European competition

Tottenham Hotspur

Season	League	P	W	D	L	F	A	Pts	Pos
1980–81	Div 1	42	14	15	13	70	68	43	10
1981–82	Div 1	42	20	11	11	67	48	71	4

ARSENAL vs SPURS

1982–83	Div 1	42	20	9	13	65	50	69	4
1983–84	Div 1	42	17	10	15	64	65	61	8
1984–85	Div 1	42	23	8	11	78	51	77	3
1985–86	Div 1	42	19	8	15	74	52	65	10
1986–87	Div 1	42	21	8	13	68	43	71	3
1987–88	Div 1	40	12	11	17	38	48	47	13
1988–89	Div 1	38	15	12	11	60	46	57	6
1989–90	Div 1	38	19	6	13	59	47	63	3

FA Cup

1980–81	3-2 v Manchester City (Final)
1981–82	1-0 v Queens Park Rangers (Final)
1982–83	0-2 v Everton (Fifth Round)
1983–84	0-0, 1-2 v Norwich City (Fourth Round)
1984–85	0-1 v Liverpool (Fourth Round)
1985–86	1-2 v Everton (Fifth Round)
1986–87	2-3 v Coventry City (Final)
1987–88	1-2 v Port Vale (Fourth Round)
1988–89	0-1 v Bradford City (Third Round)
1989–90	1-3 v Southampton (Third Round)

League Cup

1980–81	0-1 v West Ham United (Fifth Round)
1981–82	1-3 v Liverpool (Final)
1982–83	1-4 v Burnley (Fifth Round)
1983–84	1-2 v Arsenal (Third Round)
1984–85	0-0, 1-2 v Sunderland (Fourth Round)
1985–86	0-0, 0-0, 0-1 v Portsmouth (Fourth Round)
1986–87	1-0, 2-1, 1-2 v Arsenal (Semi-final)
1987–88	1-2 v Aston Villa (Third Round)
1988–89	1-2 v Southampton (Fourth Round)
1989–90	2-2, 2-3 v Nottingham Forest (Fifth Round)

Europe

| 1980–81 | Did not qualify |

1981–82	Did not qualify
1982–83	Did not qualify
1983–84	UEFA Cup: 1-1, 1-1 (4-3 pens) v Anderlecht (Final)
1984–85	UEFA Cup: 0-1, 0-0 v Real Madrid (Quarter-final)
1985–86	English clubs banned from European competition
1986–87	English clubs banned from European competition
1987–88	English clubs banned from European competition
1988–89	English clubs banned from European competition
1989–90	English clubs banned from European competition

30th August 1980

First Division

Arsenal 2

Price, Stapleton

Tottenham Hotspur 0

Attendance: 54,045

Arsenal: *Jennings, Devine, Sansom, Talbot, O'Leary, Young, Hollins, Sunderland, Stapleton, Price, Rix.*

Tottenham Hotspur: *Kendall, Smith (Taylor), Hughton, Yorath, Lacy, Perryman, Ardiles, Archibald, Villa, Hoddle, Crooks.*

John Lacy, virtually the forgotten man of Tottenham a few months ago, had made the headlines in the week, after scoring the only goal of the League Cup second-round first-leg clash against Orient. The beanpole centre-half, who had played only four league games the previous season, stole the limelight from new glamour boys Garth Crooks and Steve Archibald, but it was an Arsenal starlet who grabbed the plaudits during the home side's 2-0 win over Spurs. "Rix seems an England cert" sang the headline! Graham Rix was just another Arsenal apprentice when Alan Ball predicted he would be a star, and it was expected that he would be named in Ron Greenwood's imminent England squad. The 22-year-old set up goals for David Price and Frank Stapleton, as Arsenal returned to form following the previous week's 3-1 loss against Coventry City.

4th November 1980

League Cup fourth round
Tottenham Hotspur 1
Ardiles
Arsenal 0
Attendance: 42,511
Tottenham Hotspur: *Daines, Smith, Hughton, Miller, Lacy, Perryman, Ardiles (Roberts), Archibald, Villa, Hoddle, Crooks.*
Arsenal: *Wood, Devine, Sansom, Talbot, Walford, Young, Hollins (McDermott), Sunderland, Stapleton, Gatting, Rix.*

Little Ossie Ardiles ended the hoodoo that had been hanging over Tottenham for more than four years in November 1980. A 25th-minute goal by the Argentinean took Tottenham to the quarter-finals of the League Cup, and gave them victory over their north London rivals for the first time since 1976. So Terry Neill finally tasted defeat against his old club. Keith Burkinshaw had called for the application his players had shown when beating Coventry and drawing against Everton. Arsenal were pushed back on the defensive right from the rain- and sleet-lashed start. Ricky Villa, full of menace and controlled Argentinean aggression, drove fiercely past George Wood early on, only for referee Ron Challis to rule the goal void because of an earlier infringement. Then it was the turn of Ardiles, the other half of Tottenham's South American team. He was desperately unlucky, with a powerful drive that just cleared the crossbar. However, in the 25th minute, groans of Tottenham disappointment turned to tumultuous cheers as Ardiles scored. Villa found Garth Crooks and his shot was beaten out by Wood. Ardiles followed up, to shoot through despite a desperate attempt by Kenny Sansom to keep the ball out. Arsenal found some rhythm after that. They forced their way forward, and Frank Stapleton had a downwards header superbly saved by Barry Daines. Arsenal had plenty of possession in the second half, but Tottenham closed them down so well that they found this particular White Hart Lane experience increasingly frustrating. Steve Perryman, again pushed forward to the midfield, was an inspiring skipper as Tottenham battled to keep their lead. After good work by Sansom and Alan Sunderland, Graham Rix curled a shot narrowly over the crossbar. But Tottenham held firm. Midway through the second half, Arsenal took off John Hollins and sent on teenage substitute Brian McDermott – a scorer in the previous Saturday's win over Brighton. It was a last desperate gamble but it didn't pay off.

17th January 1981

First Division
Tottenham Hotspur 2
Archibald 2
Arsenal 0
Attendance: 32,944
Tottenham Hotspur: *Daines, McAllister, Miller, Roberts, Lacy (Yorath), Perryman, Brooke, Archibald, Galvin, Hoddle, Crooks.*
Arsenal: *Jennings, Devine, Sansom, McDermott, Walford, Young, Hollins, Sunderland, Stapleton, Gatting, Rix.*

Ossie Ardiles was missing from the Spurs line-up for this derby match, after being fined for returning late from the Gold Cup in Uruguay. All indications were that the Argentine had been forgiven by Keith Burkinshaw and his return was merely a formality, although Portuguese champions Sporting Lisbon were monitoring the situation closely, despite everything pointing to the midfield ace signing a new contract to stay in England for a further two years. On the field, it was another import who secured the points for Spurs, as Steve Archibald netted twice.

2nd January 1982

FA Cup third round
Tottenham Hotspur 1
Crooks
Arsenal 0

London Football Clubs' Struggle to Avoid Relegation.

Action from the second north London league derby as both sides struggled to avoid relegation in April 1910. The match finished one apiece, with goals from Charlie McGibbon and Jack Curtis.

47,109 PEOPLE WATCH TOTTENHAM BEAT WOOLWICH AT WHITE HART LANE.

A massive 47,109 crowd turned out to watch this Christmas Day spectacular that saw Spurs win 5-0 in December 1911.

LEFT: Peter McWilliam managed Spurs twice (1913–1927 and 1938–1942) and was in charge during the successful early 1920s when they won the Second Division title and the FA Cup.

BELOW: The Tottenham squad pose in August 1921 with the FA Cup and Charity Shield.

ABOVE: Arsenal manager Herbert Chapman looks on as the Arsenal players lift captain Alex James following their FA Cup triumph over Huddersfield in 1930.

BELOW: Two players from the successful Arsenal team of the 1930s: Charlie Jones (left) and Charlie Preedy (right). Right-half Jones won three First Division winners' medals (in 1930–31, 1932–33 and 1933–34), and played in the 1931–32 FA Cup final, while Preedy struggled to dislodge first-choice goalkeeper Dan Lewis and made just 37 league appearances during his four-year stay at the club.

Miss injured in rushing out to save.

Attending to casualties. There were many cases of fainting owing to the crush.

Nicholls (Spurs' goalie) punches the ball off the feet of an Arsenal forward.

A gate of 71,000 broke the ground record at Highbury yesterday, when the Arsenal lost their match against the Spurs 3—1, and also the League leadership. A large crowd, seen beyond the closed gates, could not even gain admission.

Highbury struggled to cope with the record crowd of around 70,000 who turned up to see Spurs win the derby match 3-1. While thousands were shut out of the ground, many inside suffered in the crush in January 1934.

Two Arsenal legends of the 1930s: Ted Drake (left) and Alex James. Drake had an amazing scoring record for the Gunners, netting 139 times in 184 appearances between 1934 and 1945. James, meanwhile, played more than 260 games for the club between 1929 and 1937.

BELOW LEFT: Arsenal's Bryn Jones and Bert Sproston (Spurs) during the Jubilee Trust Fund charity match at Highbury in August 1938. The visitors won the game 2-0 with goals from Johnny Morrison and Colin Lyman.

BELOW RIGHT: George Swindin (left) and Ted Ditchburn (right) size each other up in December 1948. These two would be the opposing goalkeepers when Arsenal and Spurs met for the first time in the FA Cup third-round tie that Arsenal won 3-0 the following month.

ABOVE: The Arsenal team with the FA Cup in May 1950. Back row, left to right: Tom Whittaker (manager), Leslie Compton, Lawrie Scott, George Swindin, Walley Barnes, Billy Milne (trainer). Front row, left to right: Archie Macaulay, Freddie Cox, Jimmy Logie, Joe Mercer, Peter Goring, Reg Lewis, Dennis Compton.

BELOW: Goalmouth action at White Hart Lane in January 1959 where Arsenal won 4-1. Spurs striker Dave Dunmore tries to put the ball in the back of the net despite the attention of Arsenal's Bill Dodgin and keeper Jack Kelsey (partly hidden).

Bill Nicholson celebrates winning the Double in 1961 with his players in traditional style.

Pat Jennings – Spurs' new signing from Watford – shows off a safe pair of hands in August 1964. Little did anyone know at the time, but the goalkeeper would go on to become a legend at both north London clubs.

The Spurs squad prepare for the 1965–66 season under the watchful eye of the press. From left to right: Frank Saul, John Sainty, Jimmy Pearce, Neil Johnson, Jimmy Greaves, Alan Gilzean, David Gillingwater, Stephen Pitt, Keith Weller, Roger Smith, Jim Robertson, Derek Possee, Cliff Jones, Jimmy Walker, Tony Smith, Terry Reardon, Maurice Norman, Alan Mullery, Dave Mackay, Jimmy Lye, Roy Low, Roger Hoy, Den Embery, Eddie Clayton, Laurie Brown, Philip Beal, Dennis Walker, Cyril Knowles, Joe Kinnear, Ron Henry, Pat Jennings, Bill Brown, Roy Brown.

ABOVE: Jimmy Greaves celebrates after scoring a goal for Tottenham Hotspur only for it to be ruled offside by the referee at Highbury during their league match with rivals Arsenal in January 1967.

BELOW: Arsenal's squad for the 1967–68 season included two men who would go on to manage both north London rivals in Terry Neill and George Graham. Back row, left to right: Gordon Neilson, Colin Addison, John Woodward, Peter Simpson, Bob Wilson, James Furnell, Don Howe, Frank McLintock, George Graham, George Johnstone, George Armstrong. Front row, left to right: Peter Storey, Bob McNab, Jon Sammels, Ian Ure, Terry Neill, David Court, John Radford, James McGill, Tommy Coakley.

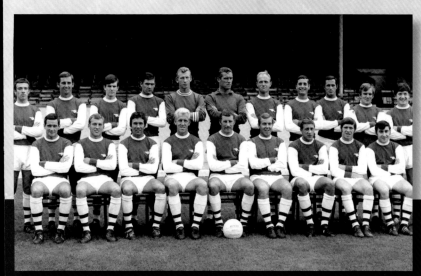

ABOVE: John Radford shoots past Spurs goalkeeper Pat Jennings to score the only goal of the November 1968 League Cup semi-final first leg.

BELOW: Jimmy Greaves scores the opening goal for Spurs in the League Cup semi-final second-leg match at White Hart Lane in December 1968. While the match finished one apiece, Arsenal went through over the two legs.

Ray Kennedy scores the only goal of the game at White Hart Lane in May 1971 that secures the First Division title for Arsenal and the first trophy of the Double.

Arsenal manager Bertie Mee and coach Don Howe show their delight at becoming only the second side to win the Double in the 20th century.

Tempers boil over in the December 1976 derby match at White Hart Lane that finished 2-2. Arsenal keeper Jimmy Rimmer is held by a linesman as Spurs' Willie Young is held back by the referee before his sending off.

ABOVE: The Highbury faithful acclaim Supermac after he scored the only goal of the game in April 1977. Sadly, Malcolm Macdonald's playing career would be prematurely cut short two years later.

BELOW: Highbury – pictured here in the 1970s – was Arsenal's home for 92 years and staged many dramatic north London derbies.

Liam Brady (left) and Ossie Ardiles compete for the ball in this midfield tussle in April 1980.

BELOW: A lighter moment in the summer of 1984 as Spurs players Mark Falco, Gary Mabbutt and Clive Allen line up for a publicity shot.

ABOVE: Garth Crooks looks for a way to break down the Arsenal defence in this First Division match at Highbury in August 1980 watched by team-mates Glenn Hoddle and Steve Archibald. Arsenal's Kenny Sansom had the last laugh though, with the Gunners winning 2-0.

A policeman tries to catch an invading spectator at Highbury in January 1985.

The crowd and players alike celebrate Gary Stevens scoring the only goal of the game at White Hart Lane on 29th March 1986.

John Lukic thwarts another Spurs attack in January 1989 as (from left) David O'Leary, Steve Bould and Tony Adams look on. Arsenal won the match 2-0 with goals from Paul Merson and Michael Thomas.

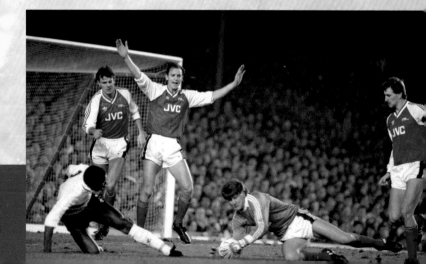

Spurs hero Paul Gascoigne celebrates with Steve Sedgley at the end of the April 1991 FA Cup semi-final at Wembley that saw Arsenal defeated 3-1.

Arsenal manager George Graham and captain Tony Adams show off the League Championship trophy to thousands of fans gathered in the streets of north London for the team's open top bus parade in May 1991.

Spurs striker Gary Lineker is presented with a special commemorative trophy to mark his final game in May 1992.

Ian Wright is at the centre of the argument at White Hart Lane in December 1992. The Arsenal striker was caught on camera in an off-the-ball incident with Spurs' David Howells.

Arsenal captain Tony Adams scores the only goal to beat archrivals Spurs in the 1993 FA Cup semi-final at Wembley.

Robert Pirès was a constant thorn in Spurs' side between 2000 and 2006 with eight goals in 12 derby appearances.

Arsène Wenger, Arsenal's most successful manager in the club's history, celebrates with yet another trophy, the 2002 FA Cup after a 2-0 win over Chelsea at Wembley.

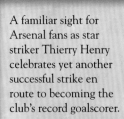

A familiar sight for Arsenal fans as star striker Thierry Henry celebrates yet another successful strike en route to becoming the club's record goalscorer.

Gareth Bale celebrates scoring Spurs' second goal in the 2-1 win at White Hart Lane in April 2010 that finally ended Arsenal's dominance of the fixture.

Harry Redknapp (left) was happier than Arsène Wenger as Spurs fought their way to a 2-1 win at White Hart Lane in October 2011 to leave Arsenal facing the worst start to a season for more years than many cared to remember.

Attendance: 38,421
Tottenham Hotspur: *Clemence, Hughton, Miller, Roberts, Villa, Perryman, Ardiles, Falco, Galvin, Hoddle, Crooks.*
Arsenal: *Jennings (Meade), Robson, Sansom, Talbot, O'Leary, Whyte, Hollins, Sunderland, Rix, Nicholas, Davis.*

The passion Paul Miller carried into any match that involved Arsenal saved him from being axed by Tottenham in November 1982. "Max", as he was known to his team-mates, stayed in the side for the third-round FA Cup confrontation at White Hart Lane. He was preferred to Paul Price. Miller and his combative defensive qualities gave the cup-holders that extra dimension, so important in the emotional encounters between the two sides about who ruled north London. Under pressure for a cup final place, Miller rose magnificently to the challenge. And Keith Burkinshaw may well have stoked up the fires again when Miller admitted that he had an obsession to beat Arsenal. When he first joined the club it was impressed on him that Arsenal were to be beaten at all levels, junior games, youth team, reserves and the first team. All his Tottenham pals knew, alongside Miller, that whatever they did they had to beat the Gunners. Miller, then 22, had made his debut against the Gunners three years before, when Arsenal won 1-0, with Frank Stapleton – the man he was marking – scoring the only goal. Even Pat Jennings, Arsenal's 36-year-old goalkeeper, was still moved by the derby matches – and by this time he'd had nearly 20 years of them. Jennings stated how much it meant to Spurs, and claimed that the intense feelings ran much deeper at Tottenham than they did at Arsenal. But it was to be Garth Crooks who would prove the destroyer of Arsenal's last cup chance. Conquering a crisis point in his own season, the striker's smile of relief was in stark contrast to the agony experienced by Jennings. Throughout his career, the months of January and December had always proved barren scoring times for Crooks, and he'd missed the first 12 league games due to a cartilage operation in the summer of 1981. It had left him trailing behind the rest of the Tottenham team, as an understandable lack of fitness aggravated the problem. However, like someone struggling with a jigsaw, it suddenly all came together for Crooks, as the holders successfully broke through the toughest possible opening defence of the FA Cup. Crooks scored the goal that started Jennings' day of despair, hit the woodwork twice, and could have potentially finished with five goals. Crooks realized he'd only been playing at about 60 per cent of his previous form but, against Arsenal, he got back the yard of pace that had been lacking since his operation – and it made all the difference. Arsenal coach Don Howe reflected on the 16th-minute Crooks shot that slid into the net past Jennings' groping hands: "Pat has been involved in talking about his contract and this can affect the most experienced players." Jennings denied that the goal had anything to do with his contract and took full responsibility when he said: "The goal was a terrible mistake on my part."

29th March 1982

First Division

Tottenham Hotspur 2

Archibald, Hughton

Arsenal 2

Sunderland 2

Attendance: 40,940

Tottenham Hotspur: *Clemence, Hughton, Roberts, Price, Villa, Perryman, Ardiles, Archibald, Galvin, Hoddle, Hazard.*

Arsenal: *Wood, Hollins, Sansom, Talbot, O'Leary, Whyte, Meade, Sunderland, Davis (Nicholas), Robson, Rix.*

The north London derby erupted in March 1982, as two men were sent off in the climax of a four-goal thriller. Before a near capacity crowd of almost 41,000, the battle to stay in the First Division title race turned from drama to controversy. Tottenham's Irish international Chris Hughton, and Arsenal's Alan Sunderland (both goalscorers), clashed in an ugly scene. Referee Ray Lewis pointed immediately to the dressing room. Later, Keith Burkinshaw said:

"If he had entered into the spirit of things he would not have done what he did. Technically he was within his rights and I thought he had a good game." According to Burkinshaw, 20 years earlier there would not have been any bookings or sendings off. It was the first sending off in defender Hughton's career; four others – Arsenal's David O'Leary, John Hollins and Stewart Robson, and Tottenham's Mike Hazard – were booked on a night of rare London excitement, when Spurs pulled back from a two-goal deficit. But for Spurs, despite the team's spirit and pulling back from two goals down, it had been a bad week, with two points lost. Arsenal had had a disappointing season being labeled "bores", but they'd scored four goals and appeared to be romping to victory. At that stage no one would have given Tottenham a chance. Arsenal scored twice in the first half and took the lead after 25 minutes, when Paul Davis created the space and the time for Sunderland to head in. Two minutes before half-time, the speed and guile of England full-back Ken Sansom provided Sunderland with a second goal – and it looked as though the crowd could pack their cases and go home. Tottenham, slammed by Burkinshaw the previous weekend for lacking spirit, came back on to an emotionally charged pitch, and reduced the arrears after 64 minutes. The impressive Hazard, who had passed a fitness test just before the game, had a shot blocked by Chris Whyte, but Scottish striker Steve Archibald was on hand to slot the ball in. Then, after 73 minutes, Hughton grabbed the equalizer. He appeared at the right moment, and the inspiring Graham Roberts headed the ball into his path. Then it was all set for a dramatic finish, which unfortunately produced not a winning goal, but a punch-up. Hughton's dismissal would not, however, rule him out of the FA Cup semi-final, as his suspension could not take effect until after Easter Monday that year.

12ᵗʰ April 1982

First Division

Arsenal 1

Hawley

Tottenham Hotspur 3

Hazard, Crooks 2

Attendance: **48,897**

Arsenal: *Wood, Hollins, Sansom, Talbot, O'Leary, Whyte, Meade, Hawley, Nicholas, Robson (McDermott), Rix.*

Tottenham Hotspur: *Clemence, Roberts, Miller, Price, Hazard, Perryman, Villa, Jones, Galvin, Hoddle, Crooks.*

The message went north in April 1982 to Merseyside that the First Division championship was still an open issue. Keith Burkinshaw had made a pre-Easter call for nine points, from matches against Ipswich, Arsenal and Sunderland, if his team were to keep the pressure on Liverpool. Ipswich and disappointing Arsenal had been beaten, and the immediate Treble was definitely on for the FA Cup, the Cup Winners' Cup and the league. There were four goals scored at the north London derby, with a streaker who appeared from Highbury's North Bank. The young girl, who made a laboured run down Tottenham's left flank late in the game, had, according to newspaper reports, as much trouble getting her bra off as Arsenal did in putting together their moves. Arsenal, who played so well in drawing 2-2 at White Hart Lane two weeks prior to the match, were never in with a genuine chance after Mike Hazard had shot Tottenham into a ninth-minute lead. Hazard, once again, was simply superb. Burkinshaw was also pleased with Ricky Villa, who shrugged off the expected abuse from Arsenal fans to play a vital part in two of Tottenham's goals. Kenny Sansom, and a not-totally-fit Graham Rix, battled with skill to lend some respectability to Arsenal's display, but Tottenham were the better side, and deserved their win. Tottenham's opening goal saw Villa send Hazard bursting through the middle, for a shot hit with ferocious power from the edge of the penalty box. It was Tottenham's first goal at Highbury since 1976. In the 53rd minute Hazard's run opened up the centre of Arsenal's defence, and he unselfishly squared the ball to Garth Crooks, who scored with ease. Arsenal pulled one back two minutes later, when Glenn Hoddle lost the ball to Rix, whose low cross was driven in firmly by John Hawley. Thoughts that Arsenal might halt the Tottenham advance lasted just two minutes. In the 57th minute, Graham Roberts and Tony Galvin combined to send Villa away. His cross was touched out by Arsenal keeper George Wood, and Crooks drove in at the far post. Tottenham were now nine points behind Liverpool, with three games in hand. Liverpool were at home to Stoke while this game was played, and Tottenham had all to play for against Sunderland the following day.

27th December 1982

First Division

Arsenal 2

Sunderland, Woodcock

Tottenham Hotspur 0

Attendance: 51,497

Arsenal: *Jennings, Hollins, Sansom, Talbot, O'Leary, Robson, Davis, Sunderland, Nicholas, Woodcock, Rix.*

Tottenham Hotspur: *Clemence, Hughton, O'Reilly, Roberts, Hazard, Perryman, Mabbutt, Archibald, Galvin (Brooke), Hoddle, Crooks.*

Arsenal defender Stewart Robson, 18, was given a "carry on" vote of confidence by manager Terry Neill, after being sent off in the humbling of Tottenham. It was the second successive home match that Arsenal had won after having a player banished. The time before, when Aston Villa were beaten 2-1, Robson replaced the ordered-off George Wood in goal, and earned a hero's rating. Cynics in the 51,497 crowd – Highbury's best of the season – claimed Arsenal would be champions if they could always play 10 against 11. At the match Robson, a former public schoolboy, had switched to the centre of Arsenal's defence at the expense of the axed Chris Whyte. He was sent off in the 55th minute of a rousing game for chopping down Steve Archibald. Five minutes earlier, he had been booked by referee Lester Shapter, after a scything tackle on Graham Roberts. Terry Neill said later: "I wouldn't argue with the decision, but there is not a trace of malice in the lad." Tottenham could not really argue about the result. Arsenal, who had been second best to their traditional rivals over the past couple of seasons, were worthy winners. David O'Leary gave one of the outstanding defensive displays of the season. Kenny Sansom and Graham Rix shone, while strikers Alan Sunderland and Tony Woodcock put Tottenham's defenders under constant pressure. Then there was goalkeeper Pat Jennings. In the words of Keith Burkinshaw, "he brought off two saves as good as any he will produce for a while". First, he spread himself to stop a Garth Crooks blast, then he turned a Crooks header on to the bar. Arsenal went in front five minutes before half-time. It started with a superb Rix ball from deep inside his own half. With Tottenham caught square, Woodcock and Brian Talbot combined to send Sunderland in for a left-foot goal, struck with ferocious power. Four minutes from the hectic end, a long Jennings clearance caught defender Gary O'Reilly wrong-footed, and Woodcock shot into the far corner.

4th April 1983

First Division

Tottenham Hotspur 5

Hughton 2, Falco 2, Brazil

Arsenal 0

Attendance: 43,652

Tottenham Hotspur: *Clemence, Hughton, O'Reilly, Roberts, Miller, Gibson, Mabbutt, Archibald, Galvin, Brazil, Falco.*

Arsenal: *Wood, Robson, Sansom, Whyte (Petrovi), O'Leary, Nicholas, Talbot, Davis, Sunderland, Woodcock, Rix.*

Arsenal reeled away from White Hart Lane in April 1983, leaving a giant-sized question mark against their ability to recover in time for the FA Cup semi-final confrontation with Manchester United.

Not since the days of knee-length shorts and heavyweight ball had Arsenal surrendered so completely in the traditional north London derby. Tottenham recorded their biggest win over them in 71 years, and Arsenal were lucky to get away with only a five-goal hiding. They were that bad. Terry Neill and coach Don Howe, let down by players whose minds seemed to be on the date with United on Saturday the following week, immediately cancelled the day off scheduled for their men. Neill controlled his anger and said: "We'll be in first thing [tomorrow] and go from there. We've not got a minute to lose. It obviously wasn't good enough and something will have to be done." Centre-half David O'Leary limped away painfully from the humiliation 20 minutes before the finish, with a recurrence of the ankle injury that kept him out for two months. With his ankle in plaster, his manager stated it was too early to talk about the semi-final. Arsenal were a world away from the side that beat Spurs 2-0 in their Yuletide encounter. Only Peter Nicholas, Stewart Robson – booked, and now scheduled to miss any FA Cup replay because of suspension – Graham Rix and Alan Sunderland matched their rivals for effort. Full-back Chris Hughton scored twice for Tottenham, and so did young striker Mark Falco, while Alan Brazil got the other. No wonder Spurs manager Burkinshaw congratulated all three of them. He praised his players and said that Falco's first goal was as good as anything he'd seen for a long time. He also remarked that Hughton was a tremendous talent. Burkinshaw further stated that Arsenal had beaten Tottenham 5-0 in his early days as manager, and that he'd waited a long time for the result to come in the other way around. The fascinating aspect of it all for Spurs was that this slaughter was achieved without Glenn Hoddle, Ossie Ardiles, Steve Perryman or Ricky Villa. An immediate return could not be guaranteed for any of them. Tottenham, when good, were very, very good. Their opening three goals came in an electrifying spell between the 10th and 18th minutes, and it was basically goodbye Arsenal. Hughton got the first with a mishit shot that trickled over the line. The second, however, was of a different calibre. Little Terry Gibson raced down the right, crossed, and Falco scored with a stunning volley. Five minutes later George Wood was beaten again, and must have had to accept much of the blame. Hughton took Brazil's pass, turned inside and beat the Arsenal keeper at the near post. With 52 minutes gone, Paul Miller's deep free-kick saw Falco score from another powerful volley. Tottenham kept up their forward march, and Brazil made it five.

9th November 1983

League Cup third round
Tottenham Hotspur 1
Hoddle (pen)
Arsenal 2
Nicholas, Woodcock
Attendance: 48,200
Tottenham Hotspur: *Clemence, Hughton, Thomas, Price (Brazil), Stevens, Perryman, Roberts, Archibald, Falco, Hoddle, Galvin.*
Arsenal: *Jennings, Robson, Sansom, Whyte, O'Leary, Hill, Sunderland, Davis, Woodcock, Nicholas, Rix.*

Television celebrity Eamonn Andrews provided the final fairy tale touch to the magnificent north London derby in November 1983, when he ran on to the pitch at the final whistle to tell Arsenal goalkeeper Pat Jennings: "This Is Your Life". The 48,200 capacity crowd at White Hart Lane for the League Cup clash, were in no doubt that, for Arsenal, this was their night. From the moment £750,000 Scot Charlie Nicholas found his capital scoring touch, his first goal since 29th August, the Gunners were on their way to a famous third-round victory. The important goal Nicholas scored in the 33rd minute was his first in London. When Tony Woodcock put Arsenal further in front two minutes into the second half, Tottenham looked buried. Even though Glenn Hoddle scored from the penalty spot four minutes later, Keith Burkinshaw was the first to admit that Arsenal had been the better side. He stated that the atmosphere had got to his men, and not one of them had played particularly well. Ray Clemence made a boob for Arsenal's first goal, and it put their tails up. Gary Stevens made a bad mistake over the second Arsenal goal. Arsenal boss Terry Neill was pleased for the fans. It was a gritty, gutsy show by an Arsenal side who never allowed Tottenham to hit the stride that had seen them overwhelm so many teams in recent matches. David O'Leary, Kenny Sansom and skipper Graham Rix were not far behind Woodcock in star quality. The signs that Arsenal were about to avenge the 5-0 First Division hammering they took at White Hart Lane were there long before the first goal was scored. Clemence, under pressure from Woodcock, failed to collect a deep ball from Colin Hill. When it broke loose towards the edge of the penalty box, Nicholas was there to lob the ball just under the crossbar. Two minutes into the second half, Alan Sunderland's pass found Woodcock. The in-form England striker left Stevens stranded, before sending a low shot wide of Clemence's left hand for his ninth goal in five games. Tottenham immediately pulled off Paul Price, sent on Alan Brazil and, after 51 minutes, found the net. Whyte handled, and Hoddle beat Jennings from the spot. Four players were booked – Tottenham pair Graham Roberts and Hoddle, plus Arsenal's Woodcock and Sunderland. But Tottenham were facing two more struggles, as UEFA were deciding whether they were responsible for the previous week's Rotterdam riots, while at home a Football League board were hearing the club's appeal against a £10,000 fine for illegal payments. It really was Arsenal's night.

26th December 1983

First Division
Tottenham Hotspur 2
Roberts, Archibald
Arsenal 4
Nicholas 2, Meade 2
Attendance: **38,756**
Tottenham Hotspur: *Clemence, Hughton (Falco), Cooke, Roberts, Stevens, Perryman, Ardiles, Archibald, Brazil, Hoddle, Dick.*
Arsenal: *Jennings, Hill, Sansom, Robson (Cork), O'Leary, Caton, Meade, Davis, Woodcock, Nicholas, Allinson.*

Don Howe was named as the runner coming up on the rails, in the great Highbury management race in December 1983. Two goals each from Charlie Nicholas and Raphael Meade saw Arsenal win at Tottenham for the second time in two months. Arsenal had won twice and scored seven goals since Howe switched to caretaker manager after the departure of Terry Neill. Howe's first major decision had proved an outright winner. He brought in Meade to partner Tony Woodcock up front against Watford, dropping Nicholas back to midfield. Meade, nearly given a free transfer in the summer of 1983, responded with a hat-trick in a 3-1 win. This time, with Tottenham conceding four goals for the second successive game, Meade and Nicholas produced some superb finishing. Arsenal went in front after 26 minutes and Nicholas, whose last league goal came in the first week of the season, saw his first shot come back off a defender, before scoring with a left-foot drive. Stevens again headed against the woodwork, before Tottenham equalized through Graham Roberts 11 minutes later. Arsenal, with the energetic David Cork brought on to mark Glenn Hoddle after Stewart Robson had gone off, went in front again after 48 minutes. Ian Allinson's ball left Tottenham's central defenders spreadeagled, and Nicholas lobbed cleverly wide of Ray Clemence. Arsenal's lead this time lasted just one minute, before Archibald struck a deserved equalizer. But Arsenal went ahead for the third time in the 74th minute. Nicholas was involved with a pass that Paul Davis controlled before crossing for Meade to head in. Tottenham put on substitute Mark Falco for Hughton, but four minutes from the finish Clemence could only push out a Nicholas shot, and Meade touched it back over the line.

21st April 1984

First Division

Arsenal 3

Robson, Nicholas, Woodcock

Tottenham Hotspur 2
Archibald 2
Attendance: **48,831**
Arsenal: *Lukic, Hill, Sansom, Talbot, O'Leary, Caton, Robson, Nicholas,*
Mariner, Woodcock, Rix (Davis).
Tottenham Hotspur: *Parks, Thomas, Hughton, Roberts, Miller,*
Perryman, Mabbutt, Archibald, Galvin, Crook (Stevens), Crooks.

Don Howe was widely tipped to be confirmed as the next Arsenal
manager in the 10 days following this victory over Spurs. The
directors had met before the previous home game against Leicester
– and everything pointed to Howe losing his tag as soccer's head
waiter. Arsenal had not planned to make a decision until the end of
the season, and Howe was told as much. The team now, however,
had the luxury of going to Birmingham with only one defeat in 10
matches, and Howe had edged in front of Terry Venables, the only
other serious contender for the job. Stewart Robson opened the
scoring just before the interval, and the score remained the same
until the 79th minute, when the goal torrent began. Charlie Nicholas
doubled Arsenal's lead, before Steve Archibald reduced the deficit.
Tony Woodcock restored the two-goal cushion, but Archibald netted
his second of the game, to provide a nervy final few minutes for the
home crowd.

1ˢᵗ January 1985

First Division
Arsenal 1
Woodcock
Tottenham Hotspur 2
Crooks, Falco
Attendance: **48,714**
Arsenal: *Lukic, Anderson, Caton, Talbot, O'Leary, Adams, Robson,*
Allinson, Mariner, Woodcock, Nicholas (Williams).
Tottenham Hotspur: *Clemence, Stevens, Mabbutt, Roberts, Miller,*
Perryman, Chiedozie, Falco, Galvin, Hoddle (Allen), Crooks.

Arsenal manager Don Howe blasted his stars, after Mark Falco's 18th goal of the season had powered Tottenham into the New Year still at the top of the First Division. Tony Woodcock put Arsenal into a 42nd-minute lead, but Garth Crooks equalized after the break. Talking of Tottenham's second-half equalizer Howe said: "It was a rubbish goal ... pathetic. If John Lukic and Tommy Caton are going to make it here they have got to do better than that." Howe took Charlie Nicholas off immediately after Falco's 74th-minute winner, replacing him with £550,000 Steve Williams, saying, "Charlie looked as if he didn't want to do battle."

17th April 1985

First Division
Tottenham Hotspur 0
Arsenal 2
Nicholas, Talbot
Attendance: 40,399
Tottenham Hotspur: *Clemence, Thomas, Bowen, Roberts, Chiedozie, Perryman, Ardiles, Falco, Leworthy, Hoddle, Galvin (Hazard).*
Arsenal: *Lukic, Anderson, Sansom, Williams, O'Leary (Mariner), Caton, Robson, Rix, Allinson, Talbot, Nicholas.*

White Hart Lane became the funeral pyre for Tottenham's dreams. Title hopes that blossomed and flourished through the dark days of winter finally died on a fine spring evening, as bitter rivals Arsenal gained an important victory. Goals by Charlie Nicholas in the first half, and Brian Talbot in the final seconds, kept Don Howe's men pushing for a place in Europe. Tottenham were left to concede that they could no longer be considered even remote rivals to Everton for the championship. They were eight points behind the relentless Merseyside machine, having played two games more, and were rapidly running out of matches. Spurs manager Peter Shreeves conceded that it had been a good night for Everton. Tottenham, in their moments of deepest despair, must have conceded the title had been lost at White Hart Lane. While no team had won more games away from their own ground, only four sides had won fewer matches at home. In a disappointing 1985, Real Madrid won at White Hart Lane to kill Tottenham's UEFA Cup chance, Sunderland succeeded there in the League Cup, and five of the previous home encounters ended in defeat. Arsenal fully deserved victory over their old enemy. Centre-half David O'Leary was forced to leave the action two minutes before half-time with an ankle injury, and was replaced by striker Paul Mariner, who played a hero's role in the heart of a superb Arsenal defence. The goal that was the beginning of the end for Tottenham came in the 21st minute from the hitman who had become a hoodoo for them. It was Nicholas at his very best. He scored for the fifth time in five games against Spurs, and this one was sheer class. Graham Rix and Steve Williams set up a move that saw Nicholas accelerate past Graham Roberts, before shooting fiercely wide of Ray Clemence. The real death blow for Tottenham wasn't the goal Talbot coolly shot after a long run in the dying seconds, it was the penalty Graham Roberts missed 10 minutes earlier. Viv Anderson was judged to have handled by referee Colin Downey in a hectic goalmouth scramble. Roberts drove his spot kick against the top of the crossbar, and the crowd knew it was all over.

1st January 1986

First Division

Arsenal 0

Tottenham Hotspur 0

Attendance: 45,109

Arsenal: *Lukic, Anderson, Sansom, Davis, O'Leary, Keown, Allinson, Rocastle, Nicholas, Quinn (Woodcock), Rix.*

Tottenham Hotspur: *Clemence, Stevens, Hughton, Roberts, Mabbutt, Perryman, Ardiles, Falco, C Allen, Hoddle, Waddle.*

Veteran keeper Pat Jennings was on call, after reserve Tony Parks went into hospital for a cartilage operation, leaving Spurs without any cover. The 40-year-old Jennings was in the squad, but Peter

Shreeves explained "Pat is in great shape and tremendous form. I wouldn't have any reservations at all if he has to play." Arsenal had moved to the fringe of the championship chase after wins over Liverpool, Manchester United and Queens Park Rangers, and had Viv Anderson back after suspension to replace Gus Caesar at right-back. In the end, Jennings was not called into action for yet another derby appearance, as the two sides played out a goalless draw.

29th March 1986

First Division

Tottenham Hotspur 1

Stevens

Arsenal 0

Attendance: 33,427

Tottenham Hotspur: *Clemence, P Allen, Thomas, Roberts, Miller, Stevens, Mabbutt, Falco, Galvin, Hoddle, Waddle.*

Arsenal: *Lukic, Anderson, Sansom, Williams, O'Leary, Keown, Hayes, Rocastle, Nicholas, Quinn (Mariner), Rix.*

Glenn Hoddle returned to form in this dogfight of a derby. The England midfielder was again totally involved in a battle that called for skill, accuracy of pass and control. Hoddle showed a growing maturity and did everything asked of him. Against an Arsenal side who were very competitive, he showed not only his elegant ability but heart for the fight too, winning the ball, getting in tackles and always being in the thick of the action. He never shirked a thing, and perhaps it was a kick from the abrasive Steve Williams that stirred him up. Chris Waddle also showed his appetite but, for all his skill, he was still criticized for being too erratic and almost irresponsible in front of the goal. At times, Viv Anderson was guilty of not getting back quickly enough after he had ventured forward. He tended to dawdle and let Spurs exploit the space he left. Hoddle inevitably set up the goal for Gary Stevens; it won the match and hit the post in a 35-yard shot that was sheer brilliance. Spurs had a real warrior in Graham Roberts, who played an inspirational game, but Hoddle easily claimed the man-of-the-match plaudits.

6th September 1986

First Division

Arsenal 0
Tottenham Hotspur 0

Attendance: 44,707

Arsenal: *Lukic, Anderson, Sansom, Robson, O'Leary, Adams, Rocastle (Hayes), Davis, Quinn, Nicholas, Rix.*

Tottenham Hotspur: *Clemence, Stevens, M Thomas, Roberts, Gough, Mabbutt, C Allen, Falco (Ardiles), Waddle, Hoddle, Galvin.*

Ossie Ardiles had a message for the critics who said he was running out of puff at the age of 34, and was finished as a First Division performer. The Argentinean superstar had given up his habit of smoking up to 40 cigarettes a day, to get himself into shape. He transformed this hurly-burly derby with his own special brand of sophistication. Ardiles had thought that his illustrious career was over after his testimonial match the previous May, but, typically, he fought back to fitness. "I'm on a monthly contract and that suits me because I wanted to prove myself, as well as the manager, that I'm physically fit," he explained. Arsenal boss George Graham, disappointed by the lack of quality in the game and by his own team's performance, marvelled at the genius of Ardiles: "It was wonderful to see him play. He gave Tottenham a new dimension."

4th January 1987

First Division

Tottenham Hotspur 1
M Thomas
Arsenal 2
Adams, Davis

Attendance: 37,723

Tottenham Hotspur: *Clemence, D Thomas, M Thomas, Ardiles*

(Claesen), Gough, Mabbutt, C Allen, P Allen, Waddle, Hoddle, Galvin.
Arsenal: *Lukic, Anderson, Sansom, Williams, O'Leary, Adams, Rocastle, Davis, Quinn (Rix), Nicholas, Hayes.*

Arsenal's significant step towards their first championship, since the Double triumph 16 years before, was all the sweeter for putting their north London rivals firmly in their place. The Gunners' jubilant fans were singing in the rain at White Hart Lane on 4th January 1987, as George Graham's team won this historic 100th league derby, and left Tottenham languishing 13 points behind them. The "Greats" of the past from the two famous north London clubs were paraded before the 37,723 crowd. But it was the new Gunners' generation that was setting the First Division alight. Arsenal were four points ahead of Everton and five ahead of Liverpool, after stretching their magnificent unbeaten run to 19 games. The punter who bet £50,000 on Graham's "babes" to win the title wasn't as crazy as startled staff in the Walthamstow betting shop thought, when he laid his bet the week before. Arsenal had the meanest defence in football, with just 13 goals conceded in 24 league games. Tottenham's Clive Allen, watched by England manager Bobby Robson, was never allowed a sniff of a chance by the majestic 19-year-old centre-half Tony Adams. As Spurs failed to turn their pretty approach work into goals, it was Adams who opened the scoring in the sixth minute of this live TV thriller. Adams must have caught the attention of the England manager, who openly admitted that he had central defensive problems. Adams stayed forward for a corner after Viv Anderson's shot was blocked on the line by Danny Thomas. Williams – abrasive and dominant in midfield alongside Paul Davis and David Rocastle – picked up the loose ball, fed Kenny Sansom on the left, and his perfect cross was headed down by Niall Quinn. Adams beat Ray Clemence to the ball, which spun off the keeper's body into the empty net. Glenn Hoddle was booked for a late tackle on Williams, before Rocastle struck the post with an outstanding effort from Quinn's cross. Williams later joined Hoddle in the book. Five minutes before half-time, a superb

Arsenal move set up the second goal, with a neat Williams back-heel to Rocastle, on to Charlie Nicholas, and a defence-splitting pass to Martin Hayes. Pleat felt Danny Thomas was to blame for not playing Hayes offside. Instead, the defender chose to chase, missing one tackle before bringing Hayes down on the edge of the area. Rocastle's back-heel led to Davis threading his shot through the defensive wall, past the stranded Clemence. Seconds before the interval, Clive Allen put Hoddle through on the right, and his accurate low cross was swept in at the far post by Mitchell Thomas. While Arsenal's players warmed to their title chances, Spurs boss David Pleat grumbled over the last-minute "penalty" that got away. Pleat claimed that referee Roger Milford had failed to spot Viv Anderson's push on Nico Claesen as Paul Allen broke on the flank. Pleat moaned that all his lads thought it was a penalty and that the referee was watching Allen and the ball. Pleat was also unhappy with his defence over both goals, and he suspected that Tony Adams was offside for the first. However, he conceded that Arsenal had played well and it hadn't been an easy game. George Graham was as cool as ever about his team's title prospects.

8th February 1987

League Cup semi-final first leg
Arsenal 0
Tottenham Hotspur 1
C Allen
Attendance: 41,306
Arsenal: *Lukic, Caesar (Thomas), Sansom, Williams, O'Leary, Adams, Groves, Davis, Quinn, Nicholas (Rix), Hayes.*
Tottenham Hotspur: *Clemence, D Thomas, M Thomas, Ardiles, Gough, Mabbutt, C Allen, P Allen, Waddle, Hoddle, Claesen (Galvin).*

Clive Allen's 34th goal of his incredible season catapulted him into the England squad named by Bobby Robson in February 1987. The hottest striker in the country had impeccable timing, because his performance at the League Cup semi-final first leg at Highbury came less than 24 hours before Robson named his players for the friendly in Madrid the following week. His phenomenal goalscoring, which Robson just couldn't ignore, included 34 goals in 33 matches, and he scored in every tie. There weren't many sweeter goals for Allen than the first of his career against the club that turned his world upside down. As the country's first £1 million teenager, Allen was sold by QPR to Arsenal and stayed for just 64 days, before – without playing a competitive match – being mysteriously dispatched to Crystal Palace. Highbury, though, did prove to be his lucky ground for semi-final goals. Meanwhile, Spurs manager David Pleat realized that George Graham's team would be stung by their first home defeat of the season, and that a single strike would open up the second leg at White Hart Lane. Pleat's main task was to control his players' natural euphoria. They had finally beaten their big rivals after enviously watching them lead the First Division for the previous three months. But it had been a costly weekend for the Gunners, who had lost their leadership of the league to Everton, as well as their proud home record. Ossie Ardiles proved a master craftsman in front of the Spurs defence, allowing Hoddle the freedom to go forward and pepper Lukic's goal with shots that included a 30-yard special which scraped the bar. Arsenal had their moments. Spurs captain Richard Gough cleared off the line in the 38th minute after a scramble in front of Ray Clemence, following a Steve Williams corner. A minute later, the Arsenal mean machine defence, once again superbly marshalled by Tony Adams, was breached. Allen swivelled and shot from 20 yards, Lukic brilliantly tipping it over. From Hoddle's corner, Gary Mabbutt's shot was saved by Lukic, and Allen poached the kind of goal that is the hallmark of all the great goalscorers. Arsenal claimed two Spurs players were offside, but the goal stood, and Allen was now only nine goals behind Jimmy Greaves' club record for a season. Three players were booked – Williams, Gough and Caesar. One fan, who ran on the pitch, was grabbed by Lukic and finally arrested.

1ˢᵗ March 1987

League Cup semi-final second leg
Tottenham Hotspur 1
C Allen
Arsenal 2
Anderson, Quinn
Attendance: **37,099**
Tottenham Hotspur: *Clemence, D Thomas, M Thomas, Ardiles (Stevens), Gough, Mabbutt, C Allen, P Allen, Waddle, Hoddle, Claesen (Galvin).*
Arsenal: *Lukic, Anderson, Sansom, Thomas, O'Leary, Adams, Rocastle, Davis, Quinn, Nicholas, Hayes (Allinson).*

George Graham blasted the critics who wrote off his young Arsenal team. After the live TV thriller, manager Graham revealed that his players had been fired up by the "experts" who said Tottenham would cruise into the League Cup final. Instead, the Gunners launched a dramatic two-goal comeback at White Hart Lane to win the semi-final second leg 2-1. With the aggregate scores level at 2-2 after extra-time, the north London giants replayed the following Wednesday. Spurs won the toss to stage the game, and the winners faced Liverpool in April 1987. Hit and miss striker Clive Allen let Arsenal off the hook in the thriller at White Hart Lane. Allen's 11ᵗʰ goal in eight games in the competition equaled the record, but it was the ones he missed rather than his 38ᵗʰ success of the season that enabled the Gunners to mount a spectacular comeback. Allen scorned four chances, before David Rocastle's low cross was swept home by Niall Quinn to complete a revival started by Viv Anderson's equalizer. The Spurs striker had proved England manager Bobby Robson's theory that Allen got bogged down in the mud. That was why he hadn't made it on to the subs bench in Madrid, and his catalogue of misses in the semi-final included a 39ᵗʰ-minute slide into a Mitchell Thomas cross after Chris Waddle started the move. The ball squirmed wide. In the 49ᵗʰ minute Waddle's cross was half cut out by Tony Adams. Allen pounced, but shot over the bar. In the 55th minute, Hoddle put him through, but John Lukic saved his closing shot. He had scored a lot of goals, but he'd missed quite a few. Pleat, who had suffered FA Cup semi-final and quarter-final defeats by Everton while at Luton, knew that his side had blown a gilt-edged chance of taking him down Wembley way. Allen's goal against Arsenal in the first leg at Highbury had given Spurs the platform from which to launch their way to Wembley, and this seemed further assured by Richard Gough's free-kick in the 15th minute, causing problems for Lukic, who dropped the ball. Allen demonstrated typical predatory instincts, weaving past Quinn and executing his deadly finish before Adam's lunging tackle. That goal meant he joined the elite band of strikers to score 11 times in the League Cup, but had he shown a little more of his normal remarkable finishing, Spurs would have been celebrating their first Wembley Cup final for five years. Arsenal, though, deserved credit for their dramatic and inspiring comeback. Charlie Nicholas began to find holes in the Spurs defence, which had gone a remarkable sequence of six games without conceding a goal. Arsenal fans launched a Roman candle on to the roof of the Spurs stand when Anderson forced the equalizer, after Rocastle's long throw was headed on by the towering Quinn. Allen shot wide from Mabbutt's outstanding, defence-splitting pass, to chalk up his fourth squandered chance, and Waddle's shot struck Lukic's legs before Arsenal struck again. Paul David found Rocastle on the right flank, and his intelligent low cross was finished off by Quinn. This enthralling, competitive and highly entertaining match moved into a dramatic extra-time, and the players were exhausted by the end. In the 100th minute Spurs might have snatched the glory they expected before the start, when Hoddle's defence-splitting pass found substitute Tony Galvin. He lobbed Lukic, but David O'Leary cleared.

4th March 1987

League Cup semi-final replay
Tottenham Hotspur 1
C Allen

Arsenal 2
Allinson, Rocastle
Attendance: 41,005
Tottenham Hotspur: *Clemence, D Thomas, M Thomas, Ardiles, Gough, Mabbutt, C Allen, P Allen, Waddle, Stevens, Claesen (Galvin).*
Arsenal: *Lukic, Anderson, Sansom, Thomas, O'Leary, Adams, Rocastle, Davis, Quinn, Nicholas (Allinson), Hayes.*

David Rocastle declared that Arsenal were the comeback kings in March 1987. The 20-year-old scored the winning goal in injury time, which put Arsenal into the final of the League Cup. Arsenal had come back off the floor to win for the second time in four days. At White Hart Lane they battled out a 2-1 victory, having trailed behind their rivals. They trailed in the decider, but came back again from a Clive Allen goal to equalize through Ian Allinson in the 82nd minute, before Rocastle booked their place at Wembley. Arsenal then faced a race against time to get Charlie Nicholas fit for the Wembley date. He had been carried off midway through the second half with damaged ankle ligaments. Arsenal, however, were assured of their place at Wembley for the first time in seven years. Tottenham were eight minutes from Wembley themselves when sub Allinson equalized, then Rocastle clinched a famous victory, as this titanic tie moved into its fifth hour. Arsenal were, for the first time, overall leaders one minute into injury time, and that was enough to send George Graham to the twin towers in his first season as Arsenal manager. Arsenal had demonstrated, over three incredible games with Spurs, that they possessed the hallmark of the 1971 Double team that featured Graham himself. Graham had refused to spend £1 million on a big name striker, and instead chose to nurture a formidable team that could boast five players aged 20 or under. Arsenal still had a chance of the Treble (but no one believed it possible). The Spurs players slumped away, some shedding tears of frustration, none more so than goalkeeper Ray Clemence, beaten twice in the last eight minutes. He could hardly believe it.

18th October 1987

First Division
Tottenham Hotspur 1
Claesen
Arsenal 2
Rocastle, Thomas
Attendance: 36,680
Tottenham Hotspur: *Parks, Stevens, Thomas, Ardiles, Fairclough, Mabbutt, Close (Samways), P Allen, Waddle, Hodge (C Allen), Claesen.*
Arsenal: *Lukic, Thomas, Sansom, Williams, O'Leary, Adams, Rocastle, Davis, Smith, Groves (Hayes), Richardson.*

Arsenal served notice to a watching nation that they had no intention of letting Liverpool run away with the league title. Kenny Dalglish's men may have been back on top of the First Division, but they would be looking over their shoulders at the team that beat them in the League Cup final. Arsenal skipper Kenny Sansom boasted to a live TV audience that there was no better team than the Gunners in the First Division. Spurs, however, were furious that Gary Mabbutt's late strike was ruled out for offside, but George Graham preferred to discuss his own team's performance. Arsenal had shown character, coming back from an early goal, and they played good football and scored two very good goals. But Arsenal's north London supremacy over their bitter rivals – this was their fourth 2-1 victory over Spurs in the previous 10 months – was still overshadowed by the great offside debate. To make matters worse, there were no television action replays, as these had been wiped out by an ITV industrial dispute. Ossie Ardiles, booked earlier for dissent, supplied the pass for Mabbutt to beat John Lukic 10 minutes from time, but the goal was immediately ruled out. David Pleat was not amused. He was sure that Mabbutt was definitely onside. He did, however, concede that Arsenal had had a good run, and were competitive and hard-working in midfield. He also claimed the rival team had a positive attitude. Nico Claesen latched on to Steve Williams' back pass and squeezed between Tony Adams and Lukic to score after just 41 seconds. Williams, both brilliant and abrasive, made amends seven minutes later, with a superb through ball for Rocastle to score on the left. The third goal came after 14 minutes of a thrilling first half, and once again the space left by the Spurs back four proved their undoing. Alan Smith supplied the killer pass to Michael Thomas. It was believed that Spurs' bitter disappointment at losing to Arsenal would convince Pleat to move into the transfer market.

6ᵗʰ March 1988

First Division
Arsenal 2
Smith, Groves
Tottenham Hotspur 1
C Allen
Attendance: 37,143
Arsenal: *Lukic, Winterburn, Sansom, Thomas, Caesar, Adams, Rocastle, Hayes, Smith, Groves, Richardson.*
Tottenham Hotspur: *Mimms, Statham, Thomas, Fenwick, Fairclough, Mabbutt, C Allen, P Allen, Ardiles, Samways, Walsh.*

Perry Groves won the north London derby battle for Arsenal, and issued a clear message to Kerry Dixon – you'll have to fight for my place. Dixon may have cost Arsenal 20 times the £65,000 they paid for Groves, but the flame-haired striker would not be forced out of the Arsenal team without a fight. Groves welcomed the pending arrival of £1.2 million Dixon from Chelsea, but was not frightened to challenge him for a place in the Gunners attack. Alan Smith was another who would not be intimidated by the arrival of Dixon, or the possibility of Graham contemplating challenging Everton for the £1.5 million-rated Tony Cottee of West Ham. Both Groves and Smith were on target against Spurs. Smith, after a barren spell, had struck a purple patch of goals, while Groves always seemed to pop up with vital contributions for the Gunners. Bubbly Groves handed Graham the personal satisfaction of a victory over his old pal Terry Venables in front of a 37,143 crowd, and was nominated by Graham as his man of the match. But his place, more than Smith's, would be at risk should the Dixon deal go through. Groves' winner ended Arsenal's TV jinx at Highbury – they had not won in front of the cameras on their own ground before. The enormity of Venables' task at Spurs was highlighted once again, but he took satisfaction from the performances of several players, including Paul Walsh and Ossie Ardiles. Arsenal got the perfect start with a goal after just 98 seconds. It was a catalogue of errors for five Spurs defenders, before Michael Thomas flung himself at the ball. It fell to Smith, who cracked a half volley past Bobby Mimms, though Spurs' new keeper might have got a hand to it. Smith set up a glorious chance for Groves in the 25th minute, but he mishit his shot well wide. The second half was greeted by a downpour, and the bearded Argentinean, Ardiles, began to revel in the conflict. Clive Allen struck a wonderful 53rd-minute goal to haul Spurs back into the game, which was set up by the brilliance of striking partner Walsh. Walsh's clever turn left Gus Caesar stranded, and his simple square pass was finished off by Allen, with a devastating strike with the outside of his boot past John Lukic. But Groves made amends for his earlier miss in the 75th minute. A long throw by Kenny Sansom bounced over Chris Fairclough and Smith, and bounced invitingly for Groves, who turned cleverly, despite the attentions of Terry Fenwick, to shoot wide of Mimms. Groves and Smith made their point, and while they would welcome the arrival of Dixon, their message was loud and clear – they were fighting hard for their places.

10th September 1988

First Division

Tottenham Hotspur 2

Waddle, Gascoigne

Arsenal 3

Winterburn, Smith, Marwood

Attendance: 32,621

Tottenham Hotspur: *Mimms, Statham (Howells), Thomas, Fenwick,*

Fairclough, Mabbutt, Walsh, Gascoigne, Waddle, Samways (Moran), Allen.
Arsenal: *Lukic, Dixon, Winterburn, Thomas, O'Leary, Adams, Rocastle
(Richardson), Davis, Smith, Merson, Marwood (Groves).*

Alan Smith increased Arsenal's domination of the current England
squad when he was added to Bobby Robson's raw recruits. Smith
became the eighth uncapped player in the 22-man squad, and the
fifth from Highbury's heroes, who beat Tottenham 3-2 in front of
Robson in September 1988. Smith, and Forest's Steve Hodge, were
summoned to the squad to face Denmark at Wembley because of
the latest injuries to Gary Lineker, John Barnes and Chris Waddle.
Brian Marwood – another Gunner – would have edged ahead of
Hodge had he not injured his groin in a game against Spurs. Smith,
an £800,000 signing from Leicester and uncapped at any level,
scored a hat-trick on the opening day of the season at Wimbledon,
and collected his fifth league goal at Spurs. He teamed up with
Paul Davis, David Rocastle – then certain of his first cap – Tony
Adams and Michael Thomas, while Spurs' £2 million new boy,
Paul Gascoigne, together with David Seaman, Mel Sterland and
Des Walker, made up the uncapped eight. Meanwhile, Gascoigne's
energy crisis pushed Paul Davis closer to an England debut against
Denmark. Gazza had the edge in power, drive, charisma and
sheer cheek, but the way he died in the second half of the match
against Arsenal worried Robson. In one of the most thrilling north
London derbies, Gazza versus Davis was a fascinating and timely
duel. Gazza started the game as favourite over Davis, a product
of Arsenal's highly efficient youth system. But, at 26 and after
skippering the Under-21s as an overage player, Davis said he felt
ready to play for England. Gazza – who cut out the Mars bars and
stuck to salads – had lost a lot of weight quickly, which appeared to
have sapped his strength, and Spurs boss Venables admitted that
he was tired. Davis, meanwhile, was calm, cool and calculating
against Spurs. He never wasted a pass and did enough to prod
Robson to pick him. A superb chipped pass from Davis on to the
chest of Alan Smith was behind the Gunners' brilliant second goal

after Nigel Winterburn had notched the opener. Chris Waddle was in devastating form and equalized just three minutes after Arsenal went ahead. But, as the goals flowed in quick time, Smith and Brian Marwood put the Gunners 3-1 ahead. Gazza's goal on his home debut inspired a Spurs revival, and convinced Venables that his team was closing the quality gap on the Gunners. Upset came when goals by Vinny Samways and Gary Mabbutt were ruled out, for being offside.

2nd January 1989

First Division
Arsenal 2
Merson, Thomas
Tottenham Hotspur 0
Attendance: 45,129
Arsenal: *Lukic, O'Leary, Winterburn, Thomas, Bould, Adams, Rocastle, Richardson (Davis), Smith, Merson, Marwood (Groves).*
Tottenham Hotspur: *Mimms, Butters, Thomas, Fenwick, Fairclough, Mabbutt, Walsh, Bergsson, Waddle, Stewart, Allen.*

Paul Merson was fast becoming a major influence as Arsenal strode towards the League Championship. Once the dust had settled on the controversy of referee Alan Seville's live TV blunder, in failing to award a blatant penalty to Spurs, it wasn't overlooked that Merson also scored a goal of sheer quality. Arsenal achieved the Double in the league over Spurs for the second successive season, to launch themselves two points clear at the top of the First Division with a game in hand. Merson not only opened the scoring for Arsenal, but made the last-minute goal for Michael Thomas, in his emergence as a key player in the battle for the most open championship in years. But referee Seville's reluctance to award Spurs a penalty two minutes from half-time was the turning point of the game. While Arsenal were top in the previous two seasons, the clamour had been for Graham to raid the transfer market for a genuine goalscorer to put the finishing touch to his title-chasing team. Graham hesitated and Arsenal blew their chances but, as they entered a new year, the Gunners now had Merson in red-hot form. He plundered his third goal in four games, with little more than a half chance, on the day Arsenal unveiled their famous old clock on the top of their new executive boxes. Arsenal were ticking over well enough to ensure that a London club took the title for the first time in 18 years, when the Gunners themselves won the championship in their Double year. Spurs pushed Arsenal to their limits and, irrespective of the penalty furore, should have done much better with a succession of second-half chances. Chris Waddle was off target with two headers, and Paul Stewart was clear through only to shoot straight at John Lukic. Terry Venables was encouraged by his team's performance, but was concerned about the wasted chances. Venables could, however, be proud of the way his team were prepared to claw their way back into the game in front of the season's second largest league attendance anywhere in the country. The Gunners were made to suffer, with Kevin Richardson handicapped by a virus – he had to come off, and was replaced by Paul Davis. Davis, who hadn't played since October – after serving a nine-match FA ban for the punch that broke Glenn Cockerill's jaw – was given an enormous cheer. England winger Brian Marwood looked jaded because of the lingering effects of a virus, and he made way for Perry Groves with nine minutes to go. Graham praised the efforts of Marwood and Richardson, and was delighted that the Gunners were putting together a good home record. He even conceded that Spurs deserved a penalty, but mentioned that Venables would need to curb the aggressive instincts of his £1.5 million centre-forward Stewart, as well as finding a way of getting more goals from him. Stewart was booked for a lunge at Tony Adams in the 29th minute, after the Arsenal captain had fouled Paul Walsh. But the penalty row raged on, and Venable was furious that Seville declined to give them a spot kick after Lukic had pulled down Chris Waddle. A slow motion replay of the incident showed that Venables was right and Birmingham official Seville was wrong. A spot kick would have put Tottenham right back in the thick of this extravagant confrontation but, as they pushed forward for the equalizer their progressive football deserved, Arsenal punished them. In a smash-and-grab raid, they got a second goal in the 89th minute through Michael Thomas. Waddle showed off his bruises, courtesy of Lukic, after the match. Even the rival goalkeeper agreed that it should have been a penalty, as did Graham.

18th October 1989

First Division
Tottenham Hotspur 2
Samways, Walsh
Arsenal 1
Thomas
Attendance: 33,944
Tottenham Hotspur: *Thorstvedt, Thomas, Van den Hauwe, Fenwick, Allen, Mabbutt, Walsh, Gascoigne, Samways (Howells), Lineker, Sedgley.*
Arsenal: *Lukic, Dixon, Winterburn, Thomas, O'Leary, Adams, Rocastle, Richardson (Jonsson), Smith (Merson), Groves, Hayes.*

Terry Venables' Tottenham won the gang war with Arsenal as they spanked the league champions at White Hart Lane. Afterwards, Venables laughed at the great result. Tottenham had waited a long time for this result, and it was Venables' first victory over the Gunners and his best pal George Graham in five meetings since he had taken over as manager two years previously. In the frenzy of this derby dogfight, with nearly 34,000 fans crammed into the ground, five players were booked. Tony Adams, Michael Thomas and Kevin Richardson went into referee Roger Milford's notebook, and Terry Fenwick and Paul Gascoigne were also cautioned. Spurs found a new dimension to their troubled season. It seemed a long time since Venables was calling for the arsenic as his £8 million side slumped to a series of alarming results. This time, however, they were caught up in the occasion, and were stronger than Arsenal, who were rattled by the panicky football being played around them and made uncharacteristic errors at the back, which resulted in a crazy 20 minutes of play that lost them the game. As Arsenal lost their way, so England winger David Rocastle lost his contact lenses. Play was halted in the second half while he rubbed his eyes and searched for them. Two goals in three first-half minutes cost Arsenal the match, and they came as crowd trouble flared momentarily in the corner by Arsenal's goal. Graham denied it cost them their concentration, but Spurs scored from two free-kicks and this changed the shape of the match. Vinny Samways got the first in the 34th minute, and Paul Walsh the second in the 37th minute. Michael Thomas replied for Arsenal in the 53rd minute. The match enabled Spurs to climb into the top half of the First Division, while Arsenal looked as if they needed reinforcements to mount a successful defence of their championship.

20th January 1990

First Division

Arsenal 1

Adams

Tottenham Hotspur 0

Attendance: 46,132

Arsenal: *Lukic, Dixon, Davis, Thomas, O'Leary, Adams, Rocastle, Richardson, Smith, Bould, Groves.*

Tottenham Hotspur: *Thorstvedt, Thomas, Van den Hauwe (Walsh), Allen, Howells, Mabbutt, Samways (Nayim), Polston, Stewart, Lineker, Sedgley.*

George Graham waited for almost 12 months before talking for the first time about the abuse Tony Adams had endured from the terrace tormentors. Since his blunder at Manchester United in the previous season, he had been subjected to "hee-haw" jibes, as it threatened to ruin Arsenal's championship challenge. Graham was convinced, however, that Adams was a thoroughbred, and finally revealed the strength of character the England centre-half had shown, ramming those taunts down the fans' throats. The giant inflatable carrot paraded at the Tottenham end was quickly deflated by Adams' brilliant winner, and Graham was ecstatic with his first-class player.

Once the dust had settled on the fierce rivalry of this red-blooded north London derby, Spurs sportingly paid tribute to Adams. Terry Venables was disappointed that Gary Lineker's shot had struck the post and flown across the goal line, while Adams saw his half-volley strike the post and go in. Adams' golden moment came seven days after he had suffered yet more criticism for allowing Wimbledon to score a late winner. But his 63rd-minute strike at Highbury helped to erase memories of that Plough Lane error, and was a precious goal in Arsenal's pursuit to retain the title. Venables had claimed before the game that Spurs shouldn't be dismissed from the race despite their long odds of 20-1. But now Tottenham's season hinged on the League Cup quarter-final replay against Nottingham Forest. Venables was pinning his hopes on Gary Lineker, following the competitive, compelling derby, which proved to be a classic. There had been chances at both ends, with Lukic making a great save with five minutes left, and Erik Thorstvedt tipping a Michael Thomas 30-yard lob over the bar. The spirit and attitude of the players was excellent, according to Venables, who naturally felt that his team didn't deserve to lose. Arsenal were such a big box office draw that it was difficult to buy tickets for matches at Highbury. As the Gunners chased the FA Cup and the League Double, their next four home games were already sold out. It all added up to yet more millions pouring into the Gunners' bank account, providing manager Graham with virtually unlimited sums to buy new players.

The 1990s

The 1990–91 season saw both north London clubs securing yet another trophy. Terry Venables led Spurs to the FA Cup final, where a goal from Paul Stewart and a Des Walker own goal gave them a 2-1 win over Nottingham Forest. Arsenal, meanwhile, had signed goalkeeper David Seaman, who played a pivotal role as the Gunners secured their second league title under George Graham. Liverpool had led the table for much of the season, but their form had deserted them following the sudden resignation of Kenny Dalglish in February 1991, allowing Arsenal to overtake them.

Terry Venables was made chief executive in June 1991, with Peter Shreeves returning to the manager's desk, before being replaced by Ray Clemence and Doug Livermore the following May. A succession of managers would try to bring success back to White Hart Lane to no avail, including Ossie Ardiles – who used a formation of five forwards not seen in English football since the 1950s, but this didn't work as Spurs finished in 15th place in the Premier League and Ardiles was sacked in October 1994 – Gerry Francis and Christian Gross.

Over at Highbury, the success just kept coming, and Arsenal found themselves in the unusual position of contesting both the League and FA Cup finals in the same season … against the same team. John Harkes opened the scoring for Sheffield Wednesday in the first Wembley showpiece, but goals from Paul Merson and Steve Morrow took the trophy back to north London. There was heartbreak for the winning goalscorer in the post-match celebrations, however, when he fell from Tony Adams' shoulders and broke his arm, thereby ruling him out of the FA Cup final. In that match, after a 1-1 draw, goals from Ian Wright and the Owls' former Spurs favourite, Chris Waddle, sent the replay into extra-time. Andy Linighan headed the winner, to ensure that Arsenal became the first English club to win both domestic cup tournaments in the same season.

Arsenal's cup successes gave them qualification for the 1993–94 European Cup Winners' Cup, and they fought their way through to the final in Copenhagen. Another priceless strike from Alan Smith secured the trophy with a 1-0 win over Parma, but they were unable to repeat the feat the following season. With John Hartson having equalized Juan Esnáider's opening goal against Real Zaragoza in Paris, midfielder Nayim tried a speculative lob from 40 yards that evaded the despairing dive of David Seaman in the last minute, to deprive Arsenal of another success. By this time George Graham had been dismissed by the club – and banned for a year by the Football Association – after admitting receiving an unsolicited gift (a "bung") from a Norwegian agent, following the signing of John Jensen and Pål Lydersen in 1992. Graham would return to north London in October 1998, when he took charge at White Hart Lane ...

His eventual permanent successor at Highbury was Bruce Rioch, who guided his team to fifth place in the Premier League in 1995–96, but was sacked during the close season over a dispute in transfer funds with the club directors. Arsenal fans had to wait until October 1996 before the official appointment of a man who would go on to become the club's longest-serving and most successful manager. But that hadn't stopped Arsène Wenger advising the board to snap up Patrick Vieira and Rémi Garde before he formally took charge of the team.

The Frenchman was an almost immediate success, with Arsenal claiming their first Premiership title in 1997–98, and finishing as runners-up to Manchester United in the next three seasons. They were also pipped at the post in the 1999–2000 UEFA Cup, when Galatasaray won 4-1 on penalties, following a 0-0 stalemate in Copenhagen.

Over at White Hart Lane, George Graham was back on the trophy trail, with a 1-0 win over Leicester City in the 1999 League Cup final. With Graham in charge of Spurs and Wenger comfortable at Highbury, the scene was set for the north London neighbours to take their rivalry into the 21st century.

Record in the 1990s

Arsenal

Season	League	P	W	D	L	F	A	Pts	Pos
1990–91	Div 1	38	24	13	1	74	18	83	1
1991–92	Div 1	42	19	15	8	81	47	72	4
1992–93	Prem	42	15	11	16	40	38	56	10
1993–94	Prem	42	18	17	7	53	28	71	4
1994–95	Prem	42	13	12	17	52	49	51	12
1995–96	Prem	38	17	12	9	49	32	63	5
1996–97	Prem	38	19	11	8	62	32	68	3
1997–98	Prem	38	23	9	6	68	33	78	1
1998–99	Prem	38	22	12	4	59	17	78	2
1999–2000	Prem	38	22	7	9	73	43	73	2

FA Cup

1990–91	1-3 v Tottenham Hotspur (Semi-final)
1991–92	1-2 v Wrexham (Third Round)
1992–93	1-1, 2-1 v Sheffield Wednesday (Final)
1993–94	2-2, 1-3 v Bolton Wanderers (Fourth Round)
1994–95	0-0, 0-2 v Millwall (Third Round)
1995–96	1-1, 0-1 v Sheffield United (Third Round)
1996–97	0-1 v Leeds United (Fourth Round)
1997–98	2-0 v Newcastle United (Final)
1998–99	0-0, 1-2 v Manchester United (Semi-final)
1999–2000	0-0, 0-0 (4-5 pens) v Leicester City (Fourth Round)

League Cup

1990–91	2-6 v Manchester United (Fourth Round)
1991–92	0-1 v Coventry City (Third Round)
1992–93	2-1 v Sheffield Wednesday (Final)
1993–94	0-1 v Aston Villa (Fourth Round)
1994–95	0-1 v Liverpool (Quarter-final)
1995–96	2-2, 0-0 v Aston Villa (Semi-final)
1996–97	2-4 v Liverpool (Fourth Round)

1997–98   2-1, 1-3 v Chelsea (Semi-final)
1998–99   0-5 v Chelsea (Fourth Round)
1999–2000 2-2 (1-3 pens) v Middlesbrough (Fourth Round)

Europe

1990–91   Did not qualify
1991–92   European Cup: 1-1, 1-3 v Benfica (Second Round)
1992–93   Did not qualify
1993–94   Cup Winners' Cup: 1-0 v Parma (Final)
1994–95   Cup Winners' Cup: 1-2 v Real Zaragoza (Final)
1995–96   Did not qualify
1996–97   UEFA Cup: 2-3, 2-3 v Borussia Mönchengladbach
          (First Round)
1997–98   UEFA Cup: 0-1, 1-1 v PAOK (First Round)
1998–99   Champions League: group stage
1999–2000 Champions League: first group stage
1999–2000 UEFA Cup: 0-0 (1-4 pens) v Galatasaray (Final)

Tottenham Hotspur

Season	League	P	W	D	L	F	A	Pts	Pos
1990–91	Div 1	38	11	16	11	51	50	49	10
1991–92	Div 1	42	15	7	20	58	63	52	15
1992–93	Prem	42	16	11	15	60	66	59	8
1993–94	Prem	42	11	12	19	54	59	45	15
1994–95	Prem	42	16	14	12	66	58	62	7
1995–96	Prem	38	16	13	9	50	38	61	8
1996–97	Prem	38	13	7	18	44	512	46	10
1997–98	Prem	38	11	11	16	44	56	44	14
1998–99	Prem	38	11	14	13	47	50	47	11
1999–2000	Prem	38	15	8	15	57	49	53	10

FA Cup

1990–91   2-1 v Nottingham Forest (Final)
1991–92   0-0, 0-1 v Aston Villa (Third Round)
1992–93   0-1 v Arsenal (Semi-final)

1993–94	0-3 v Ipswich Town (Fourth Round)
1994–95	1-4 v Everton (Semi-final)
1995–96	2-2, 1-1 (1-3 pens) v Nottingham Forest (Fifth Round)
1996–97	0-2 v Manchester United (Third Round)
1997–98	1-1, 1-3 v Barnsley (Fourth Round)
1998–99	0-2 v Newcastle United (Semi-final)
1999–2000	1-1, 1-6 v Newcastle United (Third Round)

League Cup

1990–91	0-0, 0-3 v Chelsea (Fifth Round)
1991–92	1-1, 1-2 v Nottingham Forest (Semi-final)
1992–93	0-2 v Nottingham Forest (Fourth Round)
1993–94	1-2 v Aston Villa (Fifth Round)
1994–95	0-3 v Notts County (Third Round)
1995–96	2-3 v Coventry City (Third Round)
1996–97	1-6 v Bolton Wanderers (Fourth Round)
1997–98	1-2 v Derby County (Third Round)
1998–99	1-0 v Leicester City (Final)
1999–2000	1-3 v Fulham (Fourth Round)

Europe

1990–91	Did not qualify
1991–92	Cup Winners' Cup: 0-1, 0-0 v Feyenoord (Quarter-final)
1992–93	Did not qualify
1993–94	Did not qualify
1994–95	UEFA Intertoto Cup: group stage
1995–96	Banned for fielding an under-strength side
1996–97	Did not qualify
1997–98	Did not qualify
1998–99	Did not qualify
1999–2000	UEFA Cup: 1-0, 0-2 v Kaiserslautern (Second Round)

1ˢᵗ September 1990

First Division

Arsenal 0

Tottenham Hotspur 0

Attendance: 40,009

Arsenal: *Seaman, Dixon, Winterburn, Thomas, Bould, Adams, Rocastle, Davis, Smith, Merson (Groves), Limpar.*

Tottenham Hotspur: *Thorstvedt, Bergsson, Van den Hauwe, Sedgley, Howells, Mabbutt, Stewart, Gascoigne (Thomas), Nayim, Lineker, Allen.*

Paul Gascoigne was suffering sleepless nights, as the strain of being Britain's biggest star began to affect his performances on the field. Gazza had failed to last the first week of the season before the pressure of his new-found fame took its toll against Arsenal, when he was substituted two minutes from the end. This worried new England manager Graham Taylor, who named his first squad in early September 1990 for a friendly with Hungary at Wembley. Venables substituted Gazza, explaining that the nation's World Cup hero was "tired, even before the match". The problem for Venables was how to protect the 23-year-old from the Gazzamania hype, yet maintain his level of motivation. Taylor wanted to build his new England team around Gazza but, as he was unable to cope in the first week of the new season, how would he cope four years later for the World Cup in America? Watched by Taylor's number two, Lawrie McMenemy, Gazza was reduced to walking pace at the end of a grueling north London derby, with Venables admitting that he could hardly move. The Arsenal crowd barracked Gascoigne throughout the game, and whenever Paul Davis outshone him they cried that Davis was better than Gazza. With Gazzamania rammed down the throats of Spurs' north London rivals, there was understandably little sympathy. Gazza had become the biggest box office name since George Best, who suggested that Gazza was being built up to be knocked down. He also stated that Gazza was years away from being a top world-class player. It all put Paul Davis in line for a place in the England squad, after the frantic pace of this derby. It was a remarkable comeback for the player whose career had plummeted two years before, when he broke Glen Cockerill's jaw in a controversial incident at Highbury, which had been caught on TV. The incident developed into an even wider debate about the power of TV in disciplinary issues. Davis was severely punished by the FA, and his England career was curtailed. A succession of injuries set him so far back he almost disappeared. A summer loan spell in Sweden had maintained his fitness level and his sharpness, and he underlined his personal achievements by winning the midfield battle with Paul Gascoigne. Davis outshone Gazza – to the delight of the Highbury crowd. But the Spurs team remained unbeaten and Venables was happy. Arsenal, however, felt that they deserved two penalties. First, Davis was tripped by David Howells in the 55th minute, and then Steve Bould was pulled down by Pat Van den Hauwe inside the box.

12th January 1991

First Division
Tottenham Hotspur 0
Arsenal 0
Attendance: 34,753
Tottenham Hotspur: *Thorstvedt, Thomas, Edinburgh, Fenwick, Howells, Mabbutt, Stewart, Gascoigne, Walsh, Lineker, Allen.*
Arsenal: *Seaman, Dixon, Winterburn, Thomas, Bould, Linighan, O'Leary, Davis (Hillier), Smith, Merson (Groves), Limpar.*

Gary Lineker, on the receiving end of a series of "cheat" claims, revealed how he had saved David O'Leary from a red card. Lineker felt he had been held back by O'Leary for one of the best chances the England captain had against the Gunners. But Tottenham's FIFA Fair Play award winner chose to work it to his advantage, instead of taking a dive. Lineker had been accused of diving in the past, but this time there could be no such accusation, and his final effort brought one of the many fine saves from David Seaman. Meanwhile, O'Leary didn't accept he was guilty of anything that would have warranted a red card, but, in the climate at the time, he could have been in trouble had Lineker crashed to the ground. Venables couldn't believe the number of chances his side created against the First Division's only unbeaten team, and was surprised that Lineker failed to take one of his succession of openings. But Lineker, with only one penalty in the previous seven games, stated that while he'd missed chances, he still felt it was one of his best games for a while. Credit went to David Seaman for the blinder which made him an inspired goalkeeper. His experience of facing Lineker during England training sessions helped the £1.3 million keeper keep Arsenal's unbeaten record intact. It appeared impossible for Lineker to miss, when Paul Allen put him through in the 67th minute with only Seaman to beat. But the Rotherham-born Seaman stayed upright until the last moment, committing Lineker to shoot where he anticipated, and enabling him to block the ball. Seaman had had his critics since arriving from QPR the summer before to replace the popular John Lukic, who had moved to Leeds. But he was winning Arsenal fans over and pressing his claims to displace Chris Woods as England's number one goalkeeper, with a string of faultless performances. The Tottenham shutout was Seaman's 14th clean sheet during a record-breaking 22-match unbeaten start to the season, which was keeping Arsenal hard on the heels of leaders, Liverpool. Modest Seaman, who owned up to an own goal against Wimbledon not long before this derby, was more anxious to talk about the result than his own performance. Seaman's heroics kept Arsenal within a point of Liverpool, and extinguished any lingering Tottenham hopes of remaining involved in the title race. The referee did well to prevent a full-blooded derby from boiling over, but faced controversy about his booking of Arsenal full-back Nigel Winterburn for a foul on Paul Allen. Graham insisted it was a case of mistaken identity, named Swedish winger Anders Limpar as the culprit, and would take the matter up with the FA.

14th April 1991

FA Cup semi-final (Wembley)

Arsenal 1

Smith

Tottenham Hotspur 3

Gascoigne, Lineker 2

Attendance: **77,893**

Arsenal: *Seaman, Dixon, Winterburn, Thomas, Bould, Adams, Campbell, Davis, Smith, Merson, Limpar (Groves).*

Tottenham Hotspur: *Thorstvedt, Edinburgh, Van den Hauwe, Sedgley, Howells, Mabbutt, Stewart, Gascoigne (Hayim), Samways (Walsh), Lineker, Allen.*

Soccer's most flamboyant star was due to clash head-to-head with the game's most colourful boss in the FA Cup final. The Wembley showdown the following month, on 18th May, had already billed the Gazza v Cloughie spectacular. Paul Gascoigne, playing just 35 days after a double hernia operation, inspired Spurs to a 3-1 semi-final defeat of north London rivals Arsenal at Wembley. Nottingham Forest chief Brian Clough thought that Gazza would only be stoppable if he sent him food hampers before the match. But Gazza's joy at ending Arsenal's Double bid was tinged with secret heartbreak, following the death of his 68-year-old grandfather, Fred. He played the game in memory of his grandfather, to whom he was close. It said volumes that Gazza rode his personal problem to steal the show. Terry Venables couldn't hide his admiration, and commented that Gazza's free-kick was surely the best ever seen in the history of the competition. He bent the ball, lifted it and struck it with incredible power. There were also some other great performances. Paul Stewart and Paul Allen were good, and Forest were keen to stop Gazza and win the only domestic honour that had eluded their manager. Spurs destroyed Arsenal's Double dreams and gloriously salvaged their own season of disaster. Venables bravely opted to start with Gazza just following his op, and Spurs stormed to an FA Cup final date with Clough's Forest. The cheeky talents of England's

World Cup hero were unleashed on Arsenal from the very start, with unbelievable consequences. Gazza cracked after an hour, under the strain of such a quick comeback from surgery, and inevitably had to come off, but his impact had already been devastating on the favourites. His wicked free-kick from nearly 40 yards prised open the Gunners' mean machine defence, for Gary Lineker's opening strike to put Spurs into a startling two-goal lead before his marker – Michael Thomas – knew where he was. Arsenal demonstrated their formidable commitment and passion with a spirited fightback, but Lineker's killer goal haunted skipper Tony Adams and David Seaman. Lineker's pace took him wide of Adams, but his angled drive seemed within Seaman's grasp. Yet, despite getting both hands to the shot, the most expensive keeper in the world could only guide it into the corner. Spurs may have been bust financially, but they were now bursting with the hope of Venables' first trophy after more than three and a half years at the club. Even more important than the quest for silverware was the need for cash, and the sound of coins must have surely been flooding into the coffers to ease the panic of the club's £10 million overdraft at the Midland Bank. Lineker's two formidable goals were not, however, enough to overshadow Gazza. It was a first-minute tackle on Anders Limpar that led Arsenal straight into trouble. Limpar was left seething by Vinny Samways' challenge, with full-back Pat Van den Hauwe kicking Limpar while he was on the ground. In the fifth minute Limpar got his revenge with a late challenge on Paul Stewart – and the consequences for the Gunners were dire. Gazza lined up for his shot from such a long range, and Arsenal hardly assembled a protective wall. Gazza let rip and the speed of his shot deceived Seaman. He demolished Arsenal's defence with the trickery of a double first-time flick. First, he clipped the ball to Paul Allen and, on its return, he flicked it between Steve Bould and Thomas to put Allen in the clear on the right flank. With Gary Mabbutt lurking at the far post, Arsenal striker Alan Smith cut out Allen's cross, trying to control it on his chest, but it bounced away and that was all the invitation that the predatory Lineker needed. Spurs' master goalscorer reacted a second sooner than Adams, to poke the ball past Seaman from close range. Smith scooped a shot high over the bar from Nigel Winterburn's cross, before Arsenal hauled themselves back into the game with just seconds ticking away before the interval. There was always a suspicion that Arsenal would find a way through, until Mabbutt's pass gave Lineker possession. Samways, who wore Gazza's number 8 shirt with distinction in his injury absence, made a perceptive dummy run. Lineker took full advantage to wrap up the tie with his 76th-minute goal. Samways got a standing ovation, led by his manager, when he was replaced near the end by Paul Walsh.

10th August 1991

FA Charity Shield
Arsenal 0
Tottenham Hotspur 0
Attendance: 65,483
Arsenal: *Seaman, Dixon, Winterburn, Hillier, O'Leary, Adams, Rocastle (Thomas), Davis, Smith, Merson, Campbell (Cole).*
Tottenham Hotspur: *Thorstvedt, Fenwick, Van den Hauwe, Sedgley, Howells, Mabbutt, Stewart, Nayim, Samways, Lineker, Allen.*

David Seaman aimed to end his Wembley jinx at the home of English soccer, where he faced Spurs in the Charity Shield derby. Seaman had reinforced his growing reputation by helping the Gunners to the championship, but he had unhappy memories from his two Wembley trips the season before. In late March he had been criticized on England duty when he allowed Niall Quinn's shot to go past him. Quinn's effort levelled the score, and England subsequently dropped a vital home European Championship qualifying point. Just over a fortnight later his misery was compounded at the same ground when favourites Arsenal were beaten 3-1 by Spurs in the semi-final of the FA Cup. Seaman was shocked in the opening minutes when Gascoigne's long-range guided missile free-kick flew past him into the top corner. And he got even more flak when he got his hands to Gary Lineker's second goal, and Spurs' third, but could not stop it from going into the net. The big keeper did not enjoy the best of cup campaigns. In the League Cup, Arsenal crashed out in spectacular fashion when they were hit for six by Manchester United at Highbury. Astonishingly, while Seaman and Arsenal's mean machine defence conceded only 18 goals in 38 league matches, they let in nine in just two cup matches, and they only lost three times all season. But Erik Thorstvedt, Seaman's opposite number, still rated the Gunner as the tops. Meanwhile, speculation was rife that Anders Limpar was to be axed by Arsenal, as a row between his club and country raged on. The Swedish midfielder missed the Charity Shield clash with Tottenham, after injuring his knee in an international against Norway. Arsenal boss Graham, who hadn't wanted him to play for Sweden so close to the Wembley match, said his fears had been justified. In contrast, 31-year-old Spurs defender Terry Fenwick bounced back for the match after two leg fractures failed to end his career. Fenwick replaced Justin Edinburgh after his horrendous injuries had healed.

1st December 1991

First Division
Arsenal 2
Wright, Campbell
Tottenham Hotspur 0
Attendance: **38,892**
Arsenal: *Seaman, Dixon, Winterburn, Hillier, Bould, Linighan, Rocastle (O'Leary), Wright (Limpar), Smith, Merson, Campbell.*
Tottenham Hotspur: *Thorstvedt, Fenwick, Van den Hauwe, Bergsson, Howells, Mabbutt, Stewart, Durie, Samways (Nayim), Walsh, Allen.*

Gary Lineker's family heartbreak reached out and smothered Spurs like a Sunday morning hangover on 1st December 1991, and even George Graham admitted that it was the most one-sided derby match since he had taken over as manager. Arsenal had 21 shots at goal to Tottenham's three, as they smashed their way to fourth place in the First Division with second-half goals from Ian Wright and Kevin Campbell. Tottenham, still deep in depression over the news that their star striker's baby son had leukaemia, were sent reeling to their sixth league defeat in eight matches. They had taken just four points from their last 24 matches. Worse still, as they slid towards the relegation zone, they had no idea when leading marksman Lineker would return. The news had proved exceptionally difficult for all the players, but Arsenal promptly sent them reeling again, with a performance that destroyed Tottenham and left them just four points off the bottom three. Arsenal swarmed all over Spurs, winning the midfield territory and making chance after chance, so it was no surprise that Wright eventually scored in the 69th minute. It was his ninth goal in 11 matches since his £2.5 million move from Crystal Palace. Tottenham had suffered a terrible run that had left them clinging to the hope of more Wembley glory, but they had negotiated a passage through to the European Cup Winners' Cup quarter-finals. Other than that, their entire season had come grinding to a halt. It was a painful experience for Spurs, who relied on the strength of Paul Stewart in midfield. Arsenal, on the other hand, were full of outstanding performances, with David Rocastle matching Stewart physically. The game was simply beyond Spurs. There was a lack of creativity in the team that brought their day to a sorry close.

22nd February 1992

First Division

Tottenham Hotspur 1

Stewart

Arsenal 1

Wright

Attendance: 33,124

Tottenham Hotspur: *Thorstvedt, Fenwick, Van den Hauwe, Sedgley, Howells, Mabbutt, Stewart, Durie, Nayim (Walsh), Lineker, Allen.*

Arsenal: *Seaman, Dixon, Winterburn, Hillier (O'Leary), Bould, Pates, Rocastle (Limpar), Wright, Smith, Merson, Campbell.*

In February 1992, Gary Lineker confessed that the White Hart Lane pitch had made him "look a complete idiot", as he missed two golden chances. One was such an open goal that he visibly winced when he shot over the bar from four yards, with David Seaman nowhere in sight. At the end of an amazing week when Lineker was dropped by England, only to come off the subs' bench to claim his 47th goal for his country and move closer to Bobby Charlton's record, he cited that he blamed the pitch. As White Hart Lane was vying with Old Trafford and Villa Park as the worst in the First Division, Lineker relived the nightmare of his two glaring misses. Spurs had already lost nine matches at White Hart Lane, and they now faced their most important fixture so far on their own pitch against Nottingham Forest in the League Cup semi-final second leg. The green, green grass of home certainly didn't apply to Spurs. Lineker – whose son George was quite poorly on this day – was particularly concerned with the potholes on the pitch, and ground staff confirmed that it would only get worse. With Spurs' home record in tatters and the club edging close towards the bottom, Peter Shreeves demanded commitment to the cause against the Gunners. He got it. Spurs had fire in their bellies as they tackled Arsenal, and by rights should have won. However, they let the game slip at the end, following Paul Stewart's header in the 53rd minute, which saw them take the lead. It was Ian Wright who equalized in the last minute.

12th December 1992

Premier League
Tottenham Hotspur 1
Allen
Arsenal 0
Attendance: 33,707
Tottenham Hotspur: *Thorstvedt, Austin, Edinburgh, Samways, Mabbutt, Ruddock, Howells, Durie (Barmby), Nayim, Sheringham, Allen.*
Arsenal: *Seaman, Lydersen, Winterburn, Hillier, Bould, Adams, Jensen (Limpar), Wright, Campbell, Merson, Parlour.*

Ian Wright, caught red-handed by the TV cameras, was not the only sinner in a north London derby of shame. BBC's *Match of the Day* highlighted and roundly condemned the right hook thrown at David Howells, which could have landed the Arsenal striker in the dock again. There was every chance that Wright would face a misconduct charge and a lengthy FA ban following the "trial by TV". With his England future also in question, Wright's defence could not paper over the cracks of the problems with regard to his temperament. And, unless he could get his Jekyll and Hyde character in check, he was jeopardizing his international future as a potential successor to Gary Lineker. Likeable and bubbly off the field, his winning instincts on the pitch were prone to explode into violence. He was painted as the villain in a derby that was littered with ugly running feuds, and which saw five players booked. Gordon Durie kicked John Jensen off the ball and went unpunished, then Tony Adams and Justin Edinburgh confronted each other in a snarling, spitting encounter at the end. Adams and Neil Ruddock earned their seventh bookings of the season, enough to ensure they would be banned for two games over Christmas. In a host of distasteful encounters, Wright's crime was unforgivable, but so was Durie's lunge at Jensen. The European Championship-winning Dane felt there were some very hard tackles during the game. And, as if there weren't enough incidents, Durie was confronted in the car park by an irate Spurs fan, who made unhelpful remarks. Both managers opted for diplomacy following the match, and Graham claimed that the referee's handling of the game was appalling. Buksh was in the spotlight from the very first minute, after rejecting a glaring penalty when Ray Parlour was sent crashing by Dean Austin. While Paul Allen fired in the winner after 21 minutes to clinch a rare league victory for Spurs over their bitter rivals, Jensen commented that the ref had lost control of the game in the first minute.

4th April 1993

FA Cup semi-final (Wembley)

Arsenal 1

Adams

Tottenham Hotspur 0

Attendance: 76,263

Arsenal: *Seaman, Dixon, Winterburn, Hillier, Linighan, Adams, Parlour, Wright (Morrow), Campbell (Smith), Merson, Selley.*

Tottenham Hotspur: *Thorstvedt, Austin, Edinburgh, Samways (Barmby), Mabbutt, Ruddock, Sedgley (Bergsson), Nayim, Anderton, Sheringham, Allen.*

Tony Adams became George Graham's hero in April 1993, when the Arsenal boss watched him head the Gunners' 79th-minute winner, which put them into their second cup final of the season, despite the fact that Lee Dixon was sent off in the 84th minute and automatically banned from the League Cup final. As Arsenal got sweet revenge over their north London rivals – who had beaten them in the semi-final two years previously – Graham relished another epic performance from his centre-half. At the final whistle, Graham was first on to the pitch to congratulate his skipper. It had been Adams' second goal of the season, and was enough to send his club on yet another trophy-chasing mission. They had already won the League Cup and two league titles in the six years that Graham had been in charge. Adams, driven by a personal crusade to prove he was a footballing thoroughbred, was determined to win honours for the Gunners and cement a World Cup place in Graham Taylor's England squad. The 26-year-old skipper revealed his desire for respect and recognition during duty for his country, and he managed to scale significant heights in Turkey for England just prior to the derby match. Adams had jumped, unchallenged, at the far post to head Paul Merson's 79th-minute free-kick past keeper Erik Thorstvedt, and drove home a goal that divided north London into heartbreak and ecstatic celebrations in equal measure. Even when Spurs had their best chance, David Seaman stood upright, providing a massive barrier between the net and the ball off Vinny Samways' foot. They indulged in a contest where fear of losing was paramount. There was no Chris Waddle to take centre stage and there were only rare flashes of quality from the likes of Paul Merson and Tottenham's Darren Anderton. It was a busy afternoon for referee Philip Don who, from his first controversial decision over a penalty incident to the sending off of Lee Dixon, had to deal with many undercurrents of nastiness in this scarred semi-final. Anderton burst past Adams and was sent sprawling by an Andy Linighan tackle after 28 minutes, the referee rejecting all the penalty claims. A few minutes later Paul Allen picked up the first of a profusion of yellow cards for a foul on Linighan. Dixon initially got into trouble with the referee as the first half spilled into injury time, when he tackled Nayim and felt that the midfielder over-elaborated his fall in an effort to win a penalty. Both players were booked. As the tie disintegrated into a succession of ugly brawls, Dixon was booked again in the 85th minute for bringing down Justin Edinburgh, and his dismissal put him out of the next cup final. A double substitution was made by Venables, who took off Samways and Steve Sedgley, and gave Nicky Barmby and Gudni Bergsson the chance to grab a late equalizer. Kevin Campbell limped off, to be replaced by Alan Smith, and with only a minute of normal time remaining Ian Wright was substituted.

11th May 1993

Premier League

Arsenal 1

Dickov

Tottenham Hotspur 3

Sheringham, Hendry 2

Attendance: 26,393

Arsenal: *Miller, Lydersen (McGowan), Keown, Marshall, O'Leary, Bould, Flatts (Carter), Selley, Smith, Dickov, Heaney.*

Tottenham Hotspur: *Walker, McDonald, Van den Hauwe, Hill, Mabbutt, Ruddock, Sedgley, Hendry (Hodges), Anderton, Sheringham, Allen.*

George Graham flaunted the rules on 11th May 1993 and made a mockery of this north London derby, as Spurs cruised to victory on the back of Teddy Sheringham's 22nd goal of the season. The Arsenal manager blatantly ignored Premier League regulations – to field the strongest possible side – and put out a reserve team against the Gunners' bitter London rivals. From one to 11 on the night's programme every single name changed, as Graham protected his probable FA Cup final team just four days from Wembley. It was a personal protest at the stupidity of a so-called elitist league that retained 22 clubs and left FA Cup finalists Arsenal and Sheffield Wednesday with a ridiculous pre-Wembley programme. And who could blame him? Rather than penalize Arsenal with little more than a cosmetic fine, the FA and Premier League should instead have looked within and blamed themselves. Graham sacrificed pride and Premier League points, with a far more precious prize at stake, in the most glittering knockout competition in the world. Graham had everything well planned and prepared at the club. He cited that his priority was the FA Cup final. He did what he thought was right for Arsenal. He had such a powerful squad that he could still field internationals of the calibre of Martin Keown, David O'Leary, Alan Smith and Paul Lydersen. But the side was littered with fresh-faced youngsters like Paul Dickov, who scored as a substitute against Crystal Palace, and produced a sparkling strike again. O'Leary would at least have been grateful for the profusion of matches that enabled him to make an emotional farewell in his final competitive match and his 720th appearance after 20 years at the club. O'Leary and the rest of the Arsenal reserves were contesting little more than places on the subs' bench for the Saturday. The fact that Danish international John Jensen was not involved was an indication that he would be picked for the FA Cup final. Youngster Ian Selley fought hard enough to push his claims for a place, but Spurs could easily have swamped the Arsenal reserves. Sheringham settled any lingering doubts over his claims for the Golden Boot when he notched his 22nd in the Premier League during the season. One of Spurs' promising youngsters, Danny Hill, was prominent in the move after 39 minutes, as Darren Anderton whipped over a cross for Sheringham to head past Alan Miller. The Anderton–Sheringham combination was lethal during this season, and Spurs' reserve striker John Hendry also came up with a couple of goals. Within a minute of the second half, Hill robbed Mark Flatts, and his cross was swept in by Hendry. Dickov played a delightful interchange of passes with Smith, before smashing his shot in off the post after 52 minutes. Sheringham headed against the post before Hendry got Spurs' third, five minutes from the end. But it was a hollow victory and, despite a combative and often entertaining match, more than 26,000 people inside Highbury were wondering if they had been short-changed.

16th August 1993

Premier League
Tottenham Hotspur 0
Arsenal 1
Wright
Attendance: 28,355
Tottenham Hotspur: *Thorstvedt, Austin, Campbell, Samways, Calderwood, Mabbutt, Sedgley, Durie, Dozzell, Sheringham, Howells (Caskey).*
Arsenal: *Seaman, Keown, Winterburn, Davis, Linighan, Adams, Jensen, Wright, Campbell, Parlour, McGoldrick.*

Ian Wright claimed that Arsenal would have been robbed in this north London derby if the Gunners hadn't smashed their White Hart Lane hoodoo. The striker watched in disbelief as a 35th-minute effort from Tony Adams was cleared by Colin Calderwood, as the Spurs defender stood a full yard behind his goal line. But Wright saw justice was done with an 87th-minute winner that ended Arsenal's four-year run at Spurs without a victory. Television evidence showed that the ball was well over the line, and George Graham commented it was so obviously over that he couldn't understand why the linesman didn't see it. Wright was the first to lead the protests to referee

David Elleray that the ball was over the line, and later it was stated that the linesman nearest the incident had said he had a clear view of what happened. But there was no disputing the quality of Wright's headed winner, which flashed past Thorstvedt just when it seemed the game was deadlocked in a draw. It was the Gunners who called the tune in this derby dogfight, which brought six bookings and a magnificent victory for Arsenal. Wright scored the Gunners' first goal in the Premiership that season, and it finally settled a frenetic and thrilling north London derby with just three minutes left. So much had been at stake, with Arsenal humbled and humiliated by a Micky Quinn hat-trick just two days earlier, which had left manager Graham showing signs that his cool exterior might crack. He axed Paul Merson and Anders Limpar, and called on the exuberance of Ray Parlour to quell the attacking initiatives of Vinny Samways. By also bringing in Eddie McGoldrick on wing, the transformation was breathtaking. Arsenal were full of energy and power, and took control to create a stream of chances. Sheringham's winner at St James' Park had given Ossie Ardiles a flying start to his new career as Spurs boss, in succession to Venables. However, Spurs confronted an Arsenal team that were even more fired-up – knowing that their places were at stake and their manager scrutinizing their commitment as much as their talent. Three Arsenal players were booked: Wright, Parlour and Martin Keown. But, despite his indiscipline overshadowing his special goal instincts, Wright finally struck as the Gunners were in danger of throwing away their chance of winning. Andy Linighan rose majestically to head on a McGoldrick corner, and inevitably Wright was in the right place to hook his shot past keeper Thorstvedt. Wright led the celebrations at the end, as the Gunners took over White Hart Lane with their deliriously happy supporters. The patched-up Spurs team did well to hang on as long as they did.

6th December 1993

Premier League

Arsenal 1

Wright

Tottenham Hotspur 1

Anderton

Attendance: 35,669

Arsenal: *Seaman, Dixon, Keown, Selley, Bould, Adams, Jensen, Wright, Smith (Campbell), Merson, Limpar.*

Tottenham Hotspur: *Thorstvedt, Kerslake, Edinburgh, Samways (Austin), Calderwood, Sedgley, Caskey (Hendry), Hazard, Anderton, Dozzell, Campbell.*

Ian Wright scored another wonder goal in December 1993, saving Arsenal from the worst fate of all – defeat at the hands of Spurs. His flashing left-foot volley equalized Darren Anderton's first-half strike, in a fiercely contested Highbury tussle. It meant that Wright now had scored nine of Arsenal's 18 league goals that season. His overall total was 23 (four for England, the rest for Arsenal). He was a one-man crusade, keeping the Gunners up there with the chasing pack behind Manchester United. The goal signaled Arsenal's second-half revival, after they had been exposed by Tottenham's slick passing game. Tottenham's brave display was highlighted by man-of-the-match midfielder Mickey Hazard. Described as a super player, Hazard was playing in a side, blighted by injury, that had gone nine league matches without a win. However, Darren Anderton's wonder goal for Spurs saw Wright fighting back for Arsenal. As the ball neared the Arsenal end, Anders Limpar's delicate flick-on was caught sweetly on the volley by Wright, to leave Thorstvedt rooted to the spot. In the second half, spurred on by manager Graham, Arsenal fought back, so that Thorstvedt had no chance when Wright connected with his left-foot volley. The move began with Seaman's long clearance. Alan Smith beat stand-in skipper Steve Sedgley, and Limpar chipped over Calderwood for Wright to connect just before the ball touched the ground and rob Tottenham boss Ardiles of a significant victory at Highbury. The Gunners knew they could always turn to Wright in times of crisis, and very rarely did he let them down.

2nd January 1995

Premier League

Tottenham Hotspur 1

Popescu

Arsenal 0

Attendance: 28,747

Tottenham Hotspur: *Walker, Austin, Campbell, Mabbutt, Calderwood, Howells, Popescu (Nethercott), Anderton, Sheringham, Klinsmann, Rosenthal.*

Arsenal: *Seaman, Winterburn, Dixon, Linighan, Bould, Schwarz, Selley (Smith), Jensen, Parlour, Wright, Campbell.*

By the beginning of January 1995, George Graham was facing two crucial cup games in five days, which could make or break his Arsenal career. But a goal by Spurs' star Gică Popescu left him staring at yet another disaster. Arsenal had only won two of their last 12 matches, and were just six points above the last relegation place. The cup matches that held the key to Graham's future were to be held at Millwall in the FA Cup and Liverpool in the League Cup. Arsenal also had to bear Stefan Schwarz being sent off, the second Gunner to be red-carded in successive matches. Popescu, meanwhile, had climbed off his sick bed to score the goal that doomed Arsenal. Spurs boss Gerry Francis stated that his star striker had the flu and did well to be out there at all. Graham, however, pointed to Arsenal's battling performance in an attempt to cover up the deficiencies in his own side. He even tried to defend Schwarz, first booked for clattering David Howells and then sent off for bringing down Jürgen Klinsmann. Schwarz was immediately shown the red card by referee Michael Reed, but then ran towards linesman Bill Jordan and attempted to shake his hand. The official refused and Arsenal physio Gary Lewin came on to the pitch to lead the Swede back down the tunnel. Howell had stud marks all down his groin. Spurs remained unbeaten for nine games under Francis and had kept five clean sheets – four in a row. They were now in sixth place in the Premiership, just four points behind Newcastle.

29th April 1995

Premier League
Arsenal 1
Wright
Tottenham Hotspur 1
Klinsmann
Attendance: 38,377
Arsenal: *Seaman, Dixon, Bould, Adams, Winterburn, Merson, Keown, Schwarz, Helder (Parlour), Wright, Hartson.*
Tottenham Hotspur: *Walker, Austin, Calderwood, Mabbutt, Edinburgh, Anderton, Howells, Rosenthal, Barmby, Sheringham, Klinsmann.*

Spurs were ready to offer a lucrative new contract to Jürgen Klinsmann to keep the brilliant German at White Hart Lane. Chairman Alan Sugar and manager Gerry Francis were scheduled to meet the newly elected Footballer of the Year to discuss Klinsmann's future at the club. Top of the agenda would be the massive £35,000-a-week deal being offered by German champions Bayern Munich, more than four times the basic weekly wage of £8,000 he was on at White Hart Lane. Spurs knew they would have to negotiate the remaining year of Klinsmann's contract if they were to stand any chance of keeping their 29-goal striker. Meanwhile, Klinsmann jetted off to Italy to make a TV film, after scoring his side's equalizer in the 1-1 draw at Arsenal, saying "I will make my decision at the end of the season."

18th November 1995

Premier League
Tottenham Hotspur 2
Sheringham, Armstrong

Arsenal 1
Bergkamp
Attendance: 32,894
Tottenham Hotspur: *Walker, Austin, Calderwood, Mabbutt, Campbell, Fox, Dozzell, Howells, Rosenthal (McMahon), Sheringham, Armstrong.*
Arsenal: *Seaman, Dixon, Bould, Adams, Winterburn, Merson, Platt, Keown, Helder (Hillier), Bergkamp, Hartson.*

Gerry Francis celebrated his first anniversary in charge of Spurs with a 2-1 victory over his north London rivals. They had won three of the previous six Premier League clashes, with Arsenal's only triumph coming in August 1993, thanks to a late strike from Ian Wright. But Spurs were looking for their first clean sheet since their clash with Norwich on Easter Monday ... something they again failed to achieve. Arsenal arrived with the best defensive record in the Premiership, having conceded just six goals and with seven clean sheets already registered that season. Teddy Sheringham – who had starred for England in their midweek win over Switzerland – and Chris Armstrong scored the Tottenham goals that deflated Arsenal, while a lone strike from Dennis Bergkamp denied the home side a clean sheet.

15th April 1996

Premier League
Arsenal 0
Tottenham Hotspur 0
Attendance: 38,273
Arsenal: *Seaman, Dixon, Winterburn, Keown, Marshall, Linighan, Platt, Wright, Merson (Helder), Bergkamp, Parlour.*
Tottenham Hotspur: *Walker, Edinburgh, Wilson, Howells, Campbell (Nethercott), Mabbutt, Fox, Dozzell (Anderton), Armstrong, Sheringham, Rosenthal.*

English soccer hung its head in shame again on 15th April 1996 after another shocking outbreak of violence. Rival fans hurled seats at one another in ugly scenes at the end of this north London derby. Dozens of police moved in to break up trouble at the Clock End, where 2,000 Spurs fans had sat. It was a night when hooliganism returned to the national game. The shameful scenes sent shockwaves throughout the world, as England were preparing to stage the European Championships in June. The biggest-ever security operation at a sports event would herald the start of Euro 96. But, at this London derby, officers feared the soccer showpiece of the decade could erupt into violence. The incident threatened to get out of hand, until more than 200 police and stewards moved in. There was trouble outside the ground before kick-off, when 200 fans hurled bottles of beer at each other outside the Gunners' pub. Terrified mums carried their children to safety, while the scenes posed a frightening prospect for the supporters of Holland, Germany and Italy before Euro 96. The scuffle was still in progress when Bruce Rioch and Gerry Francis were shaking hands in the one act of friendship visible to 38,273 strong crowd. There were chances on the field, but not many, and those created were just as quickly squandered.

24th November 1996

Premier League
Arsenal 3
Wright (pen), Adams, Bergkamp
Tottenham Hotspur 1
Sinton
Attendance: 38,264
Arsenal: *Lukic, Dixon, Winterburn, Keown, Bould, Adams, Platt (Hartson), Wright, Merson, Bergkamp (Parlour), Vieira.*
Tottenham Hotspur: *Walker, Carr, Wilson, Howells, Calderwood, Campbell, Anderton, Nielsen, Armstrong, Sheringham, Sinton.*

In November 1996, Ian Wright said thank you to Arsenal, with a goal and a personal message to the team he loved. After burying the penalty that gave Gunners the lead, Wright went off on a joyous lap of honour, and pulled up his Arsenal shirt to reveal a special message to his team. On his vest he had written: "I love the lads." Just a week before, Arsène Wenger revealed he had brought Wright's pay in line with other Arsenal stars, and that Wright had received the backing of the players after incidents that had threatened to put him in trouble with the FA. The goal – his 16th – and the message said it all. When Tony Adams and Dennis Bergkamp added further goals, Wenger claimed the Gunners could win the title. Adams had scored one of the best goals of his career, with the touch of a Baresi or Beckenbauer, for the new-look player took the chance to change this frantic north London derby. He struck a beautiful left-foot volley, slightly deflected off Steve Carr, past England number 2, keeper Ian Walker, with only two minutes left. Lionheart Adams gave a display that was worth 10 out of 10 in anybody's marking. Glorious goals from Adams and Dennis Bergkamp in the last couple of minutes ended Gerry Francis' record of never losing a north London derby. Certainly, Spurs never had the breaks in the first half, when Patrick Vieira got away with a suspicion of handball from a Darren Anderton cross. And Spurs themselves were the victims of a contentious penalty, awarded by David Elleray.

15th February 1997

Premier League

Tottenham Hotspur 0
Arsenal 0

Attendance: 33,039

Tottenham Hotspur: *Walker, Carr, Edinburgh, Austin, Calderwood, Campbell, Anderton, Howells, Iversen, Sinton, Rosenthal.*

Arsenal: *Lukic, Dixon, Winterburn, Keown, Bould, Adams, Parlour, Wright, Merson (Hughes), Bergkamp, Vieira.*

Darren Anderton made his Tottenham comeback in the most difficult match of all, after being absent for three months since damaging his knee in the League Cup defeat at Bolton. Colin Calderwood also returned for this encounter, although he was the only one of three

Spurs defenders to complete his suspension, with Ramon Vega and Stuart Nethercott still banned. For the second time during the 1996–97 season David Seaman missed the north London derby, this time with knee ligament damage, while David Platt was also missing with hamstring trouble. Arsenal did, however, welcome Dennis Bergkamp back from suspension, although neither side managed to score. The jury was still out on Arsène Wenger, who had proved himself a fresh and inspirational voice, but he would ultimately be judged over what he did over the course of the next two months. No foreign manager had ever won the Premiership – and that wait would continue as Arsenal could only manage third in the league.

30ᵗʰ August 1997

Premier League
Arsenal 0
Tottenham Hotspur 0
Attendance: 38,102
Arsenal: *Seaman, Dixon, Winterburn, Vieira, Bould, Grimandi, Parlour (Anelka), Wright, Petit (Platt), Bergkamp, Overmars.*
Tottenham Hotspur: *Walker, Carr, Edinburgh, Scales, Campbell, Clemence, Fox (Nielsen), Howells, Iversen (Mabbutt), Ferdinand, Sinton (Dominguez).*

A second successive goalless draw in the north London derby was not the result that anybody wanted. Spurs, however, were depleted through injury and suspension, with David Ginola ruled out with a shoulder injury and Colin Calderwood banned. Ian Wright summed up the anticipation by saying "There's nothing like a good derby tussle to set the pulses racing, and when Tottenham come to Highbury I'm always up for it, big time. Every year since I joined Arsenal, punters have told me 'Whatever you do, just make sure you beat Spurs.' It's an amazing feeling to know that you can send half the population of north London to work on Monday morning with a smile on their faces – and leave the other half wanting to phone in sick!" It is not known whether the majority of fans trudged into work or called in sick after this stalemate ...

28th December 1997

Premier League

Tottenham Hotspur 1

Nielsen

Arsenal 1

Parlour

Attendance: 38,018

Tottenham Hotspur: *Walker, Carr, Wilson, Vega, Calderwood, Campbell, Fox (Dominguez), Nielsen, Klinsmann, Clemence, Ginola (Iversen).*

Arsenal: *Seaman, Dixon (Grimandi), Winterburn, Vieira, Bould, Keown, Parlour, Anelka (Rankin), Petit, Bergkamp (Hughes), Overmars.*

Christian Gross plunged Tottenham into disarray after admitting that he might quit, after Jürgen Klinsmann's return to White Hart Lane ended in anti-climax and injury chaos. Swiss coach Gross refused to deny he would walk out just six weeks into the job if his fitness instructor, Fritz Schmidt, was refused a work permit by the Department of Employment. And, as Schmidt looked on from the stand, Spurs suffered a fresh catalogue of body blows – despite a 1-1 draw with Arsenal. Gross had signed a contract with Spurs on the condition that Fritz could come with him. As if the hold up over Schmidt's employment credentials wasn't enough, Gross had to contend with Spurs sinking into the bottom two, as England winger Darren Anderton produced another sick note and potentially needed another operation on his damaged groin. Striker Les Ferdinand joined the crocks, and was possibly out for up to a month as he struggled with a combination of stomach, thigh and dental problems, and David Ginola hobbled off with hamstring trouble that meant he might miss the following week's FA Cup third-round tie with Fulham. In addition, Klinsmann – greeted before kick-off as the messiah who would drag Spurs clear of relegation trouble

– had a disturbingly quiet game. Tottenham's next league match away to Manchester United was fast approaching, and they were faced with hitting rock bottom in the Premiership. Wenger showed the only positive approach when he pointed out that Klinsmann had much experience and that, at a time of struggle, this was extremely important.

14th November 1998

Premier League

Arsenal 0

Tottenham Hotspur 0

Attendance: 38,278

Arsenal: *Seaman, Dixon, Winterburn, Vieira, Keown, Adams, Parlour, Anelka (Boa Morte), Petit, Ljungberg (Wreh), Overmars.*

Tottenham Hotspur: *Baardsen, Carr, Edinburgh, Scales, Vega, Campbell, Anderton, Nielsen, Armstrong, Iversen, Calderwood (Sinton).*

It was tit for tat in north London in November 1998, with Spurs boss George Graham claiming that the ageing Highbury defence was on its last leg, and Nigel Winterburn retaliating that the former Arsenal manager's methods were boring and static. Arsenal chairman Peter Hill-Wood summed up the atmosphere perfectly when he said, "I'm afraid the Tottenham fixture is one I never seem able to enjoy. Everyone gets wrapped up in the tension and the games themselves are often rather fraught affairs. This one will inevitably have a little extra spice." Graham's nine-year reign at Highbury had been brought to an end in 1995 after he had been caught accepting £425,000 in unsolicited gifts – he was given half an hour to clear his desk, and received a one-year ban from the Premier League. However, by October 1998, he had returned to take charge at White Hart Lane.

5th May 1999

Premier League

Tottenham Hotspur 1

Anderton

Arsenal 3

Petit, Anelka, Kanu

Attendance: 36,019

Tottenham Hotspur: *Walker, Carr, Taricco (Sinton), Freund, Young, Campbell, Anderton, Sherwood, Armstrong, Iversen, Ginola (Dominguez).*

Arsenal: *Seaman, Dixon, Winterburn, Vieira, Keown, Adams, Parlour (Vivas), Anelka, Petit, Bergkamp (Kanu), Overmars (Grimandi).*

Arsène Wenger watched Arsenal take a huge step towards retaining their Premiership crown during a night of high drama. The Gunners' thrilling 3-1 victory over deadly rivals Spurs fired them three points clear, as United stumbled in a tempestuous 2-2 draw at Liverpool. Bookmakers immediately installed Arsenal 6/4 favourites to win the title, with United evens – the first time Arsenal had ranked ahead of their Manchester rivals that season. But Alex Ferguson was left counting a different cost at Anfield as he clashed angrily with ref David Elleray in the tunnel after Paul Ince's late equalizer. Ferguson claimed that the ref handed it to Liverpool. But Arsenal didn't have a problem dealing with their past as they wrote another glorious chapter in their history. Wenger's men not only had the psychological edge, but also a potentially vital advantage if the decision came down to a goal difference decision. It really was that close. In one of those strange twists of fate, Arsenal cleared the obstacle set out by former boss Graham, only to head for the penultimate hurdle set by Highbury playing legend David O'Leary. The reigning champions, with their talented galaxy of stars accumulated by Wenger, showed, however, that they were more than a match for Spurs. David Ginola was the Players' Player of the Year and was hopeful of being named Footballer of the Year. With Patrick Vieira, Dennis Bergkamp and Marc Overmars, the Gunners possessed one of the most adventurous teams around. They had a mean defence, and despite the fact that Spurs managed to defeat Seaman once over their two meetings that season, Arsenal conceded only 16 Premiership goals in the other 36 games. It was a phenomenal record.

7th November 1999

Premier League

Tottenham Hotspur 2

Iversen, Sherwood

Arsenal 1

Vieira

Attendance: 36,085

Tottenham Hotspur: *Walker, Carr, Edinburgh, Sherwood, Campbell, Perry, Leonhardsen (Fox), Clemence, Armstrong, Iversen, Ginola (Dominguez).*

Arsenal: *Seaman, Dixon, Winterburn, Vieira, Keown, Adams, Ljungberg, Petit (Grimandi), Kanu (Suker), Bergkamp, Overmars.*

Arsène Wenger was humiliated by another disciplinary meltdown as nine-man Arsenal crashed in this north London derby demolition. The Gunners' Freddie Ljungberg and Martin Keown were sent off at White Hart Lane, bringing the club's appalling disciplinary record to 26 red cards in Wenger's 37-month reign. Ref David Elleray booked another nine players, as Spurs chief Graham put one over the club who sacked him in the bungs scandal almost five years previously. Wenger, whose side had already lost as many games in this season as they had in the whole of the previous one, admitted that the red cards had destroyed his team. In the mayhem, Swedish star Ljungberg flicked V-signs to the crowd, and kicked a door as he stomped down the tunnel. Wenger clamed he was sent off for a head butt, but TV replays suggested he was guilty only of shoving Justin Edinburgh in the face. In addition, Emmanuel Petit was cut above the eye by Sherwood's elbow, as the match veered towards anarchy in the second half. However, none of the acrimony could wipe the smile from Graham's face, as he claimed Spurs had been superb.

19th March 2000

Premier League

Arsenal 2

Armstrong (og), Henry (pen)

Tottenham Hotspur 1

Armstrong

Attendance: 38,131

Arsenal: *Manninger, Dixon, Silvinho, Vieira, Luzhny, Adams, Parlour, Grimandi, Kanu, Henry (Winterburn), Overmars (Ljungberg).*

Tottenham Hotspur: *Walker, Carr, Taricco, Freund, Campbell (Young), Perry, Anderton, Leonhardsen, Armstrong, Iversen (Ferdinand), Ginola (Korsten).*

Arsenal took a major step towards their Champions League dream thanks to Thierry Henry and their bitter north London rivals. The Gunners leapfrogged Chelsea, and went into fourth place in the Premiership, winning a stormy derby against Spurs, with Chris Armstrong's own goal separating the sides. But Arsenal's delight at beating their fiercest opponents was marred by the sending off of Gilles Grimandi, which put them back in the dock over their shocking disciplinary record. That would come back to haunt Arsène Wenger, although at this time Arsenal were just two points behind Liverpool in the top three. They were vying for a coveted place in the Champions League. In Henry, Wenger had found a striker of genuine pace and menace, and not even the usual cluster of red and yellow cards could take the shine off Henry's dazzling contribution to Arsenal's victory over Spurs.

The 21st century

While Arsène Wenger would be a fixture at Highbury throughout the first decade of the new century and beyond, his counterpart did not fare as well. George Graham was sacked amid controversial circumstances in March 2001, and replaced by Glenn Hoddle.

The White Hart Lane hero of the 1970s and the 1980s was – despite flashes of brilliance that included taking his team to the 2002 League Cup final where they lost to Blackburn Rovers – unable to restore the club to its former glories. He was dismissed in September 2003, with Spurs having taken just four points from their opening six Premiership games. A succession of managers rotated through the White Hart Lane managerial position – with Jacques Santini, Martin Jol and Juande Ramos all trying their hand – before a semblance of stability arrived in the form of Harry Redknapp in October 2008.

Ramos – who inherited a Spurs team in the relegation zone and prone to poor defending – did have the distinction, however, of leading Tottenham to their first trophy since 1999, when they took on Chelsea in the 2008 League Cup final. Despite falling behind to a Didier Drogba free-kick, Spurs responded with a second-half Dimitar Berbatov penalty that took the game into extra-time, where Jonathan Woodgate scored the winner. Spurs also restored some north London pride under Ramos, with their first win over Arsenal since 1999 in the semi-final of that competition.

It was business as usual across at Highbury, with Wenger enjoying a decade of unprecedented success at the club. Arsenal narrowly missed out on the Double in 2000–01, when they failed to overtake Manchester United in the Premier League and fell to two Michael Owen goals; Liverpool won the FA Cup by a 2-1 margin. Undeterred, though, Wenger's side repeated the feat achieved by their 1970–71 predecessors by claiming the club's second Double the following season. The Gunners finished the league campaign a massive seven points ahead of second-placed Liverpool, and swept aside the challenge of Chelsea in the FA Cup final with goals from Ray Parlour and Freddie Ljungberg.

A second consecutive Double was not to be achieved in 2002–03, with Manchester United taking the Premier League, although Arsenal did beat Southampton in the FA Cup final, courtesy of a first-half Robert Pirès goal. The following campaign was definitely one to be remembered and recorded in history, as Arsenal's "Invincibles" completed the whole 38-game Premier League campaign without defeat, wining 26 matches and drawing 12, to claim the crown with a massive 11-point advantage over Chelsea. The Stamford Bridge club reversed the roles the following season, which, with Arsenal beating Manchester United in the FA Cup final, meant that the Gunners had once again come so close to completing yet another Double.

The 2005–06 season was an emotional one for Arsenal fans, as they prepared to say goodbye to their home. The Gunners' 4-2 victory over Wigan Athletic on 7th May 2006 saw them end 92 years of playing at Highbury, before they moved into their new 60,000-seat Emirates Stadium. In a fitting tribute to their old stadium, Thierry Henry – who had finished the season as the Premier League's top scorer with 27 goals – scored a hat-trick to bid farewell to an old friend.

The shock for many Arsenal fans, however, was that for the first time under Arsène Wenger, the club had failed to finish in the top two, but they were hoping that success in the Champions League final would provide a quick remedy for their disappointment. The stage was set for a spectacular exhibition of football, with Arsenal paired with Barcelona in the showpiece event at the Stade de France. It got even better when Sol Campbell opened the scoring late in the first half, but the Spanish giants retorted with two goals in a five-minute second-half spell that broke the Gunners. There was little recompense in the 2006–07 campaign either, with Arsenal again finishing fourth in the Premier League, and losing 2-1 to Chelsea in the League Cup final.

Fresh from his FA Cup victory with Portsmouth, Harry Redknapp was appointed Spurs manager in October 2008 and promptly led the White Hart Lane club to a second successive League Cup final. Unfortunately, though, Spurs were unable to add yet another trophy to their cabinet, as Manchester United won the penalty shootout 4-1 after the game had finished goalless. Arsenal also fell at the last hurdle in 2010–11, when they, surprisingly, lost to a soon-to-be relegated Birmingham City.

In stark contrast to Arsenal's league positions during the 21st century – which had, so far, never seen them fall lower than fourth – Tottenham were struggling to establish themselves as a consistent top 10 team, with three finishes in the bottom half of the table and their best showing being the fourth they achieved in 2009–10 and 2011–12 before the shock departure of Redknapp in June 2012. With Manchester United narrowly missing out on their 20th league title, as big-spending Manchester City claimed their first crown since 1968, only time would tell whether either of the north London giants could again challenge for the greatest prize in English football … but the disappointment would be eased as long as they won the derby matches and finished higher than their neighbours!

Record in the 21st century

Arsenal

Season	League	P	W	D	L	F	A	Pts	Pos
2000–01	Prem	38	20	10	8	63	38	70	2
2001–02	Prem	38	26	9	3	79	36	87	1
2002–03	Prem	38	23	9	6	85	42	78	2
2003–04	Prem	38	26	12	0	73	26	90	1
2004–05	Prem	38	25	8	5	87	36	83	2
2005–06	Prem	38	20	7	11	68	31	67	4
2006–07	Prem	38	19	11	8	63	35	68	4
2007–08	Prem	38	24	11	3	74	31	83	3
2008–09	Prem	38	20	12	6	68	37	72	4
2009–10	Prem	38	23	6	9	83	41	75	3
2010–11	Prem	38	19	11	8	72	43	68	4
2011–12	Prem	38	21	7	10	74	49	70	3

FA Cup

2000–01	1-2 v Liverpool (Final)
2001–02	2-0 v Chelsea (Final)
2002–03	1-0 v Southampton (Final)
2003–04	0-1 v Manchester United (Semi-final)
2004–05	0-0 (5-4 pens) v Manchester United (Final)
2005–06	0-1 v Bolton Wanderers (Fourth Round)
2006–07	0-0, 0-1 v Blackburn Rovers (Fifth Round)
2007–08	0-4 v Manchester United (Fifth Round)
2008–09	1-2 v Chelsea (Semi-final)
2009–10	1-3 v Stoke City (Fourth Round)
2010–11	0-2 v Manchester United (Sixth Round)
2011–12	0-2 v Sunderland (Fifth Round)

League Cup

2000–01	1-2 v Ipswich Town (Third Round)
2001–02	0-4 v Blackburn Rovers (Fifth Round)
2002–03	2-3 v Sunderland (Third Round)

2003–04	0-1, 1-2 v Middlesbrough (Semi-final)
2004–05	0-1 v Manchester United (Fifth Round)
2005–06	0-1, 2-1 v Wigan Athletic (Semi-final)
2006–07	1-2 v Chelsea (Final)
2007–08	1-1, 1-5 v Tottenham Hotspur (Semi-final)
2008–09	0-2 v Burnley (Fifth Round)
2009–10	0-3 v Manchester City (Fifth Round)
2010–11	1-2 v Birmingham City (Final)
2011–12	0-1 v Manchester City (Fifth Round)

Europe

2000–01	Champions League: 2-1, 0-1 v Valencia (Quarter-final)
2001–02	Champions League: second group stage
2002–03	Champions League: second group stage
2003–04	Champions League: 1-1, 1-2 v Chelsea (Quarter-final)
2004–05	Champions League: 1-3, 1-0 v Bayern Munich (First Knockout Round)
2005–06	Champions League: 1-2 v Barcelona (Final)
2006–07	Champions League: 0-1, 1-1 v PSV Eindhoven (First Knockout Round)
2007–08	Champions League: 1-1, 2-4 v Liverpool (Quarter-final)
2008–09	Champions League: 0-1, 1-3 v Manchester United (Semi-final)
2009–10	Champions League: 2-2, 1-4 v Barcelona (Quarter-final)
2010–11	Champions League: 2-1, 1-3 v Barcelona (First Knockout Round)
2011–12	Champions League: 0-4, 3-0 v AC Milan (First Knockout Round)

Tottenham Hotspur

Season	League	P	W	D	L	F	A	Pts	Pos
2000–01	Prem	38	13	10	15	47	54	49	12
2001–02	Prem	38	14	8	16	49	53	50	9
2002–03	Prem	38	14	8	16	51	62	50	10
2003–04	Prem	38	13	6	19	47	57	45	14

2004–05	Prem	38	14	10	14	47	41	52	9
2005–06	Prem	38	18	11	9	53	38	65	5
2006–07	Prem	38	17	9	12	57	54	60	5
2007–08	Prem	38	11	13	14	66	61	46	11
2008–09	Prem	38	14	9	15	45	45	51	8
2009–10	Prem	38	21	7	10	67	41	70	4
2010–11	Prem	38	16	14	8	55	46	62	5
2011–12	Prem	38	20	9	9	66	41	69	4

FA Cup

2000–01	1-2 v Arsenal (Semi-final)
2001–02	0-4 v Chelsea (Sixth Round)
2002–03	0-4 v Southampton (Third Round)
2003–04	1-1, 3-4 v Manchester City (Fourth Round)
2004–05	0-1 v Newcastle United (Sixth Round)
2005–06	2-3 v Leicester City (Third Round)
2006–07	3-3, 1-2 v Chelsea (Sixth Round)
2007–08	1-3 v Manchester United (Fourth Round)
2008–09	1-2 v Manchester United (Fourth Round)
2009–10	0-2 v Portsmouth (Semi-final)
2010–11	0-4 v Fulham (Fourth Round)
2011–12	1-5 v Chelsea (Semi-final)

League Cup

2000–01	1-3 v Birmingham City (Third Round)
2001–02	1-2 v Blackburn Rovers (Final)
2002–03	1-2 v Burnley (Third Round)
2003–04	1-1 (4-5 pens) v Middlesbrough (Quarter-final)
2004–05	1-1 (3-4 pens) v Liverpool (Quarter-final)
2005–06	0-1 v Grimsby Town (Second Round)
2006–07	2-2, 1-3 v Arsenal (Semi-final)
2007–08	2-1 v Chelsea (Final)
2008–09	0-0 (1-4 pens) v Manchester United (Final)
2009–10	0-2 v Manchester United (Fifth Round)
2010–11	1-4 v Arsenal (Third Round)

2011–12   0-0 (6-7 pens) v Stoke City (Third Round)

Europe

2000–01   Did not qualify
2001–02   Did not qualify
2002–03   Did not qualify
2003–04   Did not qualify
2004–05   Did not qualify
2005–06   Did not qualify
2006–07   UEFA Cup: 1-2, 2-2 v Sevilla (Quarter-final)
2007–08   UEFA Cup: 0-1, 1-0 (5-6 pens) v PSV Eindhoven (Round of 16)
2008–09   UEFA Cup: 0-2, 1-1 v Shakhtar Donetsk (Round of 32)
2009–10   Did not qualify
2010–11   Champions League: 0-4, 0-1 v Real Madrid (Quarter-final)
2011–12   Europa League: group stage

18th December 2000

Premier League

Tottenham Hotspur 1

Rebrov

Arsenal 1

Vieira

Attendance: **36,062**

Tottenham Hotspur: *Sullivan, Carr, Clemence, Thelwell, Campbell, Perry, Anderton, Sherwood, Rebrov (Armstrong), Ferdinand, King.*

Arsenal: *Manninger, Dixon, Silvinho, Grimandi (Vieira), Keown, Adams, Parlour, Ljungberg, Kanu (Wiltord), Henry, Pirès (Bergkamp).*

Patrick Vieira scored a last-minute equalizer to keep Arsenal's title hopes alive. Vieira had not trained for nine days after pulling a hamstring, but came off the bench to deny Tottenham victory. The point kept Arsenal within touching distance of Manchester United, and Wenger hailed Vieira as his "saviour" after his vital 89th-minute goal. The draw took Arsenal to within five points of Premiership leaders United, but the Gunners looked dead and buried after Sergei Rebrov's 31st-minute opener. Arsenal bombarded the Spurs goal in the second half, and were rewarded when Vieira rose above the defence to head Silvinho's corner into the net. But Spurs boss George Graham was furious with the goal, claiming that Vieira climbed all over Les Ferdinand to head home. "It was unbelievable," Graham said. "I cannot understand how the referee allowed the goal to stand. Vieira virtually pulled Les' shirt off his back and almost sent him to the ground. How the goal stood I'll never know and when I watched it on television afterwards it was even clearer that it was a foul. The lads are very let down because it's always sad to let in an equalizer in the last moments of a game. But I'm very proud of the way my team performed."

31st March 2001

Premier League

Arsenal 2

Pirès, Henry

Tottenham Hotspur 0

Attendance: 38,121

Arsenal: *Seaman, Dixon (Luzhny), Cole, Vieira, Keown, Adams, Parlour, Lauren (Kanu), Wiltord, Henry, Pirès.*

Tottenham Hotspur: *Sullivan, Iversen, Young, Doherty, Perry, Gardner, Freund, Thelwell, Ferdinand, Korsten (Piercy), Davies (Etherington).*

Arsenal striker Dennis Bergkamp was ruled out with an Achilles injury, but Martin Keown returned after missing 13 games with a knee injury. Giles Grimandi dropped out with flu, while Silvinho and Nelson Vivas were not in the squad after arriving back from international duty the day before. Spurs were without Sol Campbell (ankle), top scorer Sergei Rebrov (hamstring) and Stephen Clemence (groin), but the biggest news was the return of Glenn Hoddle to White Hart Lane. Arsène Wenger admitted he feared his managerial apprentice was about to come back to haunt him. The Arsenal manager had persuaded Hoddle to try his hand at running a club when Tottenham's boss-in-waiting played under him at Monaco 10 years earlier. Hoddle was just an interested observer at this match, but would be in charge of the club he graced as a player when the two sides met in the following week's FA Cup semi-final at Old Trafford. "It's a very exciting opportunity for me and I feel like I've come home," said Hoddle. "I've been a Spurs supporter ever since I walked through the turnstiles as an eight year old and I have a deep-rooted feeling for this club." By the end of the 90 minutes, Hoddle had a more realistic understanding of the task he had taken on, as goals from Robert Pirès and Thierry Henry gave the Gunners a 2-0 win.

8th April 2001

FA Cup semi-final (Old Trafford)

Arsenal 2

Vieira, Pirès

Tottenham Hotspur 1

Doherty

Attendance: **63,541**

Arsenal: *Seaman, Dixon, Silvinho, Vieira, Keown, Adams, Parlour, Lauren, Wiltord (Cole), Henry, Pirès (Ljungberg).*

Tottenham Hotspur: *Sullivan, Carr, Young, Doherty, Campbell (King), Perry, Sherwood, Iversen, Rebrov, Ferdinand (Leonhardsen), Clemence (Thelwell).*

Patrick Vieira lit up this grotesquely one-sided match, and capped a formidable week with an inspiring display. Vieira had been brooding over his future since his disciplinary problems at the start of the season, and had received flattering overtures from Juventus. The Frenchman destroyed Spurs with a storming dribble through the heart of their team late in the game, teasing substitute Ledley King, before flicking the ball wide to Sylvain Wiltord, whose cross was finished off at the far post by Robert Pirès. Arsenal squandered so many chances, as the Gunners displayed an embarrassment of riches. New Spurs manager Glenn Hoddle would have been simply mortified. Spurs skipper Sol Campbell defied the odds to start the game, but he didn't last long, and the sight of the club's most inspiring player hobbling off visibly lifted an already superior Arsenal. Spurs went ahead with a 14th-minute move that began with a free-kick, but fell apart in a comedy of errors. But Arsenal were not laughing when centre-half Gary Doherty chested the ball down for Les Ferdinand to manoeuvre into a shooting position. Although his effort was saved by David Seaman and headed away by Lee Dixon, Steffen Iversen's mishit shot was deflected into the corner by a smart glancing header from Doherty. Vieira got away with a late tackle on Carr, but was booked for a challenge on Iversen. Then Campbell was shown the yellow card by referee Graham Poll for a foul on Ray Parlour. The England defender hurt himself in the challenge and, while he was out of action, Vieira stole in ahead of Perry to head the equalizer from Pirès' 33rd-minute free-kick. After 56 minutes Hoddle changed tack by taking off Les Ferdinand and sending on Øyvind Leonhardsen into midfield, to release Rebrov and Iversen as a two-pronged attack. Arsenal then launched into a succession of counter-attacks, Sullivan saving from Wiltord, Parlour and Pirès. Inevitably, Arsenal went in front, but Spurs then had perhaps their best moments. Rebrov's volley – from an Iversen cross – looked promising but Seaman was right behind it.

17th November 2001

Premier League

Tottenham Hotspur 1

Poyet

Arsenal 1

Pirès

Attendance: **36,066**

Tottenham Hotspur: *Sullivan, Taricco, Ziege, King, Perry, Richards, Anderton, Freund (Davies), Ferdinand (Rebrov), Sheringham, Poyet.*

Arsenal: *Wright, Lauren, Cole, Vieira, Campbell, Keown, Parlour, Grimandi, Wiltord, Bergkamp (Kanu), Pirès.*

Former Tottenham skipper Sol Campbell was bracing himself for the biggest test of his career, after his defection across north London to bitter rivals Arsenal the previous summer. Campbell was branded unambitious for turning his back on Europe to move just four miles across north London, yet he insisted that it proved he *was* ambitious and not just after the money. While his contract was worth £100,000 at Arsenal, he could have earned far more than that with Barcelona or Inter Milan, who were both keen to sign him in the summer. Spurs were buoyed by the news that Christian Ziege and Sergei Rebrov had both returned unscathed from international duty, but Arsenal's Thierry Henry was ruled out with an ankle problem. Dennis Bergkamp partnered Sylvain Wiltord up front, but Freddie Ljungberg failed a late fitness test on his shoulder. The match finished 1-1, with Robert Pirès again getting his name on the scoresheet for the visitors, while Gus Poyet scored for Spurs.

6th April 2002

Premier League

Arsenal 2

Ljungberg, Lauren (pen)

Tottenham Hotspur 1

Sheringham (pen)

Attendance: 38,186

Arsenal: *Seaman, Lauren, Luzhny, Vieira, Campbell, Adams, Wiltord (Dixon), Edu (Kanu), Henry, Bergkamp (Parlour), Ljungberg.*

Tottenham Hotspur: *Keller, Anderton (Poyet), Thatcher, Gardner, Perry, Richards, Sherwood, Davies, Iversen, Sheringham (Rebrov), Etherington (Clemence).*

Freddie Ljungberg's first-half goal seemed to have secured a victory that would reclaim the top spot from Manchester United, despite the match being the least convincing Arsenal performance of recent weeks. But then, with just nine minutes remaining, referee Mark Halsey awarded Tottenham a penalty that never was. When Gus Poyet miskicked, and then fell over in front of David Seaman and somehow got a 12-yarder out of it, it was nothing more than laughable. Teddy Sheringham kept a straight face and an even surer aim to equalize from the spot kick. Halsey then promptly awarded Arsenal a penalty too. Thierry Henry tumbled under Dean Richards' light challenge, and equality of good fortune was restored, although there was still more drama to come. Henry, a regular penalty-taker despite two recent misses, had to go off after receiving treatment and could not be allowed back on until play had restarted – from the spot. He had to wait on the touchline. Edu, designated number 2, had already been substituted. Lauren shoved everybody out of the way and got on with the job – with some style too as he aimed his kick slowly and deliberately down the middle rather than relying on the bombshell blast. The result put the Gunners two points ahead of United in the race for the Premiership title, with one game in hand.

16th November 2002

Premier League
Arsenal 3
Henry, Ljungberg, Wiltord
Tottenham Hotspur 0
Attendance: **38,121**
Arsenal: *Shaaban, Luzhny, Cole, Vieira (van Bronckhorst), Campbell, Cygan, Wiltord, Silva, Henry (Jeffers), Bergkamp (Pirès), Ljungberg.*
Tottenham Hotspur: *Keller, Carr, Bunjevčević, Freund, Richards, King, Davies (Iversen), Redknapp, Keane, Sheringham (Anderton), Etherington (Poyet).*

Arsène Wenger admitted before this match that the north London derby did not mean what it once did – but promised more pain for Spurs ... and delivered! Goals from Thierry Henry, Freddie Ljungberg and Sylvain Wiltord gave the Gunners a comfortable 3-0 win in this Premier League encounter. "For us it's three points at stake," explained Wenger. "When you play United or Liverpool you know that what's at stake is your position at the end of the year. When it's

Tottenham, it's prestige and rivalry. If you are manager of Arsenal then you know that your position at the end of the year will depend on how we do in the derbies, because we play so many of them, but there is a special excitement to the rivalry against Spurs." David Seaman was still absent with a groin injury, so Rami Shaaban deputized in goal, while Sol Campbell returned, following a back injury, to help keep a clean sheet against his former club.

15th December 2002

Premier League
Tottenham Hotspur 1
Ziege
Arsenal 1
Pirès (pen)
Attendance: **36,077**
Tottenham Hotspur: *Keller, Carr, Ziege, King, Richards, Bunjevčević, Anderton (Davies), Freund, Keane, Sheringham, Poyet.*
Arsenal: *Seaman, Lauren, Cole, Silva, Campbell, Keown, Ljungberg (Touré), Parlour, Henry, Bergkamp (Wiltord), Pirès (van Bronckhorst).*

This north London derby turned on a goalkeeping mistake and, given his recent form, the first surprise was that David Seaman didn't make it. This time, the honours went to Spurs keeper Kasey Keller, who invited Arsenal back into the game with a maddeningly pointless kamikaze dive at the flying feet of Thierry Henry. Robert Pirès converted the penalty, and Arsenal gained a precious point that lifted them just clear of the closing pack. The second surprise was the sight of that bag of creaking bones, formerly known as Safe Hands, coming to the rescue of his side when Tottenham pressed for a second-half winner. His spring may have sprung, his leap may have leapt and his bolt may have decidedly been shot, but Seaman summoned up the embers of his authority at White Hart Lane to halt his team's quickening slide. For once, no one even tried to blame him for the 11th-minute Christian Ziege free-kick that whistled past his despairing left hand. Seaman had always been vulnerable at dead balls, but this time it was the quality of Ziege's strike and not the goalkeeper's leaden legs that caught the eye. Perhaps if Ashley Cole, the game's outstanding player, had not twice spared his blushes by nodding a header from Dean Richards off the line and kicking Robbie Keane's shot to safety, Seaman might have been the villain again. In the second half, Arsenal were the dominant side, but they still needed their goalkeeper to keep them in the game when their concentration lapsed. The longer the game went on, the more Seaman's experience helped to steady an Arsenal side that had seen its Premiership lead whittled away to almost nothing.

8th November 2003

Premier League

Arsenal 2

Pirès, Ljungberg

Tottenham Hotspur 1

Anderton

Attendance: 38,101

Arsenal: Lehmann, Lauren (Cygan), Cole, Silva (Bergkamp), Campbell, Touré, Ljungberg, Parlour, Kanu (Edu), Henry, Pirès.

Tottenham Hotspur: Keller, Carr, Taricco, Gardner, Richards, King, Anderton, Dalmat (Ricketts), Keane, Postiga (Zamora), Konchesky (Mabizela).

Spurs went to Highbury without a win in 10 attempts ... and left still seeking that elusive victory. Glenn Hoddle had been sacked and caretaker boss David Pleat was left with a squad bereft of quality in midfield; it was plain for all to see that Spurs would struggle to attract the high-calibre manager they needed to regain their status of being a big club. It was the visitors, however, who took the lead, when Darren Anderton opened the scoring after just four minutes, and it took Arsenal until well into the second half before they responded in kind. Hélder Postiga had missed two chances to extend Spurs' lead before Thierry Henry's powerful shot, which could only be parried by Kasey Keller. The ball rebounded to Robert Pirès, who netted a 69th-minute equalizer. Ten minutes later, Freddie Ljungberg launched a speculative shot from 25 yards, that took a deflection off Stephen Carr to loop over the stranded Spurs keeper, thus giving Arsenal the win, and keeping them at the head of the Premiership.

25th April 2004

Premier League
Tottenham Hotspur 2
Redknapp, Keane (pen)
Arsenal 2
Vieira, Pirès
Attendance: **36,097**
Tottenham Hotspur: *Keller, Kelly (Poyet), Taricco (Bunjevčević), Gardner, King, Brown, Davies, Redknapp, Keane, Kanoute, Jackson (Defoe).*
Arsenal: *Lehmann, Lauren, Cole, Vieira, Campbell, Touré, Parlour (Edu), Silva, Henry, Bergkamp (Reyes), Pirès.*

Champions without losing a game … not one! "I don't think you will ever see that again," exclaimed Arsène Wenger. "It is something very special." For most of this match, Arsenal played with imperious majesty. They made Spurs chase shadows. Their first goal made people all around the ground look at each other and shake their heads in either wonder or despair. A burst from the incomparable Thierry Henry from the edge of his own area, a sublime pass to Dennis Bergkamp inside the full-back, a first-time cross hit low to the back post where the captain, Patrick Vieira, slid in to add the final touch. The second goal was brilliant, too. Robert Pirès linked up with his skipper and Gilberto before finding Bergkamp, who had drifted off the central defenders into the hole, with time and space to see Vieira peeling away to the left. The Arsenal captain, too quick for Stephen Kelly, might have gone for goal, but he realized Pirès' support run meant he was better placed, and the left footer gave Kasey Keller no chance. It was Pirès' 19th of the season, and, between them, he and Henry had scored 44 Premiership goals – matching the entire Spurs tally for the season. The interval saw Defoe on for the overwhelmed Johnnie Jackson, as David Pleat attempted to earn credibility. Spurs were finding the fight and fire that had been lacking for too long. Jamie Redknapp pulled one back just after the hour, bending into the bottom corner from 20 yards after good work from Defoe and Brown. Pirès thudded a shot against the bar, but Spurs kept coming. Then, when Defoe's enthusiasm led to a corner, Lehmann lost his marbles to hand the home side their chance. A stunning, unfeasibly stupid push that sent Robbie Keane hitting the deck before cartwheeling in delight when he struck home from 12 yards. Even as the Spurs supporters took consolation from the point that should secure their Premiership salvation, they were left as spectators at a coronation of the finest team for a generation.

13th November 2004

Premier League

Tottenham Hotspur 4

Naybet, Defoe, King, Kanoute

Arsenal 5

Henry, Lauren (pen), Vieira, Ljungberg, Pirès

Attendance: 36,095

Tottenham Hotspur: *Robinson, Pamarot, Edman, Brown (Kanoute), Naybet, King, Mendes (Davies), Carrick, Keane (Gardner), Defoe, Ziegler.*

Arsenal: *Lehmann, Lauren, Cole, Vieira, Touré, Cygan, Ljungberg, Fàbregas, Henry, Bergkamp (van Persie), Reyes (Pirès).*

Few would have expected the avalanche of second-half goals that proliferated during this match at White Hart Lane. Martin Jol had just taken over the reins from Jacques Santini – who had surprisingly resigned after just 13 games in charge – and must have been encouraged by his team's first-half performance when Noureddine Naybet gave the home side the lead in the 37th minute.

Thierry Henry equalized on the stroke of half-time, and Lauren gave the visitors the lead with a penalty, after Noé Pamarot was judged to have fouled Freddie Ljungberg. Jermain Defoe restored parity, before the floodgates opened and Arsenal stormed into a 5-2 lead with goals from Patrick Vieira, Ljungberg and Robert Pirès. Although Ledley King and Freddie Kanoute reduced the deficit to just one goal, to set up a nailbiting finale, Arsenal hung on to claim the three points in a nine-goal thriller.

25ᵗʰ April 2005

Premier League
Arsenal 1
Reyes
Tottenham Hotspur 0
Attendance: 38,147
Arsenal: *Lehmann, Lauren, Cole, Vieira, Touré, Senderos, Fàbregas (Edu), Silva, Reyes (Aliadière), van Persie (Bergkamp), Pirès.*
Tottenham Hotspur: *Robinson, Kelly, Edman, Davis (Ziegler), Dawson, King, Davies, Carrick, Kanoute (Mido), Defoe (Keane), Reid.*

José Antonio Reyes, who had spurned a gem of a chance inside the first minute, went from villain to hero with the scintillating first-half strike that kept Arsène Wenger's team on course for second place, and put Chelsea's celebration party on hold for a few more days. The Spaniard, whose Arsenal future remained clouded after admitting the lure of Real Madrid, drilled in only his second Premiership goal since 2ⁿᵈ October, with a stunning finish that knocked the heart out of Martin Jol's limp Spurs. Arsenal should have taken a hold on this contest within 50 seconds of the start as Reyes, playing alongside Robin van Persie in an unlikely strike duo, missed an absolute sitter. Van Persie threaded a perfect ball between Ledley King and Michael Dawson to set the Spaniard clear. Reyes did all the hard work to round keeper Paul Robinson and, even on his weaker right foot, the goal was begging only for him to hit the side netting. Jermain Defoe had a great chance on 17 minutes, but shot straight at Jens

Lehmann and miskicked the rebound. Both sides spurned further chances as the match wore on, and Reyes' goal proved to be the deciding factor.

29th October 2005

Premier League
Tottenham Hotspur 1
King
Arsenal 1
Pirès
Attendance: 36,154
Tottenham Hotspur: *Robinson, Stalteri, Lee, Lennon (Reid), Dawson, King, Jenas, Carrick, Mido, Defoe (Keane), Tainio (Mendes).*
Arsenal: *Lehmann, Lauren, Clichy, Silva, Touré, Campbell, Ljungberg (van Persie), Fàbregas, Reyes (Cygan), Bergkamp, Flamini (Pirès).*

This match hit the headlines for unsavoury reasons, following a 1-1 draw at White Hart Lane. Sol Campbell escaped FA action over his bloody clash with Tottenham's Teemu Tainio – but the Spurs fan who abused him was facing a life ban. Arsenal's Campbell was involved in an amazing bust-up with a supporter after the north London derby, in which the Finnish midfielder was left with a bad cut after being caught with an elbow. Spurs also wanted to identify the person who threw a conker at Arsenal keeper Jens Lehmann during the second half. Spurs skipper Ledley King opened the scoring in the 17th minute when he headed home a Michael Carrick free-kick, but Robert Pirès followed up to equalize after Dennis Bergkamp's free-kick had been palmed straight to him by Paul Robinson. Arsenal made sure they left still boasting only one defeat in the last 20 derby matches, but they were still looking for their first away win in the Premiership as October 2005 drew to a close.

22nd April 2006

Premier League

Arsenal 1

Henry

Tottenham Hotspur 1

Keane

Attendance: 38,326

Arsenal: *Lehmann, Djourou, Flamini, Silva, Touré, Senderos (Eboué), Reyes, Diaby (Fàbregas), Adebayor, van Persie (Henry), Pirès.*

Tottenham Hotspur: *Robinson, Stalteri, Lee, Gardner, Dawson, Lennon (Murphy), Tainio, Carrick, Keane, Defoe, Davids.*

Tottenham remained four points above their north London rivals after earning a 1-1 draw at Highbury, although controversy was rearing its head over the coveted fourth place in the Premier League. Arsenal were en route to the Champions League final, with UEFA ruling that if they won the competition and finished outside of the Premiership top four then only the top three would qualify for the following season's Champions League. The match itself was passionately contested, with Robbie Keane opening the scoring in the 66th minute despite Arsenal having a man down injured. Thierry Henry, a 62-minute sub for van Persie, equalized with six minutes of normal time remaining, but the drama was not over. With Arsenal searching for a second goal, Spurs' Dutch midfielder Edgar Davids was sent off for a second bookable offence minutes later.

2nd December 2006

Premier League

Arsenal 3

Adebayor, Silva 2 (2 pens)

Tottenham Hotspur 0

Attendance: 60,115

Arsenal: *Lehmann, Eboué, Clichy, Silva, Touré, Djourou, Ljungberg, Fàbregas, Adebayor (Walcott), van Persie, Rosický (Hleb).*

Tottenham Hotspur: *Robinson, Chimbonda, Assou-Ekotto (Lee),*

Zokora, Dawson, King, Lennon, Malbranque (Jenas), Berbatov, Keane, Tainio (Defoe).

Reports of a falling out between Arsène Wenger and Thierry Henry overshadowed the preparations for this match, with the French international accused of being conceited and self-obsessed. Henry, furious at being told by Wenger that he was unfit to face Spurs, allegedly stormed out of Arsenal's training ground and accused the club of falling behind the likes of Manchester United and Chelsea in terms of spending power. His team-mates, however, did not miss him that much during this derby match, and took the lead after just 20 minutes. Emmanuel Adebayor latched on to a long pass from Kolo Touré, and calmly slipped the ball past Paul Robinson. Shortly before half-time, Pascal Chimbonda was penalized for bringing down Tomáš Rosický, and Gilberto Silva doubled the hosts' lead from the spot. Spurs conceded a second penalty in the second half, when Jermaine Jenas fouled van Persie and Gilberto again converted, to give Arsenal a comfortable 3-0 victory.

24th January 2007

League Cup semi-final first leg
Tottenham Hotspur 2
Berbatov, Baptista (og)
Arsenal 2
Baptista (2)
Attendance: 35,485
Tottenham Hotspur: *Robinson, Chimbonda, Assou-Ekotto, Zokora, Dawson, Gardner, Lennon, Huddlestone, Berbatov (Keane), Defoe (Mido), Malbranque.*
Arsenal: *Almunia, Hoyte, Traoré, Diaby (Hleb) (Flamini), Touré, Senderos, Denilson, Fàbregas, Aliadière (Eboué), Walcott, Baptista.*

Arsenal looked dead and buried, with Tottenham in cruise control towards Cardiff and the Carling Cup final, with half an hour of this pulsating semi-final to go. But Arsenal's amazing kids proved their six-goal quarter-final demolition of Liverpool was no freak, and their latest cup fairy tale was all about heart, commitment and never-say-die spirit. Arsenal's Brazilian Júlio Baptista scored twice in the last 26 minutes, and Theo Walcott could even have won it at the death in one of the most remarkable fightbacks seen in a north London derby. And it was certainly a match Baptista will never forget, as he scored three times, even if one was at the wrong end. That put Tottenham two goals up, after Dimitar Berbatov had scored after 12 minutes. This incredible match evoked memories of 20 years earlier when Arsenal came back from two goals down at half-time in a League Cup semi-final, and won the replay after the late David Rocastle inspired an extra-time victory.

31st January 2007

League Cup semi-final second leg

Arsenal 3

Adebayor, Aliadière, Chimbonda (og)

Tottenham Hotspur 1

Mido

Attendance: **55,872**

Arsenal: *Almunia, Hoyte, Traoré (Clichy), Silva, Touré, Senderos, Walcott (Rosický), Denilson, Adebayor, Aliadière, Diaby (Fàbregas).*

Tottenham Hotspur: *Robinson, Chimbonda, Assou-Ekotto, Zokora, Dawson, Gardner (Rocha), Ghaly (Huddlestone), Jenas, Keane, Defoe, Malbranque (Mido).*

Arsène Wenger masterminded a dramatic extra-time victory, with goals from Emmanuel Adebayor, Jeremie Aliadière and an own goal from Pascal Chimbonda. But what was even more remarkable was that Wenger's starting line-up included just three players who were over 25. Brazilian teenager Denilson was outstanding throughout, and when the going got tough Wenger was able to bring on some experience in the shape of 19-year-old Cesc Fàbregas. Tottenham striker Mido headed the tie into extra-time with an 85th-minute leveller, and Arsenal's neighbours briefly looked as if they might snatch a winner. But, other than those five or so nervous minutes, Arsenal were always in command. Tottenham did not push enough, and when Wenger needed to step up a gear he was able to bring on Fàbregas, Gaël Clichy and Tomáš Rosický whose cameo role as a 65th-minute substitute was hugely influential.

21st April 2007

Premier League

Tottenham Hotspur 2

Keane, Jenas

Arsenal 2

Touré, Adebayor

Attendance: 36,050

Tottenham Hotspur: *Robinson, Chimbonda, Rocha, Zokora (Defoe), Dawson, King, Lennon (Huddlestone), Jenas, Berbatov, Keane, Tainio (Malbranque).*

Arsenal: *Lehmann, Eboué, Clichy, Silva, Touré, Gallas, Hleb (Senderos), Diaby, Adebayor, Ljungberg (Fàbregas), Rosický (Baptista).*

The Gunners were in disarray following the acrimonious departure of vice-chairman David Dein, and Spurs were confident they could add to Arsenal's gloom. Arsène Wenger's team were only just piecing their form back together, after their Carling Cup final defeat and exits from the FA Cup and Champions League. Tottenham, meanwhile, had shown there was still character in the team in the previous week's 3-3 draw at Wigan, where they came from behind three times to salvage a point. A point was all they could muster from this match though, as Kolo Touré and Emmanuel Adebayor scored second-half goals that nullified Robbie Keane's opener, before Jermaine Jenas picked the ball up with seconds to go and blasted an equalizer past Jens Lehmann.

15th September 2007

Premier League

Tottenham Hotspur 1

Bale

Arsenal 3

Adebayor 2, Fàbregas

Attendance: 36,053

Tottenham Hotspur: *Robinson, Chimbonda, Lee, Huddlestone, Kaboul, Dawson, Malbranque (Bent), Jenas, Berbatov, Keane, Bale (Lennon).*

Arsenal: *Almunia, Sagna, Clichy, Flamini, Touré, Silva, Hleb (Song), Fàbregas, Adebayor, van Persie (Denilson), Diaby (Rosický).*

It may have taken 66 minutes for Emmanuel Adebayor's header to finally reward Arsenal's beautiful football – cancelling out Gareth Bale's early free-kick – and improve the north London derby scoreline, but nobody inside White Hart Lane would deny that Wenger's men played the purest football on display in the Premiership. Sublime goals from the magnificent Cesc Fàbregas and Adebayor sealed the victory: a thunderous strike from the Spaniard followed by the African's stunning volley. Yet what inspired, thrilled and captivated, was the sheer instinctive quality Arsenal showed all over the pitch. At times the team tore Spurs to shreds, and nobody summed it up more than the boy-man at the heart of everything. Fàbregas may only have been 20, but in his head he was already 32, chillingly calm among the maelstrom and utterly outstanding.

22nd December 2007

Premier League

Arsenal 2

Adebayor, Bendtner

Tottenham Hotspur 1

Berbatov

Attendance: 60,087

Arsenal: *Almunia, Sagna, Clichy, Flamini, Touré, Gallas, Eboué*

(Bendtner), Fàbregas, Adebayor, Hleb (Silva), Rosický.
Tottenham Hotspur: *Robinson, Tainio, Lee (Taarabt), Chimbonda, Kaboul, Boateng (Huddlestone), Lennon, O'Hara, Berbatov, Keane (Defoe), Malbranque.*

After flirting with the relegation zone in the run-up to this match, Tottenham were finally starting to look up, after three straight wins and two clean sheets, but they failed to make their chances count, and thereby were unable to register a first victory over their north London rivals since 1999. Emmanuel Adebayor opened the scoring just after the interval, when he latched on to a Cesc Fàbregas back-heel to curl his shot past Paul Robinson. Spurs quickly fought back, with Robbie Keane showing a deft touch of his own with a back-heel into the path of Dimitar Berbatov. The Bulgarian made no mistake, equalizing in the 66th minute, and was again in the thick of the action when he earned a penalty after a Kolo Touré trip. Keane stepped up to take the spot kick, but Manuel Almunia was equal to the task and pushed it away to safety. Wenger brought on Nicklas Bendtner with a quarter of an hour to go, and the gamble paid off when the Dane headed the winner from a Fàbregas corner just minutes later.

9th January 2008

League Cup semi-final first leg
Arsenal 1
Walcott
Tottenham Hotspur 1
Jenas
Attendance: 53,136
Arsenal: *Fabiański, Hoyte, Traoré, Silva, Djourou (Sagna), Senderos, Walcott (Randall), Denilson, van Persie (Eduardo), Bendtner, Diaby.*
Tottenham Hotspur: *Černý, Chimbonda, Lee, O'Hara, Dawson, King, Lennon, Jenas, Berbatov, Keane (Defoe), Malbranque (Boateng).*

Theo Walcott left Spurs ruing their inability to win a game that was there for the taking as Arsenal somehow stole a draw to keep their Wembley hopes alive. Dimitar Berbatov's brilliance appeared to have finally made Arsène Wenger's youth policy come unstuck, as the Pied Piper led the kid Gunners a merry dance. But for all the dominance and a host of chances, Spurs only had Jermaine Jenas' first-half tap in to show for their efforts – the England midfielder taking his opportunity to impress the watching Fabio Capello. Just as Juande Ramos looked set to become the first Spurs boss to beat Wenger since 1999, the Achilles heel that had dogged Tottenham resurfaced. Walcott got the luck of the bounce as he chased Eduardo's pass, with Lee Young-Pyo's clearance bouncing off the winger's hand and past Radek Černý.

22nd January 2008

League Cup semi-final second leg
Tottenham Hotspur 5
Jenas, Bendtner (og), Keane, Lennon, Malbranque
Arsenal 1
Adebayor
Attendance: **35,979**
Tottenham Hotspur: *Černý, Chimbonda, Lee, Tainio, Dawson, King, Lennon (Huddlestone), Jenas, Berbatov (Defoe), Keane (Boateng), Malbranque.*
Arsenal: *Fabiański, Sagna, Traoré (Eduardo), Silva, Hoyte, Gallas, Hleb, Denilson (Fàbregas), Walcott (Adebayor), Bendtner, Diaby.*

Tottenham reached the Carling Cup final in style, by humiliating bitter rivals Arsenal at White Hart Lane. Spurs had not beaten the Gunners in 21 matches, going back eight years, but boss Juande Ramos showed his magic cup touch as a 5-1 win sealed a 6-2 aggregate triumph. In just three months, Ramos did what Martin Jol could not do in three years – mastermind this magnificent win. This was not just defeat for Arsenal ... it was destruction! A Jermaine Jenas shot and a Nicklas Bendtner own goal gave the hosts a two-goal lead at the break. Robbie Keane, Aaron Lennon and Steed

Malbranque completed the rout, with Emmanuel Adebayor getting a consolation strike on 70 minutes. A semi-final at the home of Arsenal's local rivals, in front of the new England manager, was a chance for Theo Walcott to show he could deliver on the big stage. Instead, with his side badly needing inspiration, he fluffed his lines. Even before the break the frustrated Arsenal fans were calling for the introduction of Adebayor from the bench, and when the Togo striker did make a belated appearance on 65 minutes it was Walcott who made way. This was the night that all the pain, all of the hurt and all of the frustration at not beating their bitter rivals for eight long years and 21 heartbreaking games came flooding out – as Spurs earned their biggest win over them for 25 years.

29th October 2008

Premier League
Arsenal 4
Silvestre, Gallas, Adebayor, van Persie
Tottenham Hotspur 4
Bentley, Bent, Jenas, Lennon
Attendance: 60,043
Arsenal: *Almunia, Sagna, Gallas, Silvestre, Clichy, Fàbregas, Nasri (Song), Denilson, Walcott (Eboué), van Persie (Diaby), Adebayor.*
Tottenham Hotspur: *Gomes, Hutton (Gunter), Bale (Lennon), Assou-Ekotto, Woodgate, Ćorluka, Bentley, Huddlestone, Jenas, Modrić, Pavlyuchenko (Bent).*

David Bentley scored one of the greatest goals ever seen, as Spurs completed an incredible comeback. The England midfielder fulfilled his promise to make Arsène Wenger regret letting him go, with a stunning strike to kick-start a remarkable night at the Emirates. Bentley, 43 yards out, took a short pass from Jermaine Jenas, juggled the ball to set himself up, and then leashed a tremendous volley, which looped over Arsenal keeper Manuel Almunia. While Cesc Fàbregas clearly fouled Bentley, before forcing the corner that led to the equalizer, Heurelho Gomes was the villain of the piece, getting nowhere near van Persie's corner as Mikaël Silvestre nodded in. A minute after the restart, Gomes failed to deal with William Gallas' header, and when Emmanuel Adebayor scored his trademark goal against Spurs – his eighth in eight derby clashes – it looked all over. Even when Bent came off the bench to cash in, Hutton immediately gifted the ball to Adebayor, who squared for van Persie to thrash home. But Jenas robbed Gaël Clichy on the halfway line, ran to the edge of the box and curled home a beauty. Aaron Lennon's injury-time strike, when even the Spurs fans had started to give up hope, was the sensational final word of a game of sheer drama.

8th February 2009

Premier League
Tottenham Hotspur 0
Arsenal 0
Attendance: **36,021**
Tottenham Hotspur: *Cudicini, Ćorluka (Chimbonda), Dawson, Woodgate, Assou-Ekotto, Lennon (Taarabt), Jenas, Palacios, Modrić, Pavlyuchenko (Bent), Keane.*
Arsenal: *Almunia, Sagna, Gallas, Touré, Clichy (Gibbs), Eboué, Song, Denilson, Nasri, van Persie, Adebayor (Bendtner).*

Robbie Keane launched his second coming at Tottenham in the north London derby, still baffled by his treatment from Liverpool manager Rafa Benitez. The £20 million striker became surplus to requirements in just six months at Anfield, and returned to a relegation dogfight at White Hart Lane. With 24 games of the season gone, Spurs were in 14th place in the Premiership ... just one point ahead of the relegation zone, and only two off the foot of the table. The home side started brightly, but had an early penalty claim turned down by referee Mike Dean. Luck was not with Arsenal on the day, however, with Emmanuel Adebayor pulling up with a hamstring injury, and winger Emmanuel Eboué being dismissed after two needless yellow cards. Keane skimmed the crossbar with a header in the 56th minute, but neither side was able to break the deadlock.

31st October 2009
Premier League
Arsenal 3
van Persie 2, Fàbregas
Tottenham Hotspur 0
Attendance: 60,103
Arsenal: *Almunia, Sagna, Gallas, Vermaelen, Clichy, Song, Diaby, Fàbregas, Arshavin (Eboué), van Persie (Ramsey), Bendtner (Eduardo).*
Tottenham Hotspur: *Gomes, Ćorluka (Hutton), King, Bassong, Assou-Ekotto, Bentley, Palacios, Huddlestone (Bale), Jenas, Keane (Pavlyuchenko), Crouch.*

Robin van Persie was a constant thorn in Tottenham's side, scoring twice and dispossessing Wilson Palacios to allow Cesc Fàbregas' crazy solo goal, which killed off Harry Redknapp's men. The Dutchman's double made it eight goals in 13 games so far, as Arsenal rubbed Tottenham's nose in it. For 42 minutes you could have understood Robbie Keane's midweek assertion that Spurs had caught up with Arsenal – or, more to the point, had closed the gap – but then two kamikaze bits of defending suggested the game was as wide as ever. First, Bacary Sagna's low cross found van Persie, who lost his marker and slotted past Spurs keeper, Heurelho Gomes, at the near post. If that was not bad enough, from the restart Palacios was dispossessed by van Persie, and Fàbregas picked up the loose ball before going past Palacios, Tom Huddlestone and Ledley King, and firing past Gomes. Arsenal's third came when Sagna again crossed low, with van Persie scoring past Gomes to rub salt in the Tottenham wounds.

14th April 2010

Premier League

Tottenham Hotspur 2

Rose, Bale

Arsenal 1

Bendtner

Attendance: **36,041**

Tottenham Hotspur: *Gomes, Kaboul, Bale, King, Dawson, Assou-Ekotto, Huddlestone, Modrić, Rose (Bentley), Defoe (Gudjohnsen), Pavlyuchenko (Crouch).*

Arsenal: *Almunia, Eboué, Clichy, Vermaelen (Silvestre), Campbell, Sagna (Walcott), Diaby, Denilson (van Persie), Rosický, Nasri, Bendtner.*

This truly was a night for Spurs heroes – some expected, some certainly not. The Tottenham fans always assumed that Ledley King would slot back in as if he had never been away, that Michael Dawson would never buckle, that Gareth Bale would run and run down the left. Now, they also had the hunch that Heurelho Gomes would make saves that would turn a match – although not, presumably, that he would make four stellar stops in the space of six unbelievable minutes, as Arsenal so nearly pulled off the mother of all derby comebacks. Just 10 minutes into his full Premier League debut, Danny Rose etched himself into Spurs folklore. When Manuel Almunia punched Bale's corner 20 yards clear, the Spaniard must have felt he'd done his job, even as he saw the ball dropping on to Rose's left foot, but what followed was remarkable – a thunderbolt strike that flew back from where it had come with a velocity nobody saw coming, ripping into the roof of the net. Jermain Defoe showed great quality as he held off Sol Campbell in the second half, before threading a pass for Bale to finish off. Enter Theo Walcott and Robin van Persie, who was twice stunningly thwarted by Gomes, before Nicklas Bendtner touched home the England winger's low cross. There was no late salvation, as Harry Redknapp became the first Spurs boss in 21 attempts to beat Wenger in the league.

21ˢᵗ September 2010

League Cup third round

Tottenham Hotspur 1

Keane

Arsenal 4

Lansbury, Nasri 2 (2 pens), Arshavin

Attendance: 35,883

Tottenham Hotspur: *Pletikosa, Naughton, Bassong, Assou-Ekotto, Caulker, Sandro (Kranjcar), Livermore (Lennon), Palacios, Bentley, Pavlyuchenko, Dos Santos (Keane).*

Arsenal: *Fabiański, Eboué, Koscielny, Djourou, Gibbs (Clichy), Denilson, Wilshere, Nasri, Rosický (Arshavin), Lansbury, Vela (Chamakh).*

When it mattered, Arsenal's quality was too much for Spurs' youngsters. Spurs could have no complaints; they were played off the park by a Jack Wilshere-inspired Arsenal for the first half, and were always second best, even when they were handed a lifeline by the hapless Łukasz Fabiański, who somehow let Robbie Keane's shot slip through his fingers. Wilshere was in at the inception of the opener, as the ball was spread wide to Kieran Gibbs, who fed stand-in skipper Tomáš Rosický. Wilshere then popped up on the outside of the Spurs back line, threading a cross, for Henri Lansbury to mark his first Arsenal start with a tap in past Stipe Pletikosa. Arsenal were able to pass the ball with impunity, and Spurs were left chasing shadows, only for Fabiański to gift them a way back into the tie three minutes after the break. But while Spurs resisted the late siege in normal time, they fell apart at the start of the additional period, as Samir Nasri netted two spot-kick conversions in the space of four minutes, with Andrey Arshavin finishing off the scoring.

20ᵗʰ November 2010

Premier League

Arsenal 2

Nasri, Chamakh

Tottenham Hotspur 3
Bale, van der Vaart (pen), Kaboul
Attendance: **60,102**
Arsenal: *Fabiański, Sagna, Squillaci, Koscielny, Clichy, Arshavin (Walcott), Fàbregas, Nasri (Rosický), Denilson, Song, Chamakh (van Persie).*
Tottenham Hotspur: *Gomes, Hutton, Gallas, Kaboul, Assou-Ekotto, Bale, van der Vaart (Palacios), Modrić, Jenas, Lennon (Defoe), Pavlyuchenko (Crouch).*

From being 2-0 down at half-time, when Samir Nasri and Marouane Chamakh were shown little resistance as Arsenal overran Tottenham, Harry Redknapp tore into his players, made a tactical change and went for broke. Arsenal did not show either the mental or physical strength to hold off the visitors. Nasri, Cesc Fàbregas, Chamakh and Andrey Arshavin were as bad in the second half as they had been good in the first half. Tottenham's first goal was Sunday league stuff – a long ball down the middle was not dealt with, and Gareth Bale escaped to score. Fàbregas inexplicably handled Rafael van der Vaart's free-kick, and the Dutchman scored from the resulting penalty. The winner was just as bad. Van der Vaart's free-kick was not defended in the Arsenal box, and it was fitting that Younès Kaboul was on hand to score the winner.

20th April 2011
Premier League
Tottenham Hotspur 3
Van der Vaart 2 (1 pen), Huddlestone
Arsenal 3
Walcott, Nasri, van Persie
Attendance: **36,138**
Tottenham Hotspur: *Gomes, Ćorluka (Kaboul), Gallas, Dawson, Assou-Ekotto, Bale (Lennon), van der Vaart, Modrić, Huddlestone, Crouch, Pavlyuchenko (Sandro).*
Arsenal: *Szczęsny, Sagna, Djourou, Koscielny, Clichy, Nasri (Arshavin), Diaby (Wilshere), Fàbregas, Walcott (Bendtner), Song, van Persie.*

Less than five minutes had gone when Cesc Fàbregas dropped his shoulder to make space for himself in midfield, and threaded a perfect pass through the Spurs defence for Theo Walcott to run on to. Walcott was calmness personified, and took the ball on a few yards before sliding it past Heurelho Gomes to open the scoring – although Rafael van der Vaart had Spurs level within two minutes. Samir Nasri and Robin van Persie added two more first-half goals, to give the visitors a 3-1 lead, before Tom Huddlestone reduced the arrears in the 44th minute. Gareth Bale, injured in the first half, was replaced for the second period by Aaron Lennon, but it was Arsenal who next had the ball in the net, although van Persie's goal was controversially ruled out for being offside. The home side equalized when van der Vaart converted a spot kick, after Szczęsny tripped Lennon in the 70th minute, and neither team could again break the deadlock.

2nd October 2011

Premier League
Tottenham Hotspur 2
Van der Vaart, Walker
Arsenal 1
Ramsey
Attendance: 36,274
Tottenham Hotspur: *Friedel, Assou-Ekotto, Walker, King, Kaboul, Modrić, Parker (Ćorluka), Bale, van der Vaart (Sandro), Adebayor (Livermore), Defoe.*
Arsenal: *Szczęsny, Sagna (Jenkinson), Mertesacker, Gibbs, Song, Ramsey, Walcott (Benayoun), Coquelin, Arteta, van Persie, Gervinho (Arshavin).*

Arsenal's 2011–12 campaign kicked off with a string of bizarre results that saw them in 15th position in the Premiership by early October, just two points off the relegation zone, and with the fourth-worst goal difference in the league. For large parts of this pulsating north London derby, Arsenal were the better side. In Francis Coquelin and Robin van Persie they had two of the best players on the pitch, but they badly missed Jack Wilshere and Thomas Vermaelen. Per Mertesacker – thrown in as an extra forward in the closing moments – had a poor game in central defence, while Szczęsny played superbly but should have saved Kyle Walker's fiercely hit 30-yard winner. Rafael van der Vaart had opened the scoring just before half-time with a well-taken volley from Emmanuel Adebayor's cross, but Aaron Ramsey scored for Arsenal after 51 minutes.

26th February 2012

Premier League

Arsenal 5

Sagna, van Persie, Rosický, Walcott 2

Tottenham Hotspur 2

Saha, Adebayor (pen)

Attendance: 60,106

Arsenal: *Szczęsny, Gibbs (Jenkinson), Sagna, Vermaelen, Koscielny, Benayoun (Gervinho), Song, Walcott (Oxlade-Chamberlain), Arteta, Rosický, van Persie.*

Tottenham Hotspur: *Friedel, King (Dawson), Assou-Ekotto, Kaboul, Walker, Bale, Kranjcar (van der Vaart), Parker, Modrić, Adebayor, Saha (Sandro).*

Spurs had won two of their last three games against Arsenal, and Harry Redknapp was being tipped to become the first Spurs manager to win away against the Gunners for two seasons in a row for 86 years. A victory at the Emirates would also have given him the honour of being the first Spurs manager to do the Double over Arsenal for 19 years, and the signs looked good when Louis Saha and Emmanuel Adebayor opened up a 2-0 lead with just over half an hour gone. Goals from Bacary Sagna and Robin van Persie ensured that the two sides went into the interval on level terms, but it was Arsenal who kept their momentum in the second half. Tomáš Rosický put them in front for the first time in the game, while Theo Walcott made sure of the three points and amazing comeback with a brace in the 65th and 68th minutes. Spurs were left ruing the encounter that saw them surrender a two-goal lead, and become the first Tottenham team to concede five at their rivals' home since 1934.